The temple and other sites
in the north-eastern sector
of Caesaromagus

If, therefore, we could once more produce a photograph of Chelmsford as it appeared from 1,400 to 1,800 years ago, we should see the nucleus of a town with probably some few dwellings of a superior character, perhaps a Temple, possibly baths and other public buildings, with numerous other dwellings more or less substantial, some, no doubt, of a quasi-military character. The rivers, instead of being allowed to meander over the rich pasture lands, would be confined within proper limits. Certain areas of the forest land would be reclaimed and subjected to cultivation, and the old war-paths would be replaced by solid and substantial roadways. The inhabitants still engaged to some extent in the performance of military duties, but many engaged in manufactures and other peaceful occupations.

Frederick Chancellor 1857
(unpublished manuscript version)

Chelmsford Archaeological Trust
Report 9

The temple and other sites in the north-eastern sector of Caesaromagus

by
N P Wickenden

With contributions by D Andrews, S A Butcher,
V I Evison, C J Going, R M Luff, J G McDonnell,
R Reece, W J Rodwell, R Turner, P Wilthew

1992

Published by Chelmsford
Museums Service and the
Council for British Archaeology

CBA Research Report 75

Published 1992 by the Council for British Archaeology
112 Kennington Road, London SE11 6RE

British Library Cataloguing in Publication Data

Wickenden, N P (Nicholas P)
The temple and other sites in the NE sector of
Caesaromagus — (CBA research report ISSN 0589–9036; no 75)
I. Title II. Series
936.26704

ISBN 1 872414 06 0

Printed by Derry & Sons, Nottingham

The publishers acknowledge with gratitude a
grant from the Historic Buildings and
Monuments Commission for England towards
the publication of this report

Contents

Illustrations viii

Contributors ix

I Introduction

Archaeological synopsis 1

Topography and geology 1

The field recording systems and archives 1

The chronological framework 3

Acknowledgements 3

II Site D, 29–31 Rochford Road

Introduction 6

The excavated features 6

    Periods I–II: Prehistoric 6

    Period V.1: *c* AD 90–100 6

    Period V.2: *c* AD 100–120/5 9

    Period VI.1: *c* AD 120/5–mid 2nd century 10

    Period VI.2 : 2nd half 2nd century: frontage structure 13

    Period VII.1: 3rd century 13

    Period VII.2: 4th century 15

    Post-Roman activity 15

III The Temple Site: Site K, 1–8 Rochford Road

Introduction 16

The excavated features 16

    Periods I–III: Prehistoric–early Roman 16

    Period IV.1: Immediately post-Boudican 17

    Period IV.2: pre *c* AD 80 17

        Ditch 205 17

        Ditch 705 19

        The votive deposit 19

        Well 558 20

    Period IV.3: *c* AD 80–90 23

    Period IV (unphased): 1st century 25

    Period V.1: *c* AD 90–110 26

    Period V.2: *c* AD 110–120/5 27

    The 'corridor structure' (Periods V–VII.1) 29

        Discussion and the gravel spreads 31

    Period VI: *c* AD 120/5–200/10 32

        The hearths 32

        Structure 12 32

        Pit 90 33

    Period VII.1: 3rd century 36

    Period VII.2: 4th century 36

        The Romano-Celtic temple (structure 9) 36

    Period VIII: temple robbing, post *c* AD 390 39

        The stake-built structures 42

IV The Other Sites

1   Site M: 1–4 The Chase 44

Introduction 44

The excavated features 44

    Periods I–II: Prehistoric 44

    Period VI: 2nd century 44

    Period VII: 3rd–4th century 45

    Medieval and later 47

| | Comment .... | 47 |

2	Site AB: 1–12 Goldlay Road	47
	Introduction	47
	The excavated features	48
	Periods V–VI: 2nd century	48

| 3 | Site L .... | 49 |

| 4 | Site Q: Salvation Army Premises (TL 7119 0631) ... | 49 |

5	Site AS: 16–18 Baddow Road (TL 709 064)	49
	Periods V–VI: 1st–2nd centuries	49
	Period VII.1: 3rd century	50
	Period VII.2: 4th century	50
	Medieval and later	53

6	Site CF1: 16 Mildmay Road	54
	Period IV.1: 1st century	54
	Periods IV.2–V: later 1st–early 2nd century	54
	The finds	56
	Discussion	57

7	Site CR: Watching Briefs	57
	Summary	57
	1A Trench S9–S10, September 1970	58
	3 Manhole C54, after September 1970	58
	4 Manhole R52, after September 1970 (Site P1 1970, F2–4)	58
	5 Trench C53–R52, after September 1970 (Site P1, F1)	58
	The subway from Rochford Road to Baddow Road ...	58
	6 Roundabout. North subway and ramp	58
	7 (also 18) Roundabout. South subway area (Site RR 3 1970, F1–6)	59
	8 Manhole C39 and trench C39–R46	60
	10B Trench S8–S9 (east of Mildmay Road), September 1970	60
	19A Northern end of roundabout subway	60
	Central area of roundabout	60
	21 Unstratified	60
	21A Site RR 3B 1971, F1–7	60
	21B Site RR 4 1971, F1–4	61
	22 Trench C53–C54	61
	29 Site P, F5, September 1970	61
	30 Site P, F6, October 1970	61
	31 Trench R51–R52 (Site P2)	61
	32 Trench R48–C13	61
	33 Trench C12–C13 (Site P, F8)	61
	34 Goldlay Road–Lynmouth Avenue, May/June 1971	61
	35 Sewer trench (Site P, F2), July 1970	61
	36 Watermain trench (Site P, F2)	61
	37 Sewer trench (Site P, F3), July 1970	62
	38 Site P, F4, July 1970	62
	39 Site C, January 1970	62
	40 Site A	62
	41 M & S Motors, March 1970	62
	Unstratified	62

V	**The Building Materials**	
	The stone	63
	The tile	63
	mortar	63
	wallplaster	63
	tesserae	64
	burnt clay and daub	64

pigment 64

VI   The Loose Finds
The Roman coins, *by R Reece* 65
    Summary, *by R Reece, N Wickenden and R Kenyon* 69
The silver buckle, *by V I Evison* 71
The brooches, *by S A Butcher* 71
Objects of copper alloy, incorporating analyses *by P Wilthew* 73
The lead 80
Objects of iron 80
The metalworking debris, *by J G McDonnell* 82
Objects of bone 82
The glass 83
Objects of jet and shale 86
Objects of fired clay and briquetage 88
Objects of stone 89
Leather 91

VII   The Pottery, *by C J Going & W J Rodwell*
The samian, *by W J Rodwell* 92
The other pottery, *by C J Going* 93
Summary, *by C J Going* *114*

VIII   The Faunal Remains, *by R M Luff*
Introduction 116
A   Site K 116
    Introduction 116
    Relative frequency of species occurrence 117
    Distinction of sheep and goat bones 117
    Sheep slaughter patterns 117
    Metrical data 120
    Mandible morphology and pathology 120
    Sheep butchery patterns 120
    Other species 122
    Conclusion 123
B   Site D 124
C   Site AB 124

IX   Discussion
Introduction 125
1st–2nd centuries 125
    The ovens 125
    The enclosures 127
    The early religious complex 127
    Structure 11 128
The corridor structure and 3rd century occupation 129
The roads 131
Trade and industry 133
The Romano-Celtic temple 134
    The dimensions 134
    West Hill, Uley: an association with Mercury? 135
    Octagonal temples: Britain and the Continent 136
    The *temenos* 139
South of the drainage ditch, 133 139
Other religious evidence in Chelmsford 141
Sub-Roman activity and the temple aftermath 141

Bibliography 142

Index 146

Illustrations

Fig 1   The principal features of *Caesaromagus* from the early 2nd century onwards, superimposed on a modern plan of the Moulsham suburb of Chelmsford

Fig 2   General plan of the Temple area, showing the principal excavated sites and watching briefs, superimposed on the modern topography

Fig 3   The Trinovantian *civitas*, showing towns and principal roads, with a general location plan

Fig 4   Site D: Sections S1–4, 6–7,10

Fig 5   Site D: Period V. Phase 1 and 2

Fig 6   Site D: Sections S5, 8–9, 11–12; key to sections

Fig 7   Site D: Period VI. Phase 1 and 2

Fig 8   Site D: The Period VI.1 enclosure and ovens

Fig 9   Site D: Period VII. Phase 1 and 2

Fig 10   Site K: Buried old land surface and features

Fig 11   Site K: Period IV. Phases 1–3

Fig 12   Site K: Period IV.2. Distribution of 'votive' objects

Fig 13   Site K: Sections S13–29

Fig 14   Site K: Sections S45–49 (southern area)

Fig 15   Site K: Period V. Phases 1–2

Fig 16   Site K: Structures 11 and 12; ovens

Fig 17   Site K: Period VI

Fig 18   Site K: Sections S33–43

Fig 19   Site K: The storage jar hearths (Period VI)

Fig 20   Site K: Period VII. Phases 1–2. The Temple

Fig 21   Site K: the octagonal Romano-Celtic temple (Structure 9)

Fig 22   Site K: Period VIII, alteration and temple demolition

Fig 23   Site M: Periods VI–VII

Fig 24   Site M: Sections S50–53

Fig 25   Site AB: Location of trenches

Fig 26   Site AB: Sections S54–57

Fig 27   Site Q: Location of trenches

Fig 28   Site AS: Location of trenches

Fig 29   Site AS: Periods V/VI; VII. Phases 1 and 2

Fig 30   Site AS: Sections S58–60

Fig 31   Site CF1: location of trenches

Fig 32   Site CF1: Periods IV–V

Fig 33   Site CF1: Sections

Fig 34   Site CF1: Objects of copper alloy

Fig 35   Finds from the watching briefs (Site CR)

Fig 36   1, 'margined' tile; 2, roller-stamped daub

Fig 37   1, silver buckle; 2–17, copper alloy brooches

Fig 38   Copper alloy brooches, 18–26

Fig 39   Objects of copper alloy, 1–15

Fig 40   Objects of copper alloy, 16–44

Fig 41   Objects of copper alloy, 45–64

Fig 42   Objects of iron, 1–14

Fig 43   Objects of bone, 1–4

Fig 44   Glass vessels, 1–21. Beads and paste objects, 22–33

Fig 45   Objects of jet and shale, 34–39. Scale 1:1

Fig 46   Objects of fired clay and briquetage. Scale 1:3

Fig 47   Objects of stone

Fig 48   The samian

Fig 49   Roman pottery from ditch K 205, 1–26

Fig 50   Roman pottery from ditch K 205, 27–31

Fig 51   Pottery supply to Chelmsford as evidenced by ditch K 205

Fig 52   The production waste from pit D123

Fig 53   Roman pottery from pit K90.2, 1–28

Fig 54   Roman pottery from pit K90.2, 27–55

Fig 55   Pottery supply to Chelmsford as evidenced by pit K90.2

Fig 56   The composition of the assemblages from a) ditch K205; b) pit D123 and c) pit K90.2

Fig 57   The mortarium and other stamps

Fig 58   The graffiti

Fig 59   Roman pottery of intrinsic interest

Fig 60   Roman pottery of intrinsic interest

Fig 61   Graph of sheep/goat metacarpal trochlea width against condyle width

Fig 62   Relative wear stages of the third milk molar and first permanent molar at a) Harlow, b) Chelmsford temple

Fig 63   The north-eastern sector of *Caesaromagus*. Periods IV–V

Fig 64   Site K, Structure 11: reconstruction of 1st century AD temple

Fig 65   The north-eastern sector of *Caesaromagus*. Periods VI–VII

Fig 66   The late 4th century shrine at Great Dunmow, Essex

Fig 67   Romano-Celtic temple plans

Fig 68   The temples at Pagans Hill and Caerwent in their surroundings

Fig 69   The Chelmsford temple: a reconstruction

List of Tables

Table 1: Outline chronology of the sites
Table 2: Site K: octagonal temple component contexts and finds
Table 3: The coins from Site K
Table 4: The metalworking slags
Table 5: The querns
Table 6: The samian stamps
Table 7: Quantification details of the Romano-British pottery from ditch K205
Table 8: Quantification details of the Romano-British pottery from pit K90.2
Table 9: Numbers and percentages of bone fragments identified by period from Site K
Table 10: Numbers of bird bone fragments identified by period from Site K
Table 11: Minimum numbers of animals by period from Site K
Table 12: Relative percentage of meat weights from Site K
Table 13: Sheep/goat ageing data from Site K
Table 14: Identification of sheep jaw bone side by period and age
Table 15: Sheep/goat metrical data from Site K
Table 16: Relative occurrence of skeletal elements by period from Site K: sheep/goat
Table 17: Numbers of bone fragments by species for each layer from ditch K205 (Period IV)
Table 18: Relative occurrence of skeletal elements by period from Site K: cattle
Table 19: Chicken bone length measurements (mm)
Table 20: Numbers of bone fragments by period from Site D
Table 21: Comparative measurements of Romano-Celtic temples

List of Plates

Plate I   Site D, Oven 47
Plate II   Site D, Structure 1
Plate III Site K, Structures 11, 12, and ovens
Plate IV   Site K, Ditch 705 and the 'corridor' structure
Plate V   Site K, storage jar hearths
Plate VI   Site K, surviving masonry in the temple foundation trench
Plate VII Site K, surviving masonry pier base
Plate VIII Site K, robbed out foundations of the Roman-Celtic temple
Plate IX   a) copper alloy votive bar; b) bone plaque
Plate X   Iron woolcomb

Contributors

D Andrews, formerly Archaeology Section, Essex County Council, County Hall, Duke Street Chelmsford

S A Butcher, formerly Inspectorate of Ancient Monuments, HBMC(E), Fortress House, 23 Savile Row, London W1X 2HE

V I Evison, Birkbeck College, Malet Street, London

C J Going, formerly Chelmsford Archaeological Trust, 1 Writtle Road, Chelmsford, Essex, CM1 3BL

R M Luff, Faunal Remains Unit, University of Cambridge

J G McDonnell, formerly Department of Metallurgy, University of Aston, Gosta Green, Birmingham

R Reece, Institute of Archaeology, 31–34 Gordon Square, London WC1H 0PP

W J Rodwell, The Old Vicarage, Chilcompton, Downside, Somerset

B R G Turner, formerly Archaeology Section, Essex County Council, County Hall, Duke Street, Chelmsford

N P Wickenden, Chelmsford Museums Service (formerly Chelmsford Archaeological Trust), 1 Writtle Road, Chelmsford, Essex CM1 3BL

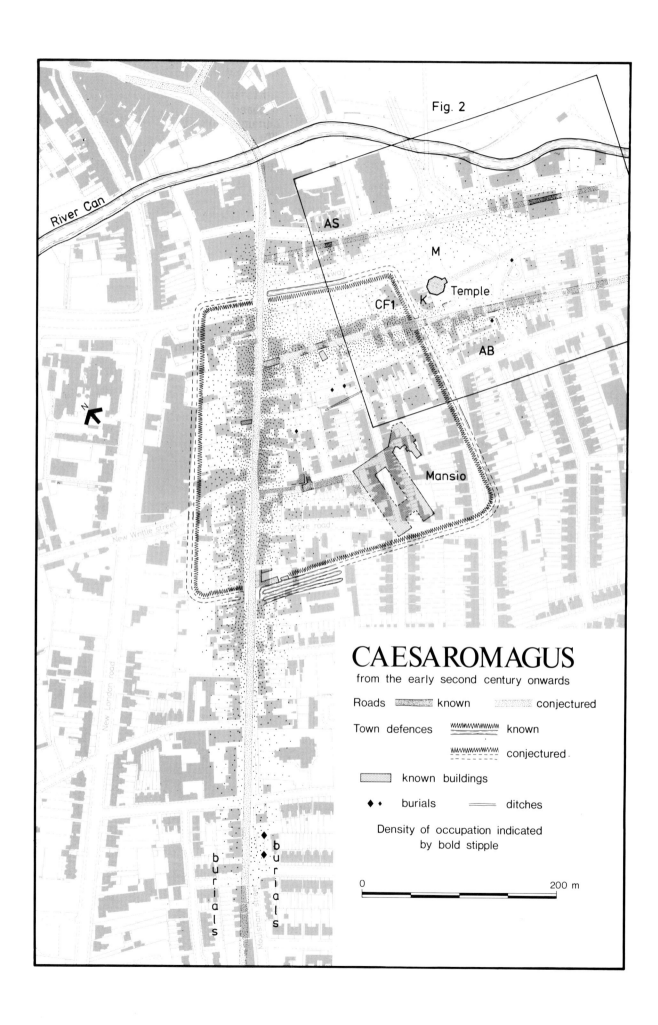

Fig. 2

River Can

AS

M

K Temple

CF1

AB

Mansio

New Writtle street

New London road

Moulsham street

burials

burials

burials

CAESAROMAGUS

from the early second century onwards

Roads ▨▨▨ known ░░░░ conjectured

Town defences ⋀⋀⋀⋀⋀ known

⋀⋀⋀⋀⋀ conjectured

▨ known buildings

◆ • burials ══ ditches

Density of occupation indicated
by bold stipple

0   200 m

I Introduction

This is the ninth in the series of *Chelmsford Archaeological Trust Reports* and the second volume which reports on sites within *Caesaromagus* — the Roman town of Chelmsford. The first was concerned with the *mansio*, town defences, and other sites in the south-eastern sector of the town (Drury 1988). Its companion volume (Going 1987) dealt with the pottery and set out a typology for Roman pottery from the town; it has been substantially referred to here. A third volume (in prep) will deal with a series of frontage sites, mainly in the north-western sector of the town.

The development of the archaeological investigation of the town generally was outlined in Drury 1988, 1–3. This volume reports on sites in the north-eastern sector of the town, which together form a coherent group. They comprise three main 'rescue' excavations (Sites K, D and M) directed by Mr P J Drury for the, then, Chelmsford Excavation Committee during 1970 and early 1971, in advance of Phase II of the Chelmsford Inner Relief Road (subsequently known as Parkway and the Baddow Road roundabout). In addition, a number of relevant small excavations and observations of contractor's works are included here. The latter were largely carried out by Messrs D Biglin and H Young. An interim report was published shortly after the excavations (Drury 1972). Two small recent excavations by the Essex County Council Archaeology Section are also included here. For the sites in relation to the general layout of the Roman settlement and the modern topography, see Figures 1 & 2.

Archaeological synopsis

The excavated sites either lie between or include two parallel metalled roads running eastwards from the main London–Colchester road. All lie outside the earthen defences of the town, constructed *c* AD 160–175 and levelled *c* AD 200–220 (Drury 1988). Site AS, excavated by the Essex County Council Archaeology Section, includes the 3rd century northern road, also found in trial trenching on Sites CR and Q (Fig 2). The southern road was located in contractors excavations and on site D, which also included part of an enclosure and frontage building remains on its southern side. Site AB yielded evidence of another building. Within the area bounded by the two roads (? an *insula*), Site M was occupied mostly by pit complexes and a surviving late Roman subsoil. The main area, Site K, contained a 4th century octagonal masonry Romano-Celtic temple, though its walls had been almost wholly robbed in the sub-Roman and medieval periods. The site appears to have had a religious significance from the 1st century AD, and part of a building with masonry foundations has been interpreted as a 1st century temple. This building lay within an enclosure defined by ditches found on Site K and at 16 Mildmay Road (Site CF1, excavated by the Essex County Council Archaeology Section) and many brooches and other copper alloy objects were associated. A subsequent building of Hadrianic date must have occupied the northern frontage of the southern road, and provides a date for its construction.

The site appears to have been deserted from the 5th century until the 13th, when there was a possible dyer's establishment on Site K (report in prep). The late Roman and post-Roman subsoils were badly truncated by flooding soon after the mid 13th century which deposited a deep alluvial silt. By the end of the 16th century, the area was under cultivation. Whilst the alluvial erosion caused much damage, the resultant silt insulated the site from serious disturbance by 19th century building.

Topography and geology

The Romano-British 'small town' of *Caesaromagus* lies in central Essex, on the southern slope of the Chelmer Valley, between 23 and 30m OD (Fig 3). Its site overlooks the confluence of the rivers Can and Chelmer, the latter joining the river Blackwater some 15 km downstream, just above the point where the Blackwater discharges into a tidal estuary. The nearby 'small town' of Heybridge probably acted as the main port of entry into central Essex in the Roman period, and indeed earlier (Rodwell 1976a, 319; Wickenden 1987). The Chelmer and Blackwater navigation, opened in 1797, enabled barges to reach Chelmsford, but the river may have been navigable to very small craft in earlier periods.

The geology of the Chelmsford area will be described in detail in a report on early prehistoric sites in the area (Healey *et al* forthcoming). Suffice it to say here that within the Roman town stoneless brickearth (loess) deposits, becoming calcareous at 1–2m, overlie first terrace gravels of the Chelmer. The brickearth stratum diminishes in thickness to the north, generally disappearing about 100m south of the river Can.

The field recording systems and archives

All field records, card indexes and other archival material are deposited in Chelmsford and Essex Museum, as are the finds. General accession numbers are shown on p 3.

2

Figure 2   Plan of the temple area, showing the principal excavated sites and watching briefs superimposed on the modern topography (based on the Ordnance Survey Map, with the consent of the Controller of HMSO; Crown Copyright reserved)

Accn number (CHMER)	Site ref	Site	Year of Excavation
1985:1	D	29–31 Rochford Road	1970
1985:2	K	1–8 Rochford Road	1970–71
1985:3	L	Machine cut trench, The Chase	1970
1985:4	M	1–4 The Chase, Baddow Road	1970
1985:5	P	Sewer trench, Goldlay Road & watching brief observations	1970–71
1985:6	Q	The Salvation Army, junction of Baddow Road & Goldlay Road	1971
1985:7	AB	Mildmay Terrace, 1–12 Goldlay Road	1972–73
1985:8	AS	16–18 Baddow Road	1978
1989:34	CF1	16 Mildmay Road	1983

Under these general accession numbers, all illustrated objects have been numbered to correspond with this report. Other material is stored primarily by category, and then in catalogue number order (see below). In 1971–2 features were generally recorded on site only by their grid coordinate; their fills (where separated) were distinguished by layer numbers, ie, L1, L2 etc. Other layers (eg, general site subsoils) were identified by coordinate and a layer number.

In order to aid post-excavation work, a card index was created for each site, which allocated catalogue entries (known as Cat nos) to each context or findspot, prefixed by the site letter. Each discrete feature/layer, eg, a pit or ditch or road surface, is referred to in this report by one of these numbers, although several catalogue numbers might be subsumed within it. Thus, for example, ditch D 173 from Site D incorporates Cats 173 and 177–180.

The site grid systems have been omitted from this publication in the interest of clarity; in many cases, however, they enable excavated objects to be more closely located than published plans might imply.

The chronological framework

The development of the Roman and medieval town, and the immediate landscape in which they were set, has been divided into thirteen periods, of which I–VIII are relevant to this report. These periods are common to all sites, but sub-divisions of them are unique to individual sites or groups of sites. The details are set out in Table 1.

The medieval and post-medieval occupation will be dealt with in another forthcoming post-Roman volume (report in prep).

The dating evidence sections

The pottery from contexts dated to each particular phase has been briefly tabulated by C J Going at the end of each phase discussion. Only the latest pieces are noted. Relevant coins, brooches etc are also listed. Those wishing further data are referred to the spot dating archive which notes salient forms and fabrics identified and the extent of their preservation. Forms (eg, G18) and fabrics (eg, **47**) are noted, based on the typologies devised for a complete study of the pottery from the *mansio* excavations (Going 1987), to which the reader is referred. A brief fabric list, however, is given below. Samian identification is by Dr W J Rodwell. Abreviations used are SG, South Gaulish, CG, Central Gaulish, EG, East Gaulish, VRW, *Verulamium* Region Ware.

The Romano-British Pottery Fabrics (after Going 1987)

2	Nene Valley colour-coat
3	Oxfordshire red colour-coat
4	Hadham oxidised red wares
5	Lyons ware
6	Lower Rhineland fabric 1
10	South East English glazed ware
12	?Local mica-dusted wares
14	Hadham white-slipped wares
21	Miscellaneous oxidised red wares
24	Nene Valley 'self-coloured' wares
26	Brockley Hill wares
27	Colchester buff ware
32	?North Kent grey wares
34	Fine Romanising wares
37	?Highgate grey wares
39	Fine grey wares
41	Black-Burnished 2
43	Alice Holt ware
44	Storage jar fabrics
45	Romanising grey wares
47	Sandy grey wares
48	Rettendon wares
50	?South Essex shell-tempered ware
51	Late shell-tempered ware
60	All samian

Acknowledgements

The excavations reported in this volume, with the exception of sites AS and CF1, were carried out between 1970 and 1973 by the then Chelmsford Excavation Committee, and its Secretary and Site Director, Mr P J Drury. Funds were provided by the Inspectorate of Ancient Monuments, Department of Environment, Chelmsford Borough Council, the Pilgrim Trust and the Essex County Council. Post-excavation work has been undertaken by Chelmsford Archaeological Trust, financed by the Historic Buildings and Monuments Commission for

Table 1 outline chronology of the main sites

Period	Date	Sites				
		K	M	D	AS	CF1
I	early prehistoric					
II	Iron Age					
—	AD 43					
III	Pre-Boudican					
—	SD 60/5					
IV		1 2 3				1 2
—	AD 90					
V		1 2		1 2		
—	AD 120/5					
VI				1 2		
—	AD 200/10					
VII	Temple	1C3 2C4 3 post-360/70	1 2	1 2	1 2	
—	AD 410/20					
VIII	Sub-Roman. Temple robbing					

England. I am grateful to all the above and to private donors for financial assistance, and to the individual site owners, their architects and builders, acknowledged in the various site reports, for their help and cooperation; all those who took part in the work, especially the supervisors, Miss J Secker, Messrs S R Bassett, S Loscoe-Bradley and P Sewter; those specialists who have contributed to this volume; Dan Biglin and the late Howard Young for their substantial contribution in recording watching briefs on the Inner Relief Road in 1970–71 (Site CR); Andrew Wallace for his assistance in spot dating the Roman pottery; and above all to Paul Drury for his invaluable help. He has commented on an earlier draft of this report, as a result of which it has been much improved, and I owe the identification of the 1st century temple on Site K to him. Any errors remain my responsibility.

The summaries of work undertaken by the Essex County Council Archaeological Section at Site AS and Site CF1 are included here thanks to the close cooperation of the Section and I am grateful to the site directors, Mr Robin Turner and Mr David Andrews respectively.

The site illustrations were drawn by Richard Bellamy, Lesley Collett, Paul Drury, Mark Duncan and Graham Reed; the small finds were drawn by Mark Duncan, Graham Reed, Frank Gardiner, John Callaghan and Susan Holden.

N P Wickenden
Chelmsford, 1989

I owe a particular debt to Peter Hawley, who organised the labour which made the 1970 excavations possible in highly adverse conditions and who is one of the best natural excavators I have ever encountered.

P J Drury

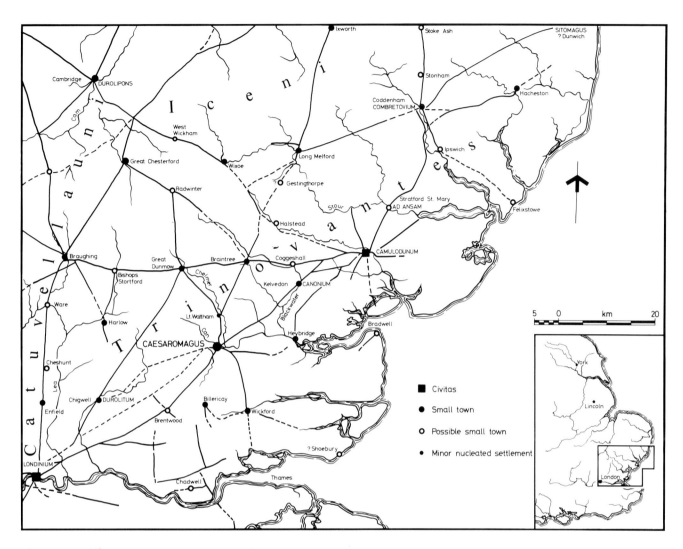

Figure 3 *The Trinovantian* civitas, *showing towns and principal roads, with a general location plan inset*

II Site D: 29–31 Rochford Road TL 710062

Introduction

In January-February 1970, five trial trenches were dug by machine (Fig 2) under the direction of P J Drury, to the south of Rochford Road, on the sites of numbers 29–31 and in neighbouring gardens, on land acquired by Chelmsford Corporation in advance of the construction of the Inner Relief Road roundabout. Since road surfaces and ditches were encountered in Trench 1 (Fig 4.S1), the area enclosed by trenches 1 and 2, and by the line of the access road from Goldlay Road to the roundabout was excavated.

Features which were subsequently excavated in the main site are dealt with below. Discrete features in the trial trenches were as follows:

Trench 2: 1st century shallow pit 292 (Figs 4.S2; 5)
Trench 3: Much post-medieval building and garden disturbances was encountered. A small gulley (302) ran perpendicular to the trench, 1.35m wide, and cut 0.45m into the gravel subsoil. It was filled with a dark grey pebbly silt. Otherwise signs of occupation were sparse. Pottery in the subsoil silt ranged from 1st to 4th century in date.
Trench 4: The natural brickearth was found at a depth of 1.05m, overlying orange gravel. Beneath approximately 0.30m of modern topsoil and rubble was a homogenous silt containing some Roman tile and a Colchester-ware mortarium (2nd century, Cat 309). One pit (307), 2.10m in diameter, was filled with a greyish brown silt with Roman tile in its primary fill.
Trench 5: Roman pottery (Cat 310), including a samian f27, and tile were found in the silt. One gulley was found, 322, approximately 0.90m wide with a shovel slot in the bottom, and c 1.05m deep.

The excavated features

Periods I–II: Prehistoric

A small number of flint flakes and a possible truncated blade indicate very limited prehistoric activity on the site; no prehistoric pottery was recovered. For further details, see Healey *et al* forthcoming.

Period V.1: c AD 90–100 (Fig 5)

The excavated area appears to have been exploited in the 1st century for its brickearth deposit overlying the gravel; amorphous lobes of two large hollows were dug and backfilled with a leached brickearth and loam admixture. Not all of these were completely excavated. Pit D 123 (Fig 4.S6) was cut c 0.50m into the natural brickearth, stopping at the underlying gravel. Its fill contained an amount of slag and a large group of hand-made, ledge-rimmed jars, dated to c AD 70–90 and almost certainly production waste from a nearby, but unlocated, pottery kiln. A few small overfired wasters were found. Large sherds of the same assemblage were also found in the surrounding brickearth hollows (42, 71 and 76; Fig 4.S3, 6), as well as re-used in the clay structure of the later ovens 47 and 92. For a discussion of the pottery, see p 97–8. D 51 (Fig 4.S6) contained a little 1st century pottery and some cremated bone. D 346 in the north yielded nothing, and was less than 0.30m deep (Fig 4.S10); it may be connected purely with pre-road consolidation (see below).

Many fragments of a carinated and ribbed bowl of green glass with a folded tubular rim (see Fig 44.7, p 85) came from the hollow lobes 51, 118 and 123, as well as from later features (pit 20, ditch 23, robber trench 74) and subsoils in the immediate area.

Dating evidence

51 (Pit) *Samian* f18/31, CG, Trajanic (Cat 68). *Other pottery* Imitation Gallo-Belgic platter (**45**); local imitation London ware bowl, crude circular stamps below small cordon below flat-topped rim, red-brown micaceous fabric, late 1st–early 2nd century (Cat 68); G18–20 jar fragments; ?N Kent grey ware poppy head beaker rim, probably Flavian-Trajanic

71 (Hollow) *Samian* f15/17, SG, Flavian; f18, SG, late Flavian (both burnt. Cat 77); f18R, 42, probably SG, late Flavian, burnt; f27, CG, Trajanic-Hadrianic (Cat 72). *Other pottery*, graffito on jar base (**39**)

118 (lobe under Oven 92) *Samian* f15/17 or 18, SG, Neronian. Stamped OFNIGR (Table 6, No.12). *Other pottery* miniature form, R2.1

123 (Pit) *Samian* f27, SG, late Flavian (Cat 98); f18/31, Trajanic (Cat 98); f27, CG, probably Hadrianic, stamped 'Immunus'. (Table 6, No.8) (both Cat 133). *Other pottery* For a discussion of the G5 jars in a local kiln fabric, see p 97–8. Other jars in the same fabric came from oven 47 (Period V) and ditch 23 (Period VI.1), which both cut Pit 123; rim of G5.1 (**50**), Flavian (Cat 97)

Pottery from 1st century features was on the whole scant. The absence of definite 2nd century or later finds suggest they were dug, or backfilled, before the early 2nd century.

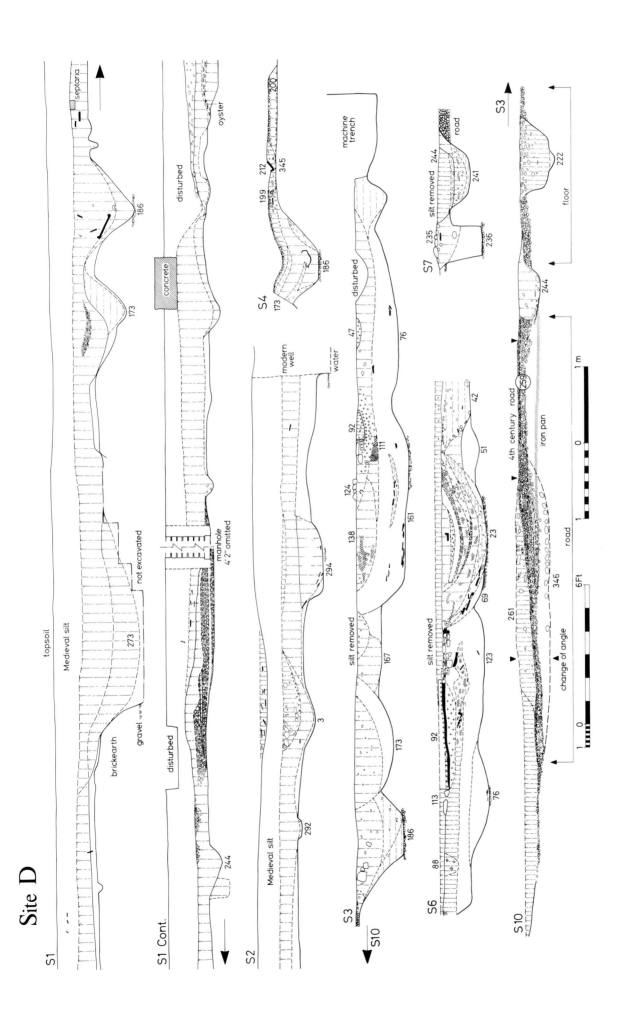

Figure 4 Site D: Sections S1–4, 6, 7, 10; for key see Fig 6

8

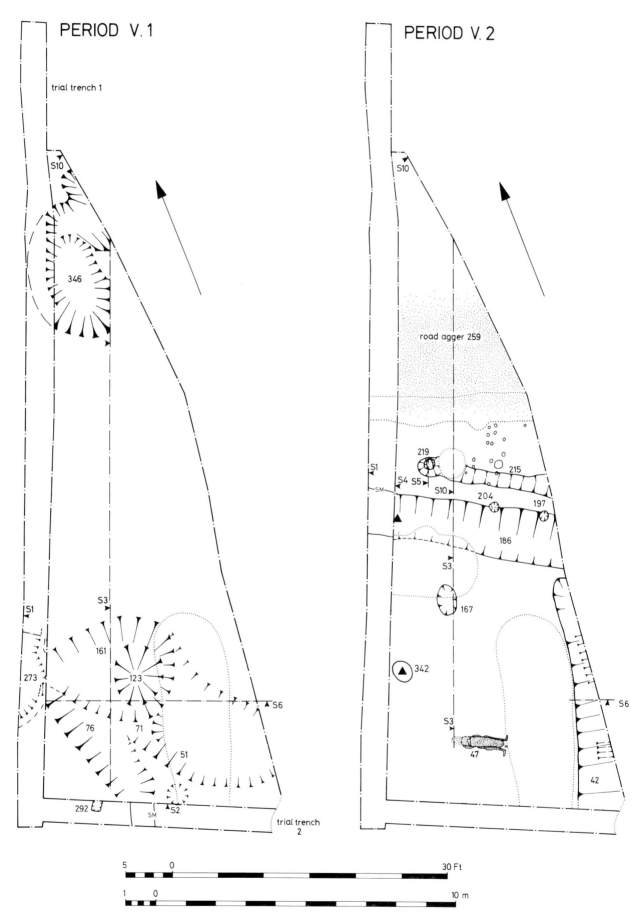

Figure 5   Site D: Period V. Phases 1 and 2

Site D

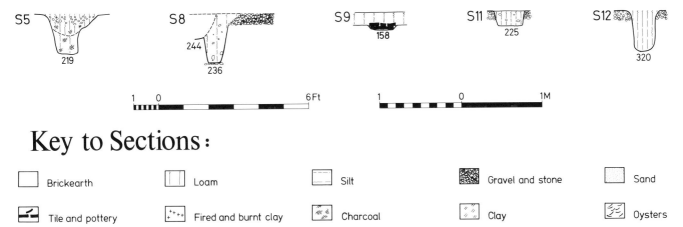

S5 219

S8 244 236

S9 158

S11 225

S12 320

1 0 6Ft

1 0 1M

Key to Sections:

Brickearth

Loam

Silt

Gravel and stone

Sand

Tile and pottery

Fired and burnt clay

Charcoal

Clay

Oysters

Figure 6   Site D: Sections S5, 8, 9, 11, 12; key to the sections

Period V.2: c AD 100 – 120/5 (Fig 5)

The road

Ditch 186 (Fig 4.S1,3,4), was the southern ditch of a road running in an east-west direction, *c* 0.65m deep, flat-bottomed, and cut down to, rather than into, the natural gravel below the brickearth. A light brownish-grey, rainwashed silt with much brickearth, clearly deposited from the north (road) side (Fig 4.S10), quickly accumulated at the end of the 1st or beginning of the 2nd century. The main fill, a clayey loam, containing a jar possibly reused as a cremation (Fig 4.S4), belongs to the early-mid 2nd century (Period VI.1). Two small post-holes (197, 204) were found along the northern lip of the ditch.

Gravel metalling (probably later in date) starts on the northern lip of the ditch (*c* 0.07m thick), and extends northwards for *c* 9.7m (32 feet). The metalling, 259, only becomes thicker, however, further north (*c* 0.23m thick) where there is a distinct camber and worn surface, 5–6m wide (Figs 4.S10; 5), before tailing off once again in the apex of the excavated triangular site. No northern road ditch was found, as was the case with the side road leading to the *mansio* (Drury 1988). The gap of 3–3.5m between the southern road ditch and the start of the *agger* is consistent with other roads in Chelmsford (Drury 1988). The road profile and width compares favourably with those of major roads published by Margary (1967, 500–501), and suggests that the Chelmsford road was designed as a main thoroughfare, rather than as a small side street. Indeed, Figs 1–3 indicate that this was the main route to the port at Heybridge, and to the Dengie Peninsula.

The road was constructed apparently on virgin ground for the main part. A shallow gulley, 215 (0.10m deep), lay just to the north of, and parallel to, ditch 186. The gulley terminates on the west in a post-hole 219 (Fig 6.S5), but their exact relationship was destroyed by a 4th century pit 222. The gulley contained some cremated bone, and

pottery dated *c* AD 90–135, consistent with a Trajanic/Hadrianic construction of the road.

Immediately prior to construction, the Period V.1 hollow, 346, was filled in with a layer of large cobbles capped by a deposit of clean brickearth (Fig 4.S10). The road agger sealed the original ground surface which survived under the gravel metalling as a leached, iron-panned brickearth (Fig 4.S10).

Whilst Slot 244 was late 3rd–4th century in date, it is feasible that is was a recut of a small gulley designed to run rainwater off the agger surface. Indeed a coin of Domitian and early Roman pottery were also found in its fill. If this were the case, then a matching gulley on the north side of the road is evident in the section of the first trial trench (Fig 4.S1).

Since the road was in continuous use, finds from its surface generally belong to its latest phase, and include Rettendon ware, a coin of Claudius II, a copper alloy pin (Fig 40.27), and, interestingly, an iron linch pin (Fig 42.2).

A shallow ditch 42 (Fig 4.S6) ran southwards from ditch 186, at an angle of 110°. Within the angle, oven 47 was constructed on the filling of pit 51. It was later dismantled and cut by ditch 23, though the sides of its firing tunnel survived up to *c* 0.10m above its floor which remained largely *in situ* as a reddened burnt clay surface, Its clay sides, *c* 0.30m apart, were fragmentary where the backing walls had been removed (Figs 4.S3; 8; Pl I).

A possible unurned cremation (Cat 342) was lying disturbed at a depth of 0.60m and comprised a circular scatter of cremated bone and charcoal. Pit 167 was dug at the end of the phase (Fig 4.S3).

Dating evidence

42 (Gulley) *Samian* f27, SG, Flavian (Cat 87); f18/31, CG, Trajanic (Cat 83); f18/31R, f18/31 x4, CG, Hadrianic-Antonine (all burnt. Cat 25). *Other pottery* decorated imitation f29 (**34/45**), ?Flavian-Trajanic (Fig 60.30); bead-rimmed dish (**47**), *c* AD

Plate I   Site D: Oven 47 (Photo: P J Drury)

125–50 (Fig 60.43); everted-rimmed jar (**47**), probably 1st–early 2nd century (Fig 60.46)
47 (Oven) *Pottery* G18–20 jars (**45**); G5, ?Flavian-Trajanic (kiln fabric)
167 (Pit) *Pottery* bead–rim dish, *c* AD 120+
186 (Road ditch) *Samian*　**L2** Scrap SG, Flavian, burnt; scrap EG, Antonine (Cat 207)
　　　　　　　　　　L3 f27, SG, Flavian (Cat 196); scrap CG, 2nd century (Cat 208)
　　Other pottery　**L4** N. Gallic or Colchester, bag-shaped beaker (H20–7) *c* AD 120+ (Cat 191)
　　　　　　　　　　L5 Bead rim dishes x 2 (**45/7**), *c* AD 120+
215 (Gulley) *Pottery c* AD 90–135. Bead rim dishes, *c* AD120+
219 (Pit) *Pottery* Scraps, 1st–2nd century
259 (Road surface) *Coin* Claudius II, AD 268–70

Period VI.1 *c AD 120/5 – mid 2nd century (Figs 7, 8)*

During the early 2nd century, Oven 47 was replaced by oven 92, on a slightly different alignment. It also overlies a key-hole-shaped hollow 111, presumably an earlier attempt at an oven, *c* 0.30m deep and filled with dark loam and charcoal (Fig 4.S3), and contiguous pits 88, 110 and 116, with similar dark fills. The floor of the new oven (Fig 8) consisted of a thin skin of brickearth, burnt red, lying on a raft of *imbrices*; the underlying soil had also been reddened by the heat (Fig 4.S3,6). The sides of the firing tunnel were 0.30m apart; the north side was intact with its backing wall of tile, stone and re-used lava quern fragments surviving to a height of *c* 0.15m; the backing wall on the south had mostly been removed and the fired clay lining had subsequently slipped. The western end

of the oven had been truncated by a later structure; the eastern area, sub-circular in plan, was made up of a raft of flint, tile, *septaria* and a fragment of storage jar, set in a brickearth matrix, burnt red. Under this surface raft were more, slightly larger, cobbles. The end had been truncated by ditch 23; the section shows the spread of oven ash and tiles cascading down the ditch side (Fig 4.S6) as this eroded.

Enclosure
The oven probably did not have a very long life, but was cut into, as noted above, by ditch 23. This was *c* 2.10m wide with a northern butt end, forming the corner of an enclosure (Fig 8) along with the butt end of ditch 173, also *c* 2.10m wide, which cut the now-filled road ditch 186. Ditch 23 (Fig 4.S6) was *c* 0.60m deep, bottoming on natural gravel, and of flattened U-shape profile. Ditch 173 (Fig 4.S3) was *c* 0.45m deep, also with a rounded profile; both were backfilled towards the mid 2nd century on pottery evidence. Ditch 23 yielded an almost complete samian platter, stamped ROPPVSFE (?Cremation), as well as another partial stamp of the same die.

A number of other features should also be dated to this phase of activity:

Pit 20; pit 88; pit 138, sealed by a later 2nd century structural cill-wall, *c* 0.30m deep and filled with a dark brown pebbly charcoally loam (Fig 4.S3); sub-rectangular pit 209, which cut the road ditch 186; post-pit 218 containing post-hole 221; pit 236 (*c* AD 140/50+) cut by later pit 235; 236 had a deep (0.60m) narrow shaft (*c* 0.20–0.37m wide) and was filled with a silty loam (Figs 4.S7;6.S8).

Dating evidence
20 (Pit) *Samian* f18–18/31, SG, Flavian-Trajanic; f18/31R–31R, CG, Antonine, stamped METTI.MA (Table 6, No 10)
23 (Ditch) *Coin* 1st-2nd dupondius. *Samian* f37, CG, early 2nd century (Cat 30); f18/31, CG, Trajanic (Cat 50); f18/31, CG, Trajanic (Cat 54); f18/31, CG, Trajanic-Hadrianic, stamped ROPPVS FE (near complete, ?Cremation, Table 6, No 15) (Cat 140). A second partial stamp of the same die came from Cat 58 (Table 6, No 16); f37, CG, Trajanic-Hadrianic, f37, CG, Hadrianic (both Cat 109); f37, CG, Hadrianic-Antonine (Cat 115); f33, CG, Antonine (Cat 139); f33a, CG, stamped VIDVCOS.F, (Table 6, No 23), *c* AD 100–120 (Cat 140)
Other pottery G5 Jars from Pit 123 (Period IV); bead rim dishes, *c* AD 120+; ?Cologne region bag-shaped beaker, ?Colchester colour coated ware, Antonine; mortarium, stamped LITVGENVSF (Fig 57.2), all Cat 54
173 (Ditch) *Samian* f27, CG, Trajanic-Hadrianic; f79, CG, late Antonine (Cat 177)
209 (Pit) *Pottery* a few sherds, probably 2nd century
218/221 (Post-pit) *Pottery* 2nd century fragments

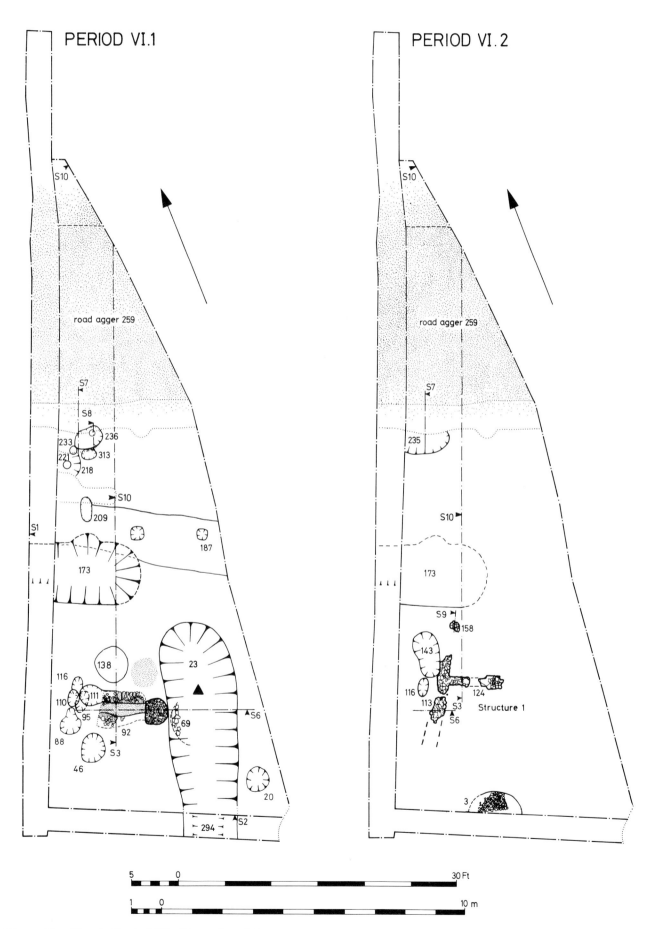

Figure 7   Site D: Period VI. Phase 1 and 2

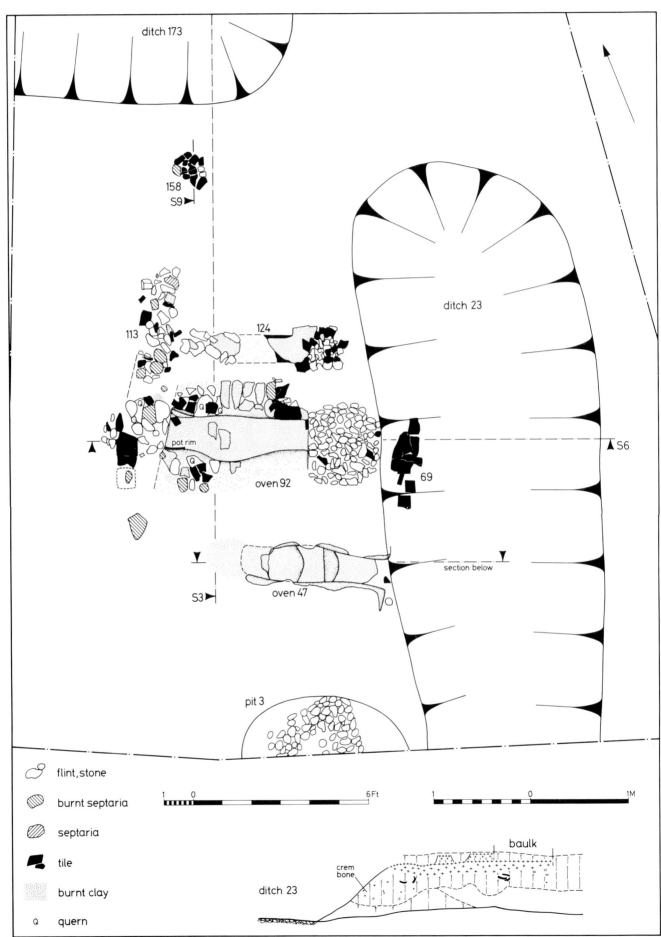

ditch 173

158
S9 ▶

113

124

oven 92

pot rim

69

ditch 23

▲ S6

section below

▼

S3 ▶

oven 47

pit 3

flint, stone

burnt septaria

septaria

tile

burnt clay

Q   quern

1   0   6Ft

1   0   1M

baulk

crem
bone

ditch 23

Figure 8   Site D: The Period VI.1 enclosure and ovens

Plate II   Site D: Structure 1 (Photo: P J Drury)

Period VI.2: 2nd half 2nd Century: Frontage Structure (Figs 7, 8)

A building (Structure 1) was constructed south of the road following the backfilling of the enclosure ditch, though its remains were fragmentary due to robbing and erosion. Ditch 173 may have remained as a hollow.

Structure 1 (Figs 7, 8, Pl II)

The structure's foundations cut away part of oven 92, and comprised a length of masonry cill-wall 124 (Fig 4.S3), 0.25m wide, which terminated at the eastern end in a wider plinth, *c* 0.38m wide; this met a second cill-wall, 113 (Fig 4.S6), at an angle, *c* 0.30m wide, but surviving to a lesser extent and mostly robbed out, the robbing trench being rather indistinct (*c* 0.50m wide, backfilled with rubble). A patch of masonry to the north, 158 (Fig 6.S9), is on the same line and is either a sole surviving trace of the continuing wall, a respond or a door jamb. However, no evidence survived for masonry continuing to the north of 158.

The masonry footings of the cill-walls comprised nodular flint, *septaria*, tile and storage jar sherds set in a matrix of brown loam and fired clay patches; two courses of tile survived generally. Since the building materials show no sign of burning, the fired clay in the matrix was presumably re-used from the ovens. Pottery evidence suggests a date for its construction in the late 2nd century. Its function is unknown; the two component walls, meeting as they do at such an angle, are not necessarily of the same phase (see p 127).

Associated pits probably include 143, an area of dark pebbly silt, from 0.15 to 0.25m below cleared level; 3, part of a large pit or ditch butt end, *c* 0.28m deep, filled with a charcoally silt and capped by a layer of cobbles, 0.05m thick (Fig 4.S2), possibly structural and later in date; 46, a nebulous hollow filled with dark loam and fired clay specks. Pit 235, further to the north, overlay pit 236, and was distinguished by its rubble fill (Fig 4.S7).

Dating evidence

3 (?Pit) *Pottery* bowl (**34**). ?Flavian-Trajanic, Fig 60.29; Fabrics **12**, **27** (Cat 7)
88 (Pit) *Pottery* ?N Kent grey ware poppyhead beaker, 2nd century
113 (Structure 1) *Pottery* a fragment of a Rettendon ware base (**48**) may date the robbing, ie post- *c* AD 280
124 (Structure 1) *Pottery* the wall structure contained fragments of storage jar (**44**), effectively undatable but probably not post-2nd century

Period VII.1: 3rd Century (Fig 9)

In the 3rd century, the southern part of the road was encroached on by Structure 2, with a new floor metalling, 220.

Structure 2

The new structure was built in a different manner to Structure 1, using wooden cill beams set in shallow slots. Slot 212, *c* 0.45m wide and *c* 0.10m deep, cut into a gravel surface 199, the underlying loam 200, and bottomed on a patch of the earlier metalling 345 (Fig 4.S4). A second slot, 225 (Fig 6.S11), ran perpendicular to 212, 2 metres to the east; this was 0.40m wide and 0.17m deep and was cut by Ditch 244. It is, however, possible that Ditch 244 originated in this phase as a small roadside gulley, or as a beam slot of the structure, thus forming a rectangular building, internally *c* 2.00m wide and at least 3.65m in length. In this case, feature 241 may have acted as a structural post-hole; it was *c* 0.45m deep.

Pit 3 (Period VI.2) was possibly capped at this point with a layer of cobbling (Fig 4.S2). Nearby was a post-hole 19, 0.40m deep below cleared level.

Demise of Structure 2

The building may have been destroyed by fire at the end of the 3rd century. Slot 212 was cut by a shallow pit, 213, which contained fragments of tile and much fired clay, presumably burnt structural daub. Pit 241 was filled with a charcoally silty loam with fired clay flecking (Fig 4.S7) and contained a coin of Gallienus, late 3rd century pottery, and human cranial fragments. Ditch 244 also yielded ten cranial fragments, suggestive of a tragic end to the building.

Dating evidence

19 (Post-hole) *Pottery* Sherds of Rettendon ware (**48**), probably late 3rd century+
212 (Slot) *Pottery* G9 Jar (**47**), 2nd century (Cat 217)
220 (Gravel metalling) *Coin* Antoninus Pius, AD 138–161 (Cat 314)
225 (Slot) *Pottery* Sherd of Fabric **48**, probably late 3rd century+
241 (Pit) *Coin* Gallienus, AD 260–268. *Pottery* Fabric **48**, fragments only of closed forms, late 3rd century+ (Cat 241,243)

14

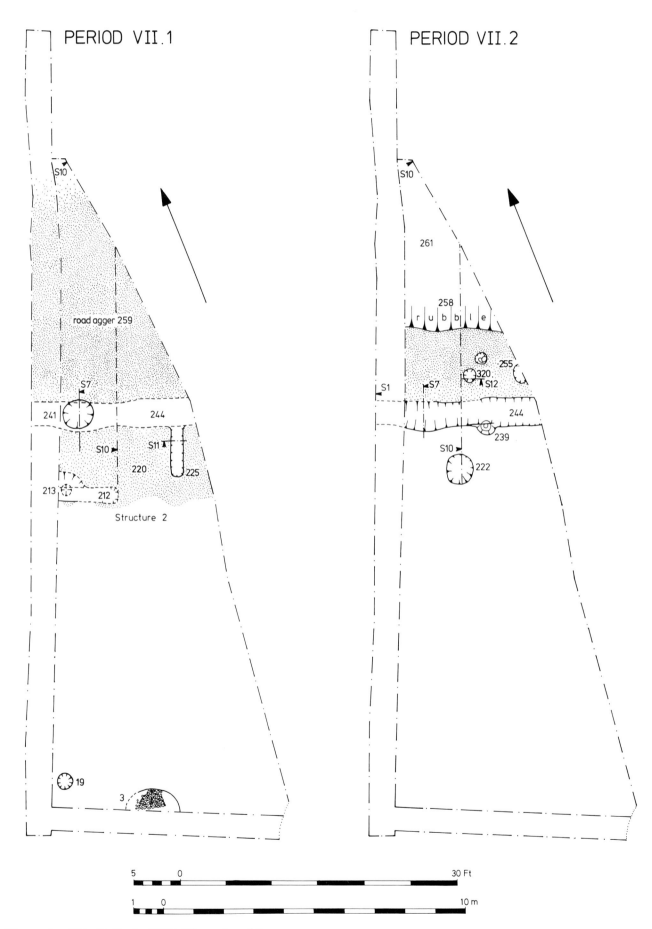

PERIOD VII.1

S10

road agger 259

S7

241 | 244

S10 ▸ S11 ▸

220 | 225

213 | 212

Structure 2

19

3

PERIOD VII.2

S10

261

258

r u b b l e

320. 255

S1 S7 ▸ S12

244

239

S10 ▸

222

5   0   30 Ft

1   0   10 m

Figure 9   Site D: Period VII. Phase 1 and 2

244 (Slot) *Coin* Domitian AD 81–96. *Pottery* Scraps, but including two sherds in Fabric **4**, probably late 3rd century+

Period VII.2 4th Century (Fig 9)

The site was virtually abandoned by the 4th Century. The road was now reduced to a narrow *agger* (Fig 4.10) as a silty loam 261 gradually accumulated over the northern part of the road surface which had sunk into an earlier feature (brickearth pit 346) in the northern apex of the excavated area (Fig 4.S10). The silty loam contained much tile and stone rubble, an abraded legionary apron strap (Fig 39.2), and two further fragments of human cranium. Ditch 244 was possibly still in use and the road metalling lay right up against its northern tip. The ditch was *c* 0.90m wide and *c* 0.20m deep with a flat (in the east) to dish-shaped bottom (Fig 4.S10), which cut earlier road metalling.

Other later Roman features include pit 222, 0.40m deep, (Fig 4.S10); post-hole 239, 0.60m deep, cutting the gravel metalling and probably ditch 244 (pottery very small, abraded sherds, and a glass bead). Several post-holes and stake-holes were excavated which cut the gravel metalling, but none contained any finds, except 320 (Fig 6.S12) (coin of the House of Constantine). They do not appear to form any patterns.

The late Roman subsoils contained coins of Arcadius and the House of Theodosius, and some late shell-tempered pottery (**51**), dated post *c* AD 360/70, indicating some late 4th century activity, and roadside usage.

Dating evidence
222 (Pit) *Pottery* Funnel-necked beaker rim (**2**), probably 4th century; closed form (**4**), probably 4th century (Cat 224); 'melon' beaker (**47**), probably 4th century (Cat 224)
239 (Post-hole) *Pottery* abraded sherd of a ?closed form (**4**), probably 4th century
261 (Hollow) *Pottery* a late, and mostly abraded group including: **2**, funnel necked beaker fragments, and a B6 (Cat 262), both probably late 4th century; **3**, a f38 base; Fabric **4**; also **47**, B6 (Cats 261 and 262), and sherds of Alice Holt storage jar (**43**), *c* AD 360+
320 (Stake-hole) *Coin* House of Constantine, AD 345–348

Post-Roman activity
The alluvial silt (*c* 0.45m thick) which truncated the late Roman levels during the early medieval period has already been referred to. Above this lay *c* 0.30m of 19th century hardcore and concrete. Only one feature survived: pit 33, a 19th century rubbish pit, containing building rubble, slate and mortar.

III   The temple site: Site K: 1–8 Rochford Road TL 710063

Introduction

Two machine-cut trial trenches were excavated by P J Drury in February-March 1970 on the site of the Thomas John's Alms Houses, 1–8 Rochford Road, in order to gauge the archaeological potential prior to the construction of the Inner Relief Road roundabout. Features found in these trenches included part of the drystone foundations of a timber building, and, in the northern extremity, a foundation trench from which all masonry had been robbed (ie the temple). The trench was then extended, and a second parallel foundation trench with some masonry still *in situ* was located (temple *cella*). Because of the obvious importance of these finds, a large area was subsequently excavated from April–July 1970, and February–April 1971, by the kind permission of the landowners, the Trustees of the Almshouses and the then Chelmsford Corporation. Thanks are due to the Trustees' clerk, Mr R A Rolfe of Messrs Balch & Balch, and the former Ministry of Public Buildings and Works who funded the excavations.

An interim report on the excavations was published in 1972 (Drury 1972). Some of the conclusions reached in it are substantially modified here.

The excavated features

Topsoil and building debris overlay an average of *c* 0.60m of alluvial silt, which in turn overlay truncated Romano-British levels or the natural brickearth. The nature and date of the alluvial action giving rise to these conditions is discussed briefly on p 141. These levels were carefully removed by JCB to a depth of *c* 0.75m, that is to the top of the Roman levels. Features were filled with a dark brown, brickearth-derived, loam, unless specific fills are noted.

Periods I–III: Prehistoric–early Roman (Fig 10)

A total of about 400 flints, mainly unworked bladelike flakes, was found in residual contexts. The artifacts show wide cultural affinity, ranging from early Mesolithic microliths to late Neolithic transverse arrowheads, and the cores show a similar chronological spread. Some 83 sherds of prehistoric pottery were found, mostly very small, abraded and formless in a flint- (or sand) tempered fabric, and generally dated to the Late Bronze Age or Early Iron Age. Thirty sherds came from a leached brickearth subsoil, 135, whilst another eleven came from contemporary stake and post-holes.

The patches of white leached brickearth apparently represent the vestiges of a buried soil, capping an area in excess of 38m long and 9m wide at its eastern end (Fig 10). This area was upstanding above the general level by *c* 0.10–0.20m, and Drury believed (1972, 14–15) that it was the remnants of a low Iron Age mound or platform, formed by scraping brickearth from the surrounding area (in the absence of ditches or quarries). There was heavy ironpanning at the interface of the natural and leached brickearth and this has been noticed on other sites in Chelmsford, noticeably Site S (Drury 1988, fig.42.S4). A large number of stake-holes (Fig 10), varying from *c* 0.07

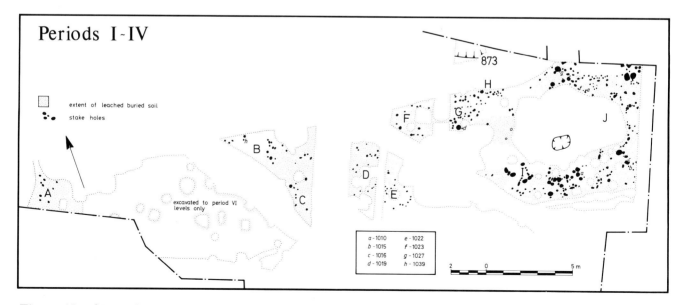

Figure 10   Site K: buried old land surface and features

to 0.30m in diameter, had been driven into the buried soil, but did not penetrate the underlying natural brickearth. Drury comments on the fact that the Roman timber structures (the 'Corridor') closely follows the outline of the 'mound' (1972,15) and suggests that this indicates that it was still visible in the early Roman period. His statement hints at what must be the true explanation of this phenomenon: the prehistoric brickearth subsoil was leached, sealed and preserved firstly by upcast from digging ditch 705, and later by the gravel floors of the Roman corridor structure (compare Fig 10 and Fig 15), whilst the same subsoil where not sealed has been totally eroded away. The same effect can be seen on Site D (Fig 4.S10).

Whilst the existence of a prehistoric mound can be discounted, the plethora of stake-holes still probably indicate prehistoric or proto-Roman occupation, contemporary with the preserved brickearth subsoil, 135. Only small areas are undisturbed by Roman and later features (Fig 10), but concentrations may outline buildings and palisades (eg A–J). At the eastern end in particular an area 4 x 8 m was marked by a number of larger stake-holes, unfortunately disturbed by medieval pitting. In the bottom of the disturbance was a steep-sided, flat-bottomed pit, 0.75m deep, filled with clean iron-stained brickearth, distinctive against the natural gravel encountered below the brickearth subsoil at this level. Those stake-holes yielding LBA/EIA pottery and/or flints were 1010, 1015, 1016, 1019, 1022, 1023, 1027, and 1039. A hollow, 873, c 0.10m deep which contained flints and charcoal, was cut by ditch 705 (Period IV), which included 1st century pottery in its fill.

Details of the prehistoric pottery and flints, and a further consideration of the stake-hole structure, will appear in Healey et al forthcoming.

Period IV Phase 1: Immediately Post-Boudican (Fig 11)

The site was reoccupied in the mid 1st century AD. Three (perhaps four) post-built structures, aligned differently and not all contemporary, have been tentatively identified. Whether they represent buildings or not is debatable, and they have all suffered serious disturbance by later features. All the post-holes lie below the earliest gravel 257 associated with Period IV.3.

Structure 3 comprises post-holes 217, 272, 300, 372, 413, 434, 929 and 972. These ranged from c 0.10m to c 0.38m in depth, and were generally filled with a light silty loam. They contained 1st century AD Roman pottery. In addition 272 contained a lump of glass paste, sub-cuboidal in shape, possibly a tessera (Fig 44.32). Structure 4, whose plan overlaps that of Structure 3, as reconstructed here, comprises post-holes 374, 389 (hollow only), 391, 511, 539 and 973. A hollow, 506, c 0.05m deep, lay inside. Their depths are shallower (c 0.05m–c 0.17m), but with similar fills.

They also contained 1st century Roman pottery, and 389 and 391 produced fragments of tegulae, and 539 a small piece of iron slag (5 gms). Structure 5 yielded Roman pottery from only one post-hole, 498; all were between 0.05m and 0.12m in depth. Two other post-holes further west appear to belong to this phase, but yielded no finds.

Possibly associated with these structures, ?forming a northern boundary, was slot 535, c 0.15m deep with a rounded profile and similarly sealed by the gravel paving. It contained a group of pottery dated c AD 60–100. However, it is more likely that this feature was a drain, delimiting the gravel path in Period IV.3.

In the southern part of the site, a number of intercutting pits were dug in the 1st century, the earliest of which, dating to this phase, was 69.

Dating evidence
The pottery from these contexts was extremely sparse and fragmentary with the exception of the material from slot 535. Only one sherd of samian (Cat 272, ?intrusive) was recovered. For the most part, contexts yielded scraps of Fabric 45 and occasionally 47, less frequently 44. Identifiable material is listed below
272 (Post-hole) Samian f33, CG, 2nd century. Other pottery Fabrics 44, 45, 4
372 (Post-hole) Pottery sherd G18 (oxidised 45), pre-Flavian-Flavian
506 (Hollow) Pottery Scrap grog-tempered storage jar
535 (Slot) Pottery Platter A1–6, jar G18 (Cat 543), G20 (Cat 544), beaker H1.3–4 (Cat 543), all Fabric 34/45; lid K (47). Flavian-end 1st century
972 (Post-hole) Samian f18, SG, early Flavian
973 (Post-hole) Samian f27, SG, early Flavian

Period IV Phase 2: Pre- c AD 80 (Figs 11–12)

Period IV.1 was of short duration, probably less than a decade. In Period IV.2 a ditched enclosure was formed, of which the northern ditch, 705, and the eastern ditch, 205, lay within the excavated area. It is possible that the gap at the north-east corner represents an entrance facing east. It is suggested that this enclosure was the earliest evidence of a religious precinct on the site, and that the area remained such, though in several different forms, for the rest of the Roman period. For a full discussion of its significance and alignment, see p 127–8.

Ditch 205
The eastern ditch, 205, ran for 7m inside the excavated area cutting through the earlier Structure 3, and was 2.23m at its widest point. It was c 1.06m deep on average, reaching a maximum of 1.32m (Fig 13.S13–16). It was filled with a primary deposit of washed-in brickearth, V; above this were the main fill layers of accumulated dark

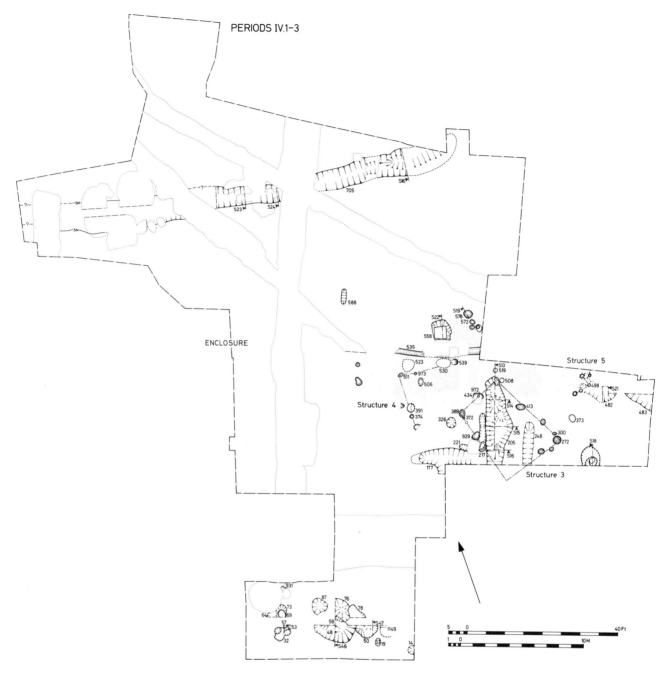

Figure 11   Site K: Period IV. Phases 1–3

silts, IV, with lenses of gravel, fired clay and charcoal; above these was a brickearth loam, III, possibly deliberate infilling, sealing the ditch before gravel metalling was laid down over it (II).

Quantities of pottery were found in the ditch fill and are discussed in detail elsewhere (p 93–7). The earliest primary deposits indicate a construction date before c AD 60–75; the main fill accumulating for perhaps a decade, up to c AD 75/85. The gravels which subsequently seal the ditch (I, II) can then be dated immediately after c AD 75/85. Other important and relevant objects were also found in the ditch, including in the weathering primary fills some fuel ash slag, a twisted iron shaft (?ladle or shovel; Fig 42.3), a decayed copper alloy stud, a

complete copper alloy incised ?votive bar (Fig 39.5; cf Wickenden 1986), a two–piece Colchester brooch (Fig 37.12) of the mid 1st century AD, a part of a melon bead (Fig 44.23), a fragment of a buffware oil-lamp with decorated discus (Fig 46.1, 1st Century AD), two fragments of a buffware lamp chimney with stamped decoration (Fig 46.13), a wheel graffito on a jar (Fig 58.7), an 'X' graffito, an imitation Gallo-Belgic platter stamp, INDATIOS (No 6, p105–6), and a number of tile fragments (*tegulae, imbrices* and bonding tile) lying on the bottom of the butt end; in the main silts were found a glass flask handle and a further three copper alloy brooches — two Nauheim derivatives of the mid 1st Century AD and a hinged head-stud brooch with enamel decoration (Figs 37.4–5; 38.24). For a discussion on the distribution of the brooches and lamp chimney fragments, see below. It is clear, however, that the lamp chimney, votive bar and perhaps the oil lamp can all have liturgical connotations.

The ditch also yielded a sizable assemblage of animal bone (see Section VIII, especially Table 17). This included a minimum number of 48 sheep (based on mandibles), with 7 male skulls and 2 female, an ox horn core, and an isolated dog skull. A distinct lack of waste bones and a preponderance of meat-bearing bones was noticed. In addition, 49% of the sheep from Period IV deposits (mainly ditch 205) were killed in their first year; 57.3% of the mandibles exhibited a secondary foramen, and 42% had a calculus deposit, possibly indications of a particular breed.

It is possible that ditch 205 did not continue much further to the south, but turned a corner to the west just south of the limit of excavation. The main evidence for this is the L-shaped ditch 221, 0.20m deep, and containing 1st century pottery, slag and tile; and ditch 177, c 1.05m wide x 0.71m deep, filled with a homogeneous weathered brickearth containing pottery dated c 60–100 in its lower fill (and later than 80 in its upper), slag and *tegulae* fragments. Together, ditches 221 and 177 might mark a western return angle for ditch 205, but this is not certain.

To the east of 205 is another smaller gulley, 248, unfortunately not clearly definable. Other nearby features include post-hole 326 (0.20m deep; pottery c AD 65/70–120), and hollows 523 and 530 (0.05m deep cut into the brickearth subsoil, below the gravel metalling, containing pottery c AD 60–120).

Ditch 705

The northern ditch, 705, ran for c 36.2m inside the excavated area (Fig 13.S17, 23–5); it was substantially disturbed by later features, but was c 1.72m wide and c 0.30–0.50m deep on average. The butt end was deeper, c 1.06m, and here its primary fill was of clean brickearth clay mixed with gravel, possibly a deliberate lining over the natural gravel so that the ditch would retain water (Drury 1972, 16). Its main fill was similar to that of 205, comprising a grey ashy, sludge-like, brickearth-derived loam, with lenses of charcoal, into which later gravel surfaces had sunk. Finds from the main fill included pottery dated c AD 60–100, slag and furnace lining, a copy of Claudius I and a plate brooch, probably Claudian-Neronian in date (Fig 38.26). The faunal assemblage (see Section VIII) includes remains of cow, ponies, a large horse, a human ankle bone, and an infant tibia.

Ditch 705 was cut by several later features including slots 678, 771 and 812 (Period V.1) slot 644, hollow 717, well pit 820 and hearths 708, 733, 808 and 1034. The line of ditch 705 forms the northern edge of the surviving leached brickearth, already described. It would indicate that the upcast from the ditch was spread over the ground surface rather than forming a distinct bank.

The votive deposit (Fig 12)

The four brooches in the silting fill of ditch 205, as well as the two fragments of a lamp chimney referred to above are part of a group of 13 brooches, other objects of copper alloy and fragments of the same lamp chimney which were scattered in the early soils to the east of the ditch. These layers comprise:
a) the earliest subsoil, 258, (Fig 13.S20), immediately above the natural brickearth
b) the first orange gravel metalling (257, Period IV.3, c AD 80/90; Fig 13.S19–21; Fig 18.S40), of good quality, but thin and sporadic as it tails away
c) the loamy soil (260) beyond the southern limit of the metalling, east of ditch 205.

The brooches consist of a Nauheim derivative (Fig 37.3, soil 260; two Hod Hill types (Fig 37.7, earliest silt 258; Fig 37.6, silt 465 (see Fig 13.S20)), four two-piece Colchester examples (Fig 37.10, soil 260; Fig 37.11, silt 258 (on natural brickearth); Fig 37.15, soil 260 (on brickearth); Fig 38.20, silt 240 below later gravel metalling 237); an enamelled sprung brooch with toothed bow (Fig 38.23, soil 260); and a lozenge-shaped plate brooch (Fig 38.25, silt 465). Two brooch pins came from the same layers (silt 258; Hollow 483).

Other objects of copper alloy include a pin (Fig 40.41, soil 260); a decorated 1st century stud of a well-known military type (Fig 39.3, primary gravel paving 257, which also produced a coin copy of Claudius I and pottery, dated c AD 60–100); two finger-rings (Fig 39.12, soil 260; Fig 39.13, silt 465); and a complete bracelet (Fig 40.16, soil 260.) In addition, 2 coins of Vespasian and one of Domitian were found in the silt, 465, over the primary metalling, and the gravel layers laid over ditch 205 in Periods V–VI also contained a two-piece Colchester brooch (Fig 38.19, Cat 403); a pin (Fig 40.35) and a decorated finger-ring (Fig 39.11, Cat 356) with Flavian parallels.

For further objects from Site CF1, from a ditch which must represent the western boundary of the enclosure, see Figure 34 and p 56.

Whilst some of this material comes from the lowest gravel 257 (IV.3), and the silt over it, it has been dealt with at length since it obviously forms a considerable early Roman discrete assemblage. The 13 brooches (including those in ditch 205) can all be dated between the middle and the last quarter of the 1st Century AD, as can the coins, 'military' stud and the decorated finger-ring. Many are in near mint condition. When and whence did all these objects originate? They were clearly being deposited before or during the accumulation of the silts in ditch 205 (c AD 60–80) and before the laying down of the primary gravel metalling (Period IV.3, c AD 80–90), *but also immediately after this event.*

It is probably impossible to reconstruct the process of deposition, but one feature might be a clue. Pit 193, lying under the top gravel (237) and silt beneath (240) was probably contemporaneous with the primary gravel metalling, 257, IV.3. It contained a post pipe, c 0.43m in diameter, set in a compact packing of flints and *septaria* nodules in a matrix of imported estuarine clay to a depth of *c* 0.90m (Fig 13.S18). The post pit itself was *c* 1.67m x at least *c* 1.52m x *c* 1.00m deep. It is clear from Figure 12, which shows a distribution of the objects under discussion that pit 193 is in a central position; its unique method of construction and the closeness of the group of objects, clearly complete when deposited, led Drury (1972, 19) to suggest this pit held 'a relatively tall pole, with some means of attaching votive objects to the lower parts'. If these objects then are votive, and connected with the post pit, it implies that the latter must have been in existence during the life of ditch 205, hence the three fibulae in the fill of the ditch; hence also the 'votive' bar in its primary fill, and the fragments of lamp chimney, of a type which often has ritual connotations (Lowther 1976, 48). As stated earlier, other fragments of the same vessel were found in the same levels as the votive objects (Cats 415, 422 and 467). For the two vessel fragments to be found in the primary brickearth weathering in ditch 205, the lamp chimney must have been broken *c* AD 60–75.

We can then surmise that the post pit, if ritual and the origin for these various objects, was in use during Period IV.2. Pottery from the fill of the post-hole, that is after the feature went out of use, is dated *c* AD 80–175; but since layers 237 and 240 seal the post-hole, a probable date for its demise is *c* AD 90 (the start of period V), and this is corroborated by the fact that there are no 2nd century brooches from the site at all. The character of the religious veneration appears to have altered, and votive objects were no longer being dedicated.

Two shallow depressions lying beneath the earliest gravel 257 might also be connected: hollow 483, *c* 0.15m deep, contained a brooch pin (already mentioned) and a fragment of a buffware oil-lamp, probably the same as that from ditch 205; hollow 482, *c* 0.20m deep, lay over the post-holes of Structure 3 (Period IV.1) and contained 1st century pottery scraps, and some lightly fired clay (Fig 13.S21).

Well 558

To the north of the gravelled path, 257, was a well, 558, *c* 1m square externally and *c* 2.25m deep, sunk into thick orange ballast, of timber caisson construction, made up of oak planks, 0.05m x 0.30m, dovetailed at the corners, each of which had a diagonal rung housed into the top edge (Fig 13.S22). The technique is now well documented from excavations in Essex: a 2nd century example was recorded at Great Dunmow (Wickenden 1988b, F 207); a possible one, though with its lining removed, at Heybridge (Wickenden 1987, F 79); a later 3rd century example noted in sewer trenches (Site CR, No 37, p 62 below); 2nd century and later examples from Sites V 1975 and AG 1975 in Chelmsford (report in prep) and two 4th century examples from Wickford (in prep, Wells 1 and 4). See also a 3rd century timber-lined well from Little

Waltham (Drury 1978, fig 31) of different construction. This, however, is the earliest occurrence for this construction to date in Essex. A secondary framework of re-used timbers was subsequently inserted due to rotting of the original caisson. Finally the well was cleared of sludge (which survived in pockets next to the framing), and deliberately backfilled with tips of orange gravel and hardcore. Drury (1972, 19) adds 'whether, in the light of the pole noted earlier, this was a ceremonial "deconsecration", involving the removal of votive objects, or whether it was simply to prevent excessive subsidence, is impossible to deduce.'

The well floor was formed of *tegulae*, broken *in situ*, and some larger flint pebbles. The lowest fills, to the top of the inserted secondary frame comprised the gravel tips, much tile (including box flue), pottery dated *c* AD 75–120, and some leather trimmings. The main fills, also deliberate, comprised tips of sandy gravel brickearth and rubble, clearly thrown in from the north-east. The rubble comprises much tile, faced flint, squared *septaria*, greensand and mortar, clearly hardcore from a dismantled masonry structure. Pottery from these tips can be dated to AD 60–120. Finally the well was sealed by the later gravel metalling of the path, 237, dated to Period VI.1 (*c* AD 120/5).

The well appears to have been contemporary with the post pit 193 and gravel path 257, being on the same alignment as the latter. It was probably constructed early in Period IV.2 (*c* AD 65–75), requiring attention to the framing after about two decades in the acidic gravel subsoil. Indeed the whole caisson appears to have become distorted to a parallelogram. The secondary base frame, of *c* 0.22m x 0.05m oak timberwork, was fitted within the existing structure, but was sunk *c* 0.15m deeper into the gravel. Within the angles, posts, *c* 0.15m x 0.10m with pointed ends, were driven into the gravel; these were re-used timbers, since the sharpening of their points cut old weathered surfaces, and they had mortices unrelated to their final use. The deliberate filling probably took place sometime in Period V (*c* AD 90–120/5).

In the southern part of the site, the following pits belong to this phase: 14, 19, 32, 48 (Fig 14.S46), 50 (Fig 14.S47), 53, 57, 59, 64, 78, 87, 931 and 1149. All contained 1st century pottery, several contained tile, and 87 contained part of a broad strap bracelet, characteristically 1st century in date (Fig 39.15). The larger central features, none deeper than *c* 0.38m, were probably all brickearth extraction pits. Feature 19 was a small double post-hole, sealed by a square slab of stone.

Dating evidence
32 (Pit bottom only) *Samian* f15/17 or 18, SG, Neronian (Cat 33). *Other pottery* jar rims G5 x2 **(50)**. Intrusive Hadham sherd (**4**.
48 (Pit) *Samian* f18, SG, Neronian-Flavian (Cat 55). *Other pottery* Imitation f30 (**34**), probably Flavian (Cat 55)

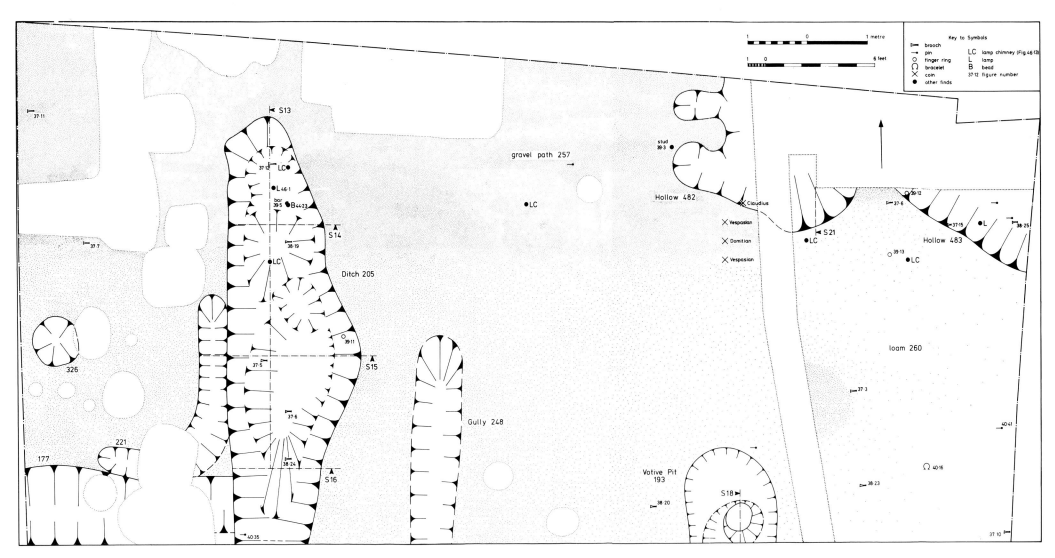

Figure 12   Site K: Period IV.2. Distribution of 'votive' objects

50 (Pit) *Coin* Lucius Verus, AD 161–68 (Cat 1048). Intrusive in top fill
78 (Pit bottom) *Samian* f29, SG, early Flavian (Cat 79). *Other pottery* Cats 77 and 79 contain 4th century material and Cat 1055 a coin of Valens, all in upper sinkage fills
177 (Ditch) *Samian* f29, SG, Neronian, for decoration see Fig 48.1 (Cat 186); f18, SG, Neronian-Flavian (Cat 203); f18, SG, early Flavian (Cat 807). *Other pottery* A1.5 platter (**45**) with multiple stamps (see Fig 57.5), Flavian (Cat 185); rough-cast beaker, Lyons ware (**5**), pre-Flavian, Fig 59.1; Jar G5 (**47**), 1st century-early 2nd century
193 (Post-pit) *Pottery* necked jar sherd (**45**), 1st -early 2nd century
205 (Ditch) For the coarse pottery from L V–III, see p 93–7

> L **V** (primary silt) *Copper alloy bar*, Fig 39.5 (Cat 454)
> *Colchester brooch*, Fig 37.12 (Cat 496)
> *Oil lamp fragment*, Fig 46.1 (Cat 495)
> *Melon bead*, Fig 44.23 (Cat 1155)
> *Lamp chimney fragments*, Fig 46.13 (Cat 408)
> *Samian* f15/17 x 4, SG, early Flavian (Cats 408, 409, 454, 495); f18, SG, Neronian (Cat 495); f22, SG, early Flavian (Cat 410); ff 24/5, 27, SG, early Flavian (Cat 451); f27 x 2, SG, early Flavian (Cats 454, 495); f29, SG, Flavian (Cat 408)
> **LV/IV–III** *Pottery* platter stamp, INDATIOS (No 6, p 105–7), *c* AD 70–85 (Cats 494, 495)
> L **IV** *Samian* f18, SG, Neronian-Flavian, slightly burnt x 3 (Cats 284, 359); f18, SG, Neronian-Flavian (Cats 290, 962); f27, SG, Neronian (Cat 284)
> L **IV–III** (main silt) *Brooches*, Fig 37.4,5; 38.24 (Cats 284, 290, 222)
> *Glass handle*, Fig 44.14 (Cat 450)
> *Samian* f 15/17, SG, Flavian (Cat 450); f18 x 2, SG, Neronian- Flavian (Cats 406, 407); f27, SG, Neronian-Flavian (Cat 222); f29, SG, Flavian (Cat 406)
> L **II–I** (Gravel, sealing ditch, Period V/VI)
> *Coin* Antoninus Pius, AD 138–161 (Cat 354)
> *Brooch*, Fig 38.19 (Cat 403)
> *Pin*, Fig 40.35 (Cat 354)
> *Finger-ring*, Flavian, Fig 39.11 (Cat 356)
> *Samian* f18 x 3, SG, Flavian (Cats 287, 401, 402); ff18/31, 33, CG, Hadrianic (Cat 278); f27 x 2, SG, Flavian (Cats 400, 404); f37, SG, *c* AD 70–85 (Cat 405). *Other pottery* neckless beaker (**21**), 1st Century, Fig 59.23 (Cat 446)

221 (Ditch) *Pottery* necked jar rim (**45**), Cat 303.
258 (Earliest Roman subsoil; Cats 258, 467, 473, 480, 518, 532). *Brooches* Hod Hill, Fig 37.7 (Cat 532); Colchester, Fig 37.11 (Cat 518); pin. *Samian* f15/17, SG, Flavian (Cat 467). *Pottery* A1.5 platter (**45**), Cat 467; neckless jar (**45**), with graffito]NDIX[(Fig 58.6); VRW mortarium (Cat 480); Fabric **27**
260 (Early Roman soil) *Brooches* Nauheim derivative, Fig 37.3 (Cat 293); Colchester, Fig 37.10 (Cat 1072); Colchester, Fig 37.15 (Cat 1106); enamelled toothed, Fig 38.23 (Cat 293); *Bracelet*,

Fig 40.16 (Cat 1072); *Finger-ring*, Fig 39.12 (Cat 414). *Samian* f27, 29, SG, Early Flavian (unworn footring) (Cat 414); f18, SG, Flavian (Cat 293)
326 (Post hole) *Pottery* G16–20 jar sherds (**45**), probably 1st century
483 (Hollow) *Samian* f18, 31, 33, SG, CG, 1st-2nd centuries *Other pottery* G16–20 jar sherds (**45**); misc. oxidised sherd, closed form, probably Flavian-early 2nd century; oil lamp sherd. *Brooch* pin
523 (Hollow) *Pottery* scraps, including Fabric **45**, and a handmade variant. Probably pre- to early Flavian
530 (Hollow) *Pottery* scraps, including Fabric **45**; a closed form in a fine white ware. Probably pre- to early Flavian
558 (Well) *Samian* f27, 31, CG, Hadrianic-Antonine (Cat 570). Filled in Period V
705 (Ditch) *Coin* Claudius I, AD 43–54; *Brooch*, plate, Fig 38.26. *Samian*, f24/25, f29, SG, pre-Flavian (Cat 773); f15/17 or 18, f27, SG, Flavian, includes one burnt sherd (Cat 850); f15/17 or 18, f15/17R or 18R, SG, Flavian (Cat 852); f18, SG, Neronian (Cat 853). *Other pottery* Colchester buff closed form, ?1st Century AD, Fig 59.25 (Cat 773); multiple-cordoned jar (**34**), 1st century AD, Fig 59.34 (Cat 853); carinated bowl (**34**), 1st century AD, Fig 60.36 (Cat 772); necked jar (**47**), Flavian, Fig 60.52 (Cat 724)

Period IV Phase 3: c AD 80–90 (Fig 11)

In this period, as discussed above, a gravel pathway, 257, 4–5m wide, was constructed, approximately aligned on the Period IV.2 enclosure (Fig 13.S19–21; Fig 18.S40). It was also located in a machine-cut trench to the east (Site L, p 49 below) and was thus at least 75m long. It is possible that slot 535 (see Period IV.1) formed a drainage channel to the north. The path, dated to *c* AD 80–90, was laid over the fill of ditch 205 and stops within the Period IV.2 enclosure without approaching any obvious feature. It has already been seen that it was in contemporary use with the votive pit, 193 and its associated group of votive bronzes. Drury (1972, 19) wrote 'it seems possible that it was the area itself, or perhaps a group of trees within it, or a feature which left no trace in the ground, which formed the focus of attention; or that the pathway continued to a feature or structure in the area under the existing cottages to the west, its extension having been eroded away where it would have passed over a natural rise in the ground'. The idea of a group of trees (ie a sacred grove) is compelling; it is clear, for instance, that when the masonry temple was built in the early 4th century, parts of the ground surface had to be made up with hardcore where there were lobed hollows — 'possibly the site of a group of trees' (*ibid*, p 22).

The gravel surface was resurfaced (more than once) with interleaving accumulations of silt (see Fig 13.S20: 464, 465), especially where the silts of the underlying ditch 205 subsided. These later

24

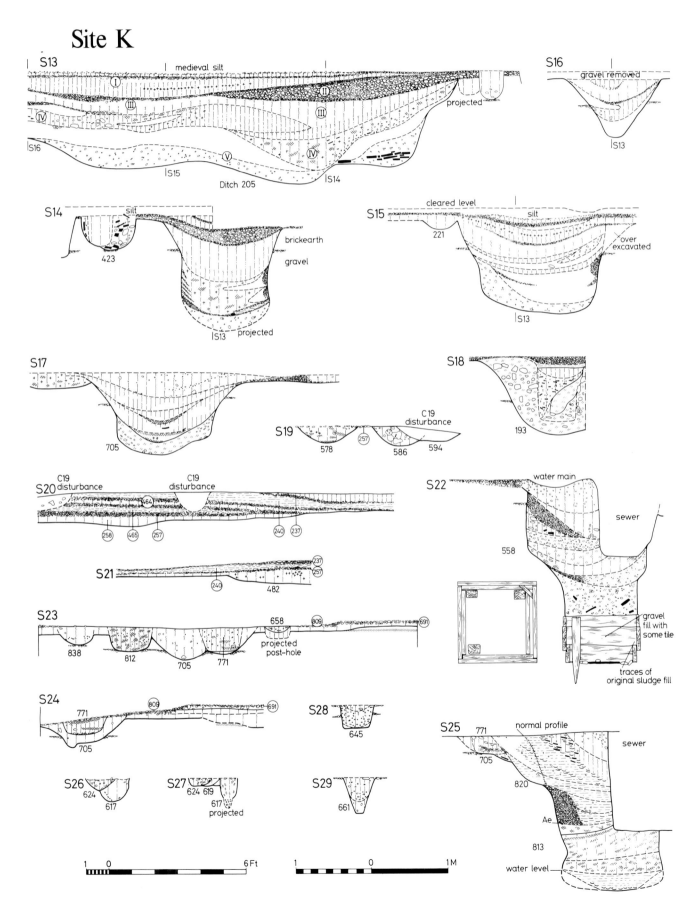

Figure 13   Site K: Sections S13–29. For key to sections see Fig 6

Site K

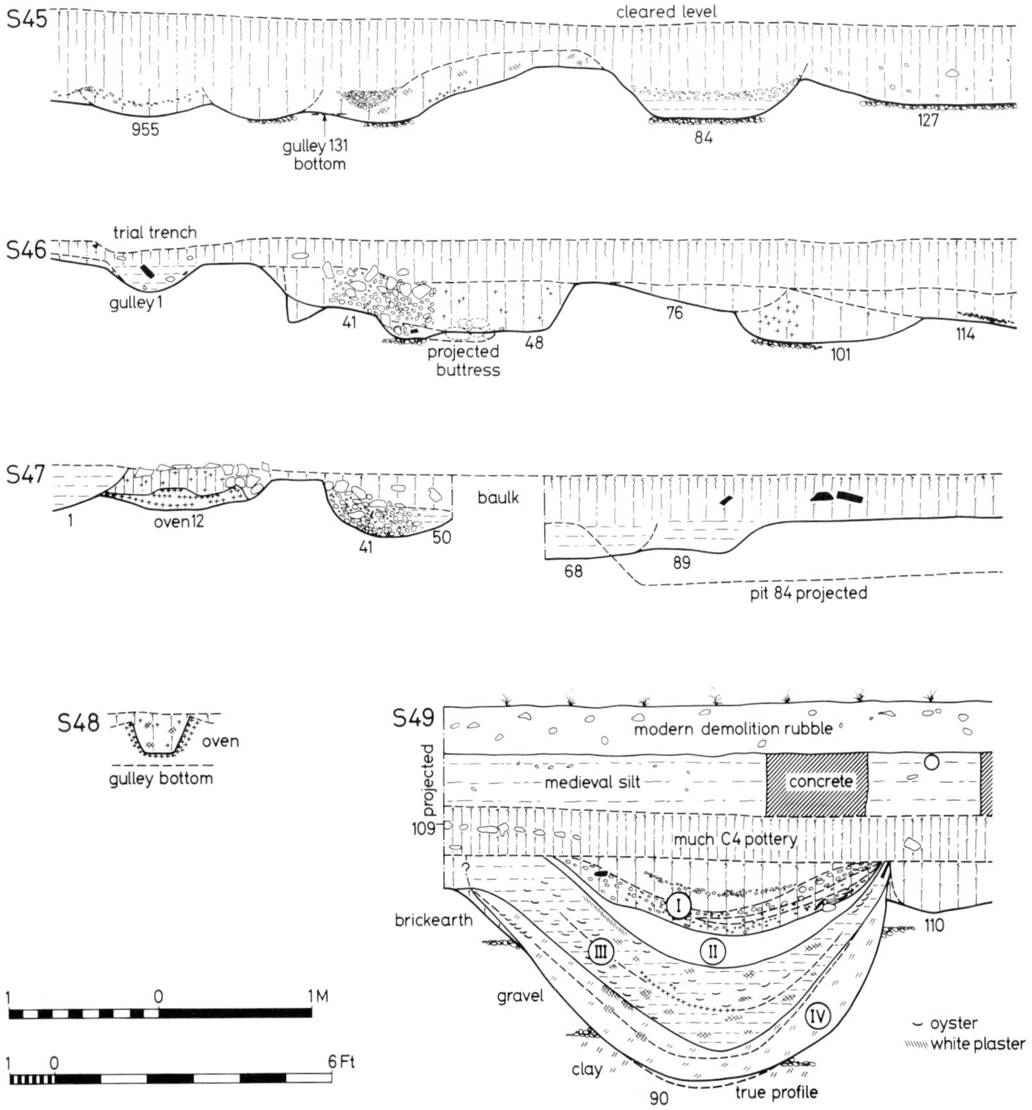

Figure 14   Site K: Sections S45–49 (southern area). For key to sections, see Fig 6

surface was thinner and less compact; the last surface was laid *c* AD 120/5 (Period VI.1).

Perhaps contemporary with the pathway 257 was a post-hole 373, *c* 0.20m deep and filled with the silt which accumulated over the entire gravelled area (240, V). A group of seven small post-holes lay partly over the fill of ditch 205, and were cut *c* 0.38m into the natural brickearth. Only two contained any pottery, 508 (*c* AD 60–120) and 519 (1st century).

In the southern part of the site pit 76 cut pit 59 and probably belongs to this phase (Fig 14.S46).

Dating evidence
257 (Gravel path) *Coin* Claudius I, AD 43–54 (Cat 479). *Military stud*, Fig 39.3 (Cat 479). *Samian* f18, SG, Neronian-Flavian (Cat 457); f27g, f29, SG, Neronian-Flavian (Cat 477); chip, SG, 1st century (Cat 936). *Other pottery* Fabric **27** (Cat 422); Fabric

45: Globular jar (Cat 460); G15 (Cat 479); G16/20 (Cats 466, 479); Lid K1 (Cat 479); early shell-tempered ware (**50**), G5 Jar rim (Cat 479). Probably later Flavian
373 (Post-hole) *Pottery* sherd, Fabric **45**. Probably 1st century
465 (Silt over Gravel 257) *Coins* Vespasian x 2, AD 69–79, Domitian, AD 81–96 (all Cat 476). *Brooches* Hod Hill, Fig 37.6; plate, Fig 38.25 (both Cat 1105).
508 (Stake-hole) *Pottery* scrap, probably 1st century
519 (Stake-hole) *Pottery* misc. oxidised sherds, probably 1st century

Period IV (unphased): 1st century

Other features dated to *c* 60–100, and belonging to Period IV are: Cremation 1 (563), a small pit,

0.15m deep, containing cremated bone and potsherds; Cremation 2 (564), a small pit, 0.48m deep, also containing cremated bone and pottery; post-hole 572, adjacent to the two cremations, and containing pottery and two *tegulae* fragments; a small adjacent hollow, 578, containing burnt clay and pottery (Fig 13.S19); and slot 588, ?for a beam, *c* 0.33m wide x 1.22m long, x *c* 0.05m deep.

Dating evidence
563 (Cremation 1) *Pottery* Jar sherds (**45**); G5 jar sherds (**50**) ?Flavian.
564 (Cremation 2) *Pottery* Body sherds only of misc oxidised ware, **44**, **45** and **47**. Probably 1st century.
572 (Post-hole) *Pottery* Body sherds only of Fabrics **44**, **45** and **47**. Probably 1st century.
578 (Hollow) *Pottery* G15/20 jar (**45**); misc oxidised sherds, probable flagon; Fabric (**47**), probable jar. 1st century.
588 (Slot) *Pottery* Poppy head beaker-rim, ?N Kent grey ware. Flavian+.

Period V Phase 1: c AD 90–110 (Fig 15)

In the southern part of the site, Structure 11 was built over the backfilled Period IV brickearth pits (Fig 16). It was defined by a plinth, 41, *c* 0.40m wide formed of one or two courses of dry-laid flints (Fig 14.S46–7).

In some cases where these disturbances occurred a foundation trench for the cill was cut through their filling to the underlying natural. In others no precautions were taken and subsidence ensued.

The structure comprised a rectangular cell, *c* 6.70m externally x at least 2.3m with a central external buttress (since there is no sign of it continuing as a wall running north), with a western (apparently curving) extension running outside the southern limit of excavation; to the east the main wall continues, forming a second, smaller room. Though the wall is cut by a 3rd century pit, 47, and its angle return lost, a small section of its eastern line survives. The whole structure is aligned on ditch 205, and hence with the entire early religious precinct, in contrast to the later Structure 12 (see below). It is interpreted as an apsidal-ended temple (or ?other public building) with internal division and external buttressing (see p 128–9).

Within the structure were two, probably successive, clay-lined ovens. The first oven was almost completely destroyed by a later gulley, 1, and the only surviving remnant is the reddened clay sides of the pit, filled with black, loamy ash, and a little fired clay (Fig 14.S48). But the second, 12, parallel to it and to the structure, survived more completely, despite also being cut by the later gulley (Fig 14.S47). Its tunnel was formed out of flint walls, with some *tegulae* and bonding tile fragments, set in a hollow in the natural brickearth, and lined with brickearth fired *in situ*. It was filled with ash, fired clay and tile fragments in a brown, silty loamy matrix. Two possible refloorings are visible in section (Fig 14.S47). It is

Plate III Site K: Structures 11, 12 and ovens (Photo: P J Drury)

difficult to ascertain whether the oven and structure were contemporary.

North of the post-medieval drainage ditch, three vertical-sided slots share a common fill and form, though their function is unknown. All cut the fill of ditch 705 (*cf* Fig 13.S24–5) and are therefore later than the end of Period IV.2 (*c* AD 80); all were filled with practically pure charcoal deposits in a silty loam matrix. Slot 678, more than 0.52m deep, contained several large flint nodules and pottery (1st–early 2nd century) including fragments of storage jar, possibly intrusive from the hearth 708 which partly overlay it; slot 771 (Fig 13.S23–4) *c* 0.30m deep, contained tile, a butchered horse radius, and pottery dated *c* AD 60–110/20 and was cut by the later well pit, 820; slot 812 (Fig 13.S23), also *c* 0.30m deep and dated by its pottery to the 2nd century, was cut by the Period V.2 circular well, 813 and sealed by the gravel 829. Charcoal from these features was also found in the surrounding subsoil, and in the brown silty loam fill of three less regular, shallower (*c* 0.20m) gulleys: 849 comprises two slots with seven post settings (including 854) within them, joined together by a larger post-hole; 823, *c* 1m further south and possibly curving to meet 849; and 836, probably a continuation of 823, only *c* 0.08m deep and terminating in a post-hole, 838, *c* 0.20m deep (Fig 13.S23). This latter post-hole was cut by the construction of well 813. Pottery in the fills of these features was 1st to 2nd century in date.

Dating evidence
41 (Structure 11) *Samian* platter footring, SG, late Flavian; chips, SG, pre-Flavian (Cat 42). *Other pottery* plain rimmed dish (**41**), Cat 42; jar G5 (**47**); Fabric **45** (both Cat 44). One oxidised sherd (??**4**), Cat 42. Probably post AD 120
129 (Pit) *Samian* 2 chips, SG, CG, ?2nd century. *Other pottery* Scraps **47**, and misc. oxidised Fabric. 2nd century+

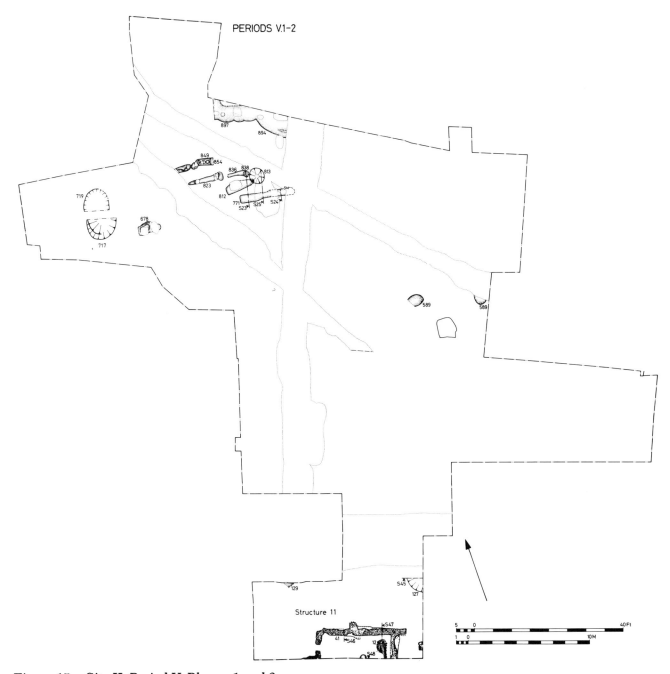

Figure 15   Site K: Period V. Phases 1 and 2

678 (Slot) *Pottery* G16/20 (**45**), probably 1st century (Cat 704); G5 (**50**), probably 1st century (Cat 704); G20 (**47**), probably 2nd century

771 (Slot) *Samian* f27, SG, Flavian. *Other pottery* G16/20 (**45**), 1st–early 2nd century; G5 (**50**), probably 1st century; a white-slipped oxidised fabric — either VRW or ?Hadham region. End 1st–early 2nd century

812 (Slot) *Samian* f18, 29, 30, 36, 37, SG, late Flavian. *Other pottery* Globular beaker (**34**); G16/20 (**45**); necked bowl (**47**). Probably 2nd century

849 (Gulley) *Pottery* Flagon sherd, VRW; platter A1–5 (**45**), probably 1st century; jar G9 (**47**), ?Hadrianic-Antonine

Period V Phase 2: c AD 110–120/5 (Fig 15)

A circular, timber-lined well, 813, which cut slot 836 and two of the charcoal-filled slots, 771 and 812, was dug, *c* 1.25m in diameter by *c* 2.00m deep; none of the lining (probably a re-used barrel) survived, and the filling contained a considerable quantity of material which would not have been out of place in a domestic context, including animal bone (2 sheep skulls) and shells, tile, triangular loomweights, briquetage and pottery (Fig 13.S25). The lowest layers of fill, V–IV, below the water level, were slightly undercut and filled with a dark brown peaty silt; charcoal around the edges may be

Structures 11 and 12 ; ovens

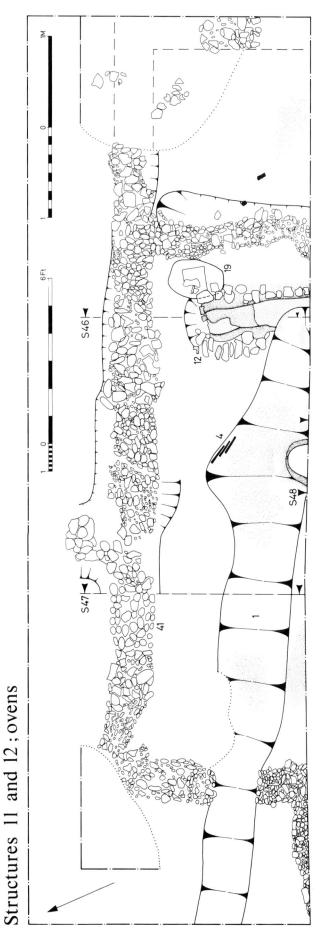

Figure 16 Site K: Structures 11 and 12; ovens

the remnants of the charred framing. The main fills, II, comprised silty, loamy sludges, with an appreciable amount of oyster shell, which clearly were the result of gradual accumulation, rather than deliberate filling. An area of brickearth and gravel subsoil, III, appears to have slipped into the well shaft during silting. The resultant hollow, 820, yielded a dog burial and a partial human infant burial. A storage jar hearth, 808, partly overlay the upper well silts, and part of the shaft was also cut away by a modern sewer trench. The pottery in the fills would suggest that the well was dug in this period, and started accumulating rubbish after *c* AD 110/120; L II was accumulating *c* AD 130–150.

Feature 719 was a shallow elliptical hollow, which partly overlay the Period IV ditch 705, filled with a charcoally silt containing 1st–early 2nd century pottery, slag and a fired clay firebar or fire dog (Fig 46.8).

Also dated to Period V are two amorphous shallow, ?clay pits, 894 and 897, dug to a maximum depth of *c* 0.18m into the brickearth; 897 contained areas of charcoal and slag in its silty backfill. Two further shallow hollows, 589 and 590, only 0.05m and 0.13m deep respectively, contained 1st–2nd century pottery. Finally it is probable that a general silt layer, 240 (Fig 13.S20–21), accumulated over the early gravels over most of the site in this phase, indicating perhaps a cessation of religious activity before the construction of the 'Corridor' structure (below) and the introduction of a new religious emphasis, with a focus perhaps to the west, outside the excavated area.

Dating evidence
240 (Silt) *Coin* illegible *as*, 1st-2nd centuries (Cat 253). *Brooch* Fig 38.20 (Cat 219). *Samian* f27, SG (Cat 463); f37, SG (Cat 364), both Flavian. *Other pottery* mainly scraps, jar G9, (**45**), *c* AD 120/30+. Intrusive sherds from Cats 247 (**3**), and 219 (?**4**, and six sherds of medieval and post-medieval wares)
590 (Hollow) *Pottery* necked jar (**45**), 1st-2nd centuries; Fabrics 44 and 47
719 (Hollow over Ditch 705) *Samian* f18, SG, early Flavian large pieces (Cat 760); f27, SG, Flavian. *Other pottery* C10, London ware; G16–20, H10 (**45**), including Fig 60.35; ?S Gallic amphora sherd. Flavian-?early 2nd century; some almost certainly derived from the underlying ditch 705 (period IV.2).
813 (Well) **L V** (organic primary sludge) *Pottery* closed form (**45**), flagon base, VRW, Flavian or later; white mica-dusted sherd, Flavian-early 2nd century (all Cat 845)
  L IV (brickearth loam) *Samian* f18, SG, pre-Flavian (Cat 818); f15/17, 27, 29, SG, early Flavian (Cat 819; Fig 48.2). *Other pottery* carinated cup (**45**), Fig 60.32; G18/20 and necked jars (**45**); necked jar (**47**); neckless jar H1 (**47**), Fig 60.51; Ring and dot beaker sherd, H6. Flavian-early 2nd century (all Cat 819)
  L II (rubbish fills) *Samian* Scrap, SG, 1st century; Ritt 12, SG, Flavian; f29, SG, late

Flavian (Cat 814); f15/17, ?CG, Trajanic, slightly burnt (Cat 816). *Other pottery* Rim imitation f30 (**34**), Cat 950; bead rimmed dishes x 4 (**41**), post AD 120, Cat 816; necked and neckless jars (**45**), Cat 814; jar G5 (**47**), Cat 814; jar (**50**), Cats 816, 950; mortarium (**27**), stamped (see Fig 57.1) *c* AD 150–80 (Cat 816); mortarium, VRW, probably 2nd century (Cat 814)
  L I (sinkage fill) *Pottery* Scraps (**45, 47**). 1st–2nd centuries (Cat 813)
820 (Slippage around well) *Samian* ff18, 36, SG, Flavian. *Other pottery* necked jar (**45**); platter A1–5 (**39**), globular beaker (**39**), both Cat 822; G5 (**50**), Cats 820, 822; mortarium (**27**), probably 1st century. Generally Flavian-early 2nd century
897 (Clay pit) *Samian* f15/17 or 18, SG, early Flavian; f15/17, SG, Flavian. *Other pottery* bowl-jar (**45**), see Fig 60.33; lead-glazed carinated cup (**10**); ring-necked flagon (**27**); mortarium, VRW. Generally 1st–2nd century

The 'Corridor' structure

The three slots, 823, 836 and 849 lay outside, but on the same alignment as, a long corridor-type structure, at least 37m long in its most extensive phase, and an average of *c* 6.80m wide. The floor was gravelled and was resurfaced several times (see below); the form of the structure is unknown but its walls are delimited by long shallow slots; these are clearly long-lived and of different phases, some replacing others. The slots are probably shallow foundation trenches for timber walls, though they are feasible eaves-drip gullies. They are not everywhere present, eg, where the later masonry temple has destroyed them, and along part of the line of ditch 705, where it is possible that they were missed in the top fill of the ditch.

The gravel floors of the structure sealed an area of leached brickearth (prehistoric subsoil) and preserved it to a depth of *c* 0.10–0.20m (see above, and Fig 10). Slot 638, *c* 0.13m deep, formed the northern wall of the structure and lay immediately outside (*c* 0.30m) the gravel flooring (Fig 13.S23). It had one post-hole within it (*c* 0.20m deep) and terminated in another, 758, *c* 0.33m deep; both contained pottery of the 1st–early 2nd centuries.

The southern wall of the structure comprises a slot on the west (no finds), slots 619, 617 and 624 which emerge to the east of the sewer trench as slots 627 and 637. Slot 619 (Fig 13.S26) was probably the earliest, 0.10m deep, and contained pottery of the 1st–early 2nd century; two adjacent lengths of it were noted, one being cut by the masonry temple and one by slot 624. Slot 617 appears to be next in the sequence (Fig 13.S26-7), and was probably dug whilst 619 was still operative, since its western end — which terminates in post-hole 615 — was tailor-made to fit round 619; 617 was *c* 0.20m deep and contained Flavian-Hadrianic pottery. To the east of the sewer trench, the slot probably continues as 637 which had two smaller slots within it, 0.38m deep,

Plate IV   Site K: Ditch 705 (left) and the 'corridor' structure, looking east (Photo: P J Drury)

possibly for upright planks or fencing (a and b), and terminated in post-hole 655 (1st–early 2nd century pottery), also *c* 0.36m deep. A wider slot (c) also cut 637, *c* 0.22m deep with vertical sides, and is perhaps to be connected with the two square post-holes which lie either side of it to the north.

Lastly, slot 624 (Fig 13.S26–7) cut both earlier slots 619 and 617; it contained 2nd–3rd century (and intrusive late 4th century) pottery, and probably emerged east of the sewer trench as 627 (1st–early 2nd century pottery).

The three square post-pits just to the north of slot 637 have already been mentioned. Only 645 (Fig 13.S28) contained any finds (pottery dated 2nd century+); all were *c* 0.20–0.30m deep and filled with a gravelly silt. Drury indicates that 'the gravel paving was laid around the posts after erection implying an open-sided "verandah" form of construction' (1972, 20), though it is virtually impossible to suggest how they were incorporated into the structure. Part of a similar square post-hole, 623 (pottery 1st–2nd century) lay to the south of slot 627, and was cut by it. Other possibly associated post-holes include 649, *c* 0.35m deep, almost conical in shape; 661, *c* 0.46m deep, also conical (Fig 13.S29); 734 and 979, both *c* 0.30m deep and filled with a very gravelly loam (979 produced 2nd century pottery); other unnumbered post-holes may belong, but produced no finds.

Further west, three post-pits from a possible 4-post building (Structure 6), *c* 4.5m x 2.5m, survive (the fourth eradicated by a post-Roman feature): 627 (1st–2nd century pottery), *c* 0.50m deep, contained a post-pipe, *c* 0.20m in diameter; 662, *c* 0.28m deep, contained a post-pipe *c* 0.30m in

diameter; there were indications that the post had been removed by rocking. The third post-pit contained no finds and had been truncated by post-Roman ditches; it was cut *c* 0.30m into the weathered brickearth.

Further west, a number of post-holes seem to be related to the structure, although their relationship is not always clear. A line of four, including 635 and 651, lay approximately 1.5m in from, and parallel to, slot 658. Pit 635 contained a post-pipe and two 1st–2nd century sherds; 651 contained a post-pipe, *c* 0.30m in diameter and contained 2nd century pottery. Both were *c* 0.38m deep. Two other post-holes 650 and 656, form a pair: 650 was overcut in digging and was truncated by the sewer trench; 656, adjacent to it, contained tile and flint packing. Both yielded pottery *c* 1st–3rd century in date.

Two other lines of post-holes may form a separate building (Structure 7), trapezoidal in plan; only two post-holes contained any finds: 593 (1st–early 2nd century pottery, tile and a piece of thick copper alloy sheeting (Fig 41.63)) and 974 which yielded tile fragments.

Further to the west, an extension appears to have been made running north sealing hollow 719. Slot 644 may be the eaves-drip gulley, or foundation slot, for this north-western extension. It contained charcoally loam, 1st century pottery, an intrusive piece of post-medieval bottle glass, and pit 666, 0.25m deep, which was sealed by gravel 609. The eastern wall of this extension was probably formed by post-holes 640, 730, 742, and 764; those between 640 and 730 having been obliterated by the medieval pit 679; but note also the extent of gravel

608 (below). Pit 640 contained a post-pipe, *c* 0.23m in diameter x *c* 0.58m deep which yielded 1st–2nd century pottery. Pit 742, containing 1st–mid 2nd century pottery, was cut by 730 and 764; 730, 0.46m deep, contained pottery (post- AD 120) and 10 nails; 764 was 0.18m deep with flint nodule packing and pottery.

An extension of the excavation to the north produced a further building apparently constructed on a pre-existing gravel metalled area (Structure 8). It was in excess of 5.60m long, and *c* 2.10m wide on the south, extending to 3.00m further to the north at which may have been its centre. The entrance appears to have been on the east, via a porch extended outwards. The lines of the walls were defined by closely laid flints and *septaria* around the exterior of the building, the walls presumably rising from ground-laid cills. External post-holes may indicate the provision of external support in the lines of roof trusses. In view of the fact that this structure was to be sealed under the central reservation of the new road, it was cleared, recorded and backfilled.

Discussion and the gravel spreads

The exact nature of this 'corridor' type structure, its chronological development and its relationship to the 'internal' post-holed Structures 6 and 7, is virtually impossible to reconstruct with any degree of certainty, as Drury recognised (1972, 19–20), though Drury does interpret it as a perhaps partly open-sided, roofed structure, 'within which a probably enclosed structure was sited on an apparently significant alignment.' (*ibid*, 20). The date, from the wall slot fills and internal post-holes, indicates primary construction around the turn of the century, *c* AD 90–100 (Period V.1), after the demise of ditch 705. In this phase, the entire area was gravelled (809; Fig 13.S23–4), extending from the southern slots (619, etc) across ditch 705, suggesting that the post-in-slot features in Period V.1 (849, 823,836) may be part of the complex in this phase. Slot 836 is cut by the Period V.2 well, 813. Thus at least two of the vertical-sided, charcoal-filled features, 771 and 812, would lie within the structure. The gravel was subsequently covered by a second metalling, 691, containing 1st–2nd century pottery (Fig 13.S23–4). Both metallings appear to preserve the outline of an eastern building, probably with a timber floor and walls rising from a ground-laid cill, within which there was a thin scatter of pebble only. This was aligned almost due east-west in contrast to the main corridor structure.

Above the second metalling (691), a thin silt accumulated, 690, containing 2nd century pottery; the gravel was patched up, 717, where the fill of the hollow 719 had subsided. Above the silt, a third gravel metalling, 609 (pottery dated *c* 130–160) was laid, mainly on the west, where the 2nd and possibly 3rd century focus of interest was. Again a loam, 611, accumulated, and a final gravel, 608,

was laid, forming a distinct northern arm, *c* 3.70m wide. Pottery in this uppermost gravel was given a date bracket of 1st–3rd century. It is thus difficult to give an end date for this structure. It appears to be an essentially 2nd century phenomenon, though it may possibly have extended into the 3rd century; the coin list cannot *per se* be cited as evidence of a 3rd century decline since numbers of the 1st, 2nd and 3rd centuries are consistently low, but see also p 129. The upper gravel levels had eroded away, possibly removing traces of the 3rd century occupation; nevertheless, two centuries seem a long period for the survival of these structures, and it may well be that further important and successive structures lie to the west outside the excavated area.

Dating evidence

Pottery was generally sparse and scrappy. The following features are dated broadly to the 1st–2nd centuries on the presence of Fabrics **44**, **45** and **47**: Slot **619**; and posts **623**, **635**, **640**, **645**, **650**, **656**, **657**, **662**, **666**, and **758**

593 (Post-hole) *Pottery* G18/20 (**45**); **27**

624 (Slot) *Pottery* beaker H32–3 (**2**); closed form (**4**); E5 (**47**); G27 rim (**51**). *c* AD 360+

627 (Slot) *Pottery* beaker H1 (?**4**); G16/20 (**45**). 1st–2nd centuries

637 (Slot) *Pottery* Fabrics **39**, **44**; G5 rim (**50**), probably 1st century; bowl resembling C16 (**45**), probably 2nd century

644 (Slot) *Samian* Curle 11, SG, Flavian; f29, SG, Flavian. *Other pottery* scraps Fabrics **44**, **45**, **47**; bucket L1.1 (**50**), pre-Flavian–Flavian

651 (Post-hole) *Samian* f33, CG, ?Hadrianic. *Other pottery* scraps Fabrics **44**, **45**; bowl fragments (**47**), ?2nd century+

655 (Post-hole) *Pottery* scraps Fabrics **45**, **50**, 1st–early 2nd centuries?

658 (Slot) *Pottery* Fabrics **44**, **45**, **47**; G5 rim (**50**); mortarium (**27**). 1st–early 2nd centuries

730 (Post-hole) *Samian* f15/17, SG, Flavian. *Other pottery* bead-rimmed dish, B2–3, (**47**), Hadrianic–Antonine

734 (Post-hole) *Samian* f38, CG, Antonine

742 (Post-hole) *Pottery* G16–20 (**45**); J.3.1–2 rim (**27**), Flavian; VRW scrap. 1st–2nd centuries

764 (Post-hole) *Pottery* scraps fabrics **44**, **45**; dish B2.1 (**47**). Antonine–early 3rd century

875 (Post-hole) *Pottery* platter A1–5 (**45**); scraps Fabrics **44**, **50**, 1st century

979 (**Post-hole**) *Pottery* beaker-rim, H20, ?N Gaulish. ?Hadrianic or later

Gravels

809 (Primary gravel) *Samian* f18, SG (Cat 860); f27 x 3, SG, (Cats 867, 907); f36 x 2, SG, (Cats 835, 884). All Flavian. *Other pottery* G16–20 (**45**); G20 (**47**); G5 rim (**50**); Fabric **27**. Late 1st–early 2nd century

691 (2nd gravel) *Samian* f18 x 3, SG, Neronian–Flavian (Cats 801, 904). *Other pottery* G16–20 (**45**); G20 (**47**); G5 rim (**50**); Fabric (**27**). Late 1st–early 2nd century

690 (Silt) *Samian* f15/17, SG; Curle 11, SG, f18 x 2, SG, one burnt (Cat 905). All Flavian. *Other pottery* beaker H3 (**27**), Flavian; G16–20 (**45**); G5, G20 (**47**). 1st–2nd centuries

717 (Gravel patch) *Pottery* scraps Fabrics **45**, **47**, **50**. 1st–2nd centuries

609 (3rd gravel) *Samian* f29, SG, Flavian. *Other pottery* Flagon J3, VRW, late type, Hadrianic–Antonine

611 (Silt) *Samian* ff27, 36, SG, Flavian. *Other pottery* scraps Fabrics **44**, **45**; neckless jar (**47**). ?2nd century

608 (Final gravel) *Samian* f18, SG, ?pre-Flavian, burnt (Cat 833); f27 x 2, SG, late Flavian (Cat 867); f37, CG, Hadrianic or Antonine (Cat 867). *Other pottery* platter A1–5 (**45**), ?residual (Cat 859), G20 (**47**) (Cat 829), Fabric **27**, VRW. ?2nd century+

Period VI: c AD 120/5–200/10 (Fig 17)

The general upper gravel paving, 237, of the temple approach pathway seems to have been laid c AD 120/5, sealing the silt 240 (Fig 13.S20–1), and indicating a renewed sphere of activity on the site, contemporary with the 'corridor structure' and possibly with a focus of attention outside the excavated area to the west. South of the post-medieval ditch 133, a new building was constructed at this time (see below), apparently aligned with the road leading south-eastwards out of the town, excavated on Site D. Clearly, much new development was underway at this time, and the same picture of Hadrianic reorganisation has already emerged from a study of the *mansio* (Drury 1988). The change of use on Site K had a dramatic impact on the samian supply (at least on the samian being thrown away), which almost completely vanishes under Hadrian (see p 92). Finds from the gravel were often contaminated, since later levels had been scoured away and redeposited by later alluvial action; despite this, most pottery was dated to the later 1st and 2nd centuries. Other finds include a copper alloy *spathomela* shaft (Cat 528, unillustrated); and a pin with an applied, faceted head (Cat 218, Fig 40.31).

Pit 138 contained pottery of the 2nd century, but also traces of mortar and plaster, which might indicate a later, post-temple phase (Fig 18.S38).

The hearths (c AD 140–170) (Figs 17, 19; Pl V)
Overlying ditch 705 were three hearths, 708, 733 and 1034 (Fig 19.S31), comprising halves of large storage jars, set into the ground. Similar features have been recorded at other sites in Chelmsford, eg, AG, AJ, V and M (p 46).

They were crushed and disturbed, but not heated to any great temperature; 708 (Fig 19.S32) also cut the charcoal-filled slot 678. A smaller patch of storage jar sherds, 659, probably derived from 708. Cutting 733 (Fig 19.S30) was a small post-hole, 741, c 0.41m in diameter x c 0.35m deep containing 2nd century pottery. A charcoal-filled fire-pit, 723,

Plate V   Site K: storage jar hearths (Photo: P J Drury)

was associated with the hearths; this contained pottery, dated c AD 120–175, but was also contaminated by a clay pipe stem; the loam levels lying over it also contained 2nd century pottery. Another similar hearth structure, 808, lay over the disused well, 813, and contained pottery dated c AD 140–170. Nearby, a crushed storage jar base, 1035, may be the remains of a fifth hearth. All would appear to date from the mid 2nd century AD, and all lie just outside the 'corridor' structure, to the north of slot 658.

Two other crushed vessels, 606 and 878, may have been votive deposits; 606 was the base of a large storage jar set upright, whilst 878 was a Flavian–Hadrianic high-shouldered jar (Fabric **45**) crushed *in situ* in a small pit.

Structure 12 (Figs 16, 17)
In the southern part of the site, Structure 11 was replaced by Structure 12, marked by a gulley, 1, c 0.60–0.75m wide x c 0.20m wide (Fig 14.S46–8). This ran for more than 9m cutting through Structure 11 and oven 12 and its predecessor which it almost completely robbed away, causing a bulge and filling the gulley with fired clay and over-fired tiles. At its western end, the gulley turned south for c 1.30m and adjacent to this, and apparently cutting it, was a pit, 2, possibly a rainwater sump, if we assume that the basis for Structure 12 is an eaves drip gulley — its irregular and rounded

Figure 17   Site K: Period VI

profile and lack of masonry fragments is inconsistent with that of a foundation or robber trench. The demise of both the gulley and the sump can be dated by the pottery in their fill to c AD 150–180; in addition the sump contained a human infant facial bone, and a copper alloy bracelet terminal (Fig 38.18). The position of the road frontage to the south gives a maximum size for the building of 9m x 11m.

The alignment of Structure 12 is different to that of its predecessor and marks a new development. It is clear from Figure 2 that it is aligned on, and was probably a frontage structure on, the Roman road leading south-eastwards out of the town. Since Structure 11 was not on this alignment but on that

of the Period IV enclosure, whose ditches by the mid 2nd century had silted up and been gravelled over, it can be assumed that the road in question was constructed some time after the construction of the first building but before the construction of its replacement. A date of c AD 120–125 might be suggested, when the town, and especially the *mansio*, was undergoing some considerable Hadrianic redevelopment (Drury 1988, 130, 133).

Pit 90

Brickearth and rubish pits continued to be dug until the late 4th century, but very few actually encroached on these structures, so that it seems possible that the building complex fronting the

Site K

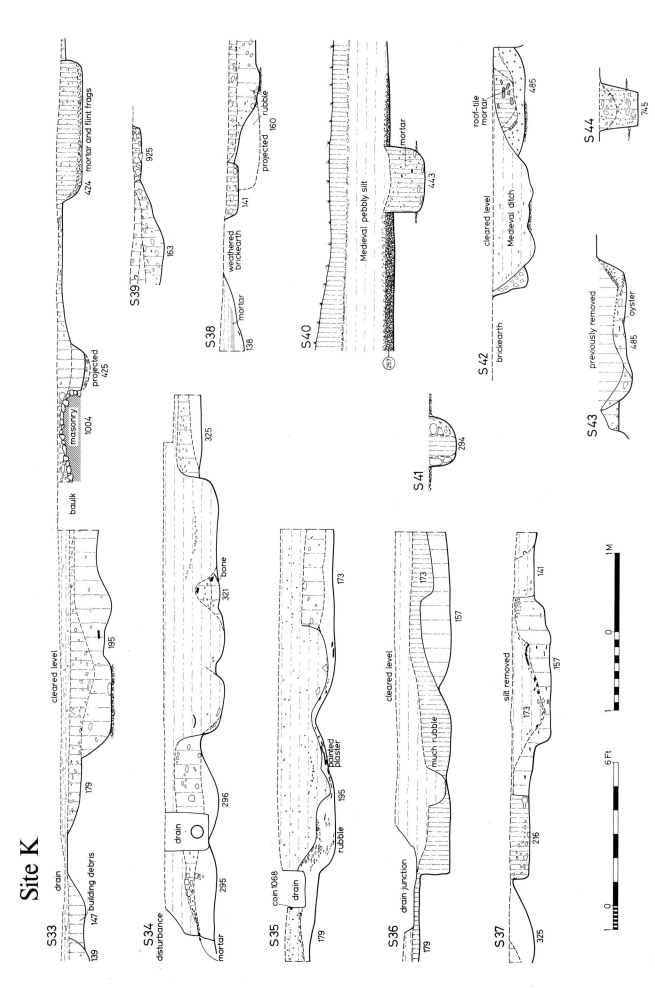

Figure 18 Site K: Sections S33–43. For key to sections, see Fig 6

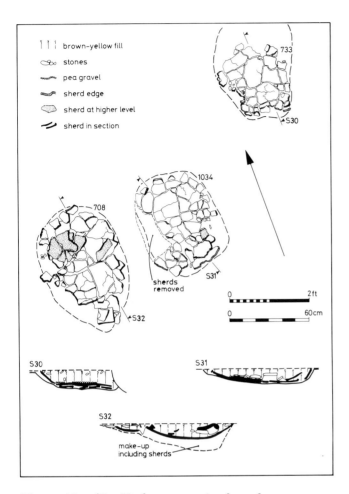

Key:
⌶ ⌶ ⌶	brown-yellow fill	
	stones	
	pea gravel	
	sherd edge	
	sherd at higher level	
	sherd in section	

Figure 19   Site K: the storage jar hearths

street survived beyond the 2nd century. The other main feature in this phase was a large clay-lined pit, 90, of parabolic profile, *c* 1.70m deep, which probably acted as a water-storage tank (Fig 14.S49). The latest primary fill, IV, was a weathered clayey brickearth containing few finds, but stained in the middle from contact with the main fill; this was a grey silty material, III, containing much pottery, animal bone, including bird and fish, oyster shell and lenses of fired clay and charcoal — all clearly tips of domestic rubbish once the pit had gone out of use. The animal bone assemblage is discussed in Section VIII. It yielded a maximum number of 35 sheep including 3 female skulls, a young mature pig and 5 chickens, as well as a partial dog burial. In general, the bone indicates a waste assemblage different to that of Period IV (ditch 205).

This rubbish accumulation was deliberately sealed virtually level with the ground by a dump of nearly clean brickearth, II, possibly to prevent smell. This, however, soon subsided as the rubbish fills decayed and settled, and a brown pebbly loam, I, accumulated in the sinkage hollow. Copper alloy objects include a decorated chatelaine fitting (Fig 39.7), two pins (Fig 40.36–7) and a *ligula* from L III; and a *ligula*, pin, three studs (Fig 40.45–6) and a coin of Claudius I from L I. The pottery has been

fully quantified and is discussed elsewhere (p 99–104). It would indicate a date for its main fill, III, *c* AD 130–160; and for the subsidence fill, I, *c* AD 130–170, though contaminated by much later material. Given these parameters, the pit was probably in use as a water tank sometime towards the end of the Period V, or the beginning of Period VI

Other pits dated to this phase are 35 (*c* AD 130–200), 65, 67 (*c* 140–200), 74, 84 (Fig 14.S45) (mainly 4th century in date, but residual finds suggest an origin — or obliterated feature — in the 2nd century), and 89 (*c* AD 60–200; Fig 14.S47)

Dating evidence

1 (Gulley) *Samian* ff 31, 45, CG, Late Antonine (Cat 3); f31R, CG, Late Antonine (Cat 11)
2 (Pit) *Samian* f18, SG, early Flavian (good condition), f33, CG, 2nd century (both Cat 9)
67 (Pit) *Samian* f18, SG, Neronian–Flavian
74 (Pit) *Pottery* bowl (**34/45**), ?Flavian–Trajanic, Fig 60.27
90 (Pit) For full quantification, see p 99–104
138 (Pit) *Pottery* bowl-jar E5 (**45**), 2nd century
237 (Upper gravel path) *Copper alloy* spatula probe terminal (Cat 528); crenellated bracelet (Cat 252), ?4th century; pin with applied, multifaceted head, ?4th century (Cat 218). *Samian* f18 x 2, SG, pre-Flavian–Flavian (Cats 345, 347); f?36, SG, Flavian (Cat 568); f18/31, LMDV, Trajanic (Cat 218); f31 x 2, CG, Antonine (Cats 239, 292); f33, CG, Antonine (Cat 237); f37, CG, Antonine (Cat 239); f37, EG, late Antonine (Cat 246). *Other pottery* platter A1/5 (**45**), pre-Flavian (Cats 322, 513); bowl B2 (**47**), *c* AD 120+ (Cat 366); plain-rimmed dish (**47**), *c* AD 120/30 (Cat 388); white-slipped ?Hadham scraps, early 2nd century+ (Cats 246, 255, 455); Oxford white ware mortarium (Cat 252); ?Hadham oxidised ware (Cat 239); N Gallic beaker H20, probably post- AD 120 (Cat 255); Flagon (**27**) (Cats 347, 352, 368); Fabric (**50** (Cat 345)

The gravel appears to be Hadrianic–Antonine in date although the scouring effect of the medieval alluvial silts which removed all later stratigraphy has intruded later material into Cats 237, 239, 246, 292, including four 4th century coins: House of Constantine x 2 (Cats 239, 252), Urbs Roma (Cat 239) and Constantine I (Cat 239)
723 (Fire pit) *Pottery* scraps including ?N Gaulish colour-coat beaker, H20/7, *c* AD 120+
733 (Hearth) *Pottery* Scraps of Fabrics **45**, **47**, 1st–2nd centuries. Storage jar G44 (**44**), 2nd century
741 (Post-hole) *Pottery* platter A1.5 (**5**); sherds of Pelichet 47 amphora, ?S French fabric. 2nd century.
808 (Hearth) *Samian* f27, SG, early Flavian. *Other pottery* storage jar G44 (**44**), lid (**45**), dish B2 (**47**), Hadrianic–Antonine. Generally *c* AD 140–170
NB It is apparent that the supply of Central Gaulish samian to the site had largely dried up by the mid 2nd century. Virtually no East Gaulish samian was found.

Period VII.1: 3rd century (Fig 20)

The 3rd century was a period of general inactivity across the whole site, a conclusion based on both ceramic and coin evidence — a phenomenon noted in other Roman towns in Essex (p 129). The coin list indicates a possible hiatus of activity from c 220 to 250, whilst ceramically, distinctive early to mid 3rd century forms, such as folded beakers or incipient-flanged rimmed bowls, are almost wholly missing. It has already been observed that samian supply dries up in the Trajanic period. It has been suggested above (p 31) that the 'corridor' structure was probably essentially 2nd century and that its 3rd century successor, if we need to look for one at all, lay outside the excavated area, to the west. However, it should also be borne in mind that many Antonine pottery types may have continued in use well into the 3rd century, so that genuine 3rd century contexts may exist, unrecognised.

Inside the excavated area, north of the post-medieval drainage ditch, 133, not one purely 3rd century feature can be isolated. South of the ditch, 3rd century features comprised Structure 47, which cut Structure 41 and hence contained much disturbed walling material, pottery dated c AD 180–230 and a copper alloy pin with glass head (Fig 40.32); 110, Fig 14.S49, containing a denarius of Julia Domna (AD 196–211); 128, and 131, a ?gulley, largely cut away by the 4th century pit 114 (Fig 14.S45). Later 3rd century pits are: 7 (pottery c AD 275+; coin of Valerian, AD 253–260; and a copper alloy penannular brooch pin); and 49/85 (pottery c AD 250–400, coin of Tetricus II, AD 270–273, Valerian 253–260, Claudius II 268–270 and Valens 364–378; copper alloy ferrule, Fig 41.55).

Period VII.2: 4th century (Figs 20–2)

The Romano-Celtic temple (Structure 9)

Make-up for the foundations (Fig 20)
The date of the construction of the octagonal structure, a temple of Romano-Celtic type, is difficult to postulate, since the surrounding contemporary ground surface has been scoured away by the medieval alluvial silt, and since the masonry was extensively robbed. In the south and west quarters of the temple, certain areas had been excavated prior to the temple's construction, the excavations being backfilled with almost clean brickearth and rubble. However, these important make-up levels were themselves disturbed in robbing operations (cf Fig 18.S34–6), rendering them less useful. The single coin of AD 313–317 cited by Drury (1972, 24) as being securely stratified in the make up, is in fact in the uppermost layer (Cat 1067) and a query had been attached to its stratification at the time of excavation. Drury also uses the massive increase in the number of 4th century coins on the site to corroborate a construction date of c 320–5. Whilst

'*all* British sites show a major loss of coin between 330 and 378' (Reece 1980, 118), and hence a huge increase in coin numbers in the 4th century cannot be equated *necessarily* with a corresponding major increase in the economy or population, the coin list does indicate a considerate rise in the level of activity c AD 320–330 (p 71).

Thus, despite the dangers of the chronology, a Constantinian origin for the temple can still be justified. The two closest British parallels (see Section IX) are Pagans Hill (late 3rd century) and Weycock (early 4th century) (Lewis 1966, 51, tab 6).

The rubble-filled make-up excavations (Fig 20) took the form of many lobed hollows, reflecting the line of the southern and south-western walls of the temple (Fig 18.S33–39). They include: 157, 161–3, 172, 173, 195, 263, 273, 301, 321, 324, 325, 331, 342 and 393, whilst they could represent a collection of pits, they may equally represent the site of a group of trees grubbed up prior to the commencement of building work possibly even a sacred grove which had acted as an earlier focus of activity (ie, the earlier gravelled pathway and 1st century votive objects). The rubble used to backfill these hollows included much tile (bonding tile, *tegulae*, *imbrices*, and a margined floor tile from 161; some of it was mortared, and some burnt), flint, chalk, and *septaria* nodules, Kentish ragstone, greensand and limestone, as well as mortar and a weak lime concrete, in a clean brickearth matrix. In addition painted wallplaster was found in Cats 195, 330, 342, 392 and 918. The group from 195 (see Fig 18.S35) includes yellow, red, green, yellow/red, red/green, red stripe and white with yellow and red colours. Since 195 forms part of the pre-construction make-up, this plaster must either be derived from an earlier building on site (?the temple's predecessor) or from an earlier building elsewhere in *Caesaromagus*.

Pottery from these levels consisted of a few featureless sherds, mainly grey wares; none were by necessity 4th century in date. Other finds included a copper alloy pin (Cat 161), and a mid 1st century hinged brooch (Fig 38.22).

Other levels of a similar depth and character (containing building materials in an almost pure brickearth matrix) in the vicinity did yield sherds of late Nene Valley, Oxfordshire red colour-coat, oxidised Hadham, and late shell-tempered wares, including disturbances post AD 350/70. These layers are: 147 (coin, Valentinian I; flange-rimmed dish (**47**), Fig 60.47), 156, 184 (coin, Constantine II), 227, 304, 330 and 377. These should probably be regarded as intrusions into the pre-temple make-up levels, at the time of the robbing of the temple (see below).

Dating evidence
161 (Hollow) *Samian* Rim of vase of uncertain form, EG, late–2nd century (Cat 163)

The temple construction (Figs 20, 21, Pls VI, VII)
The temple itself, then, was probably constructed in the first quarter of the 4th century, possibly c AD

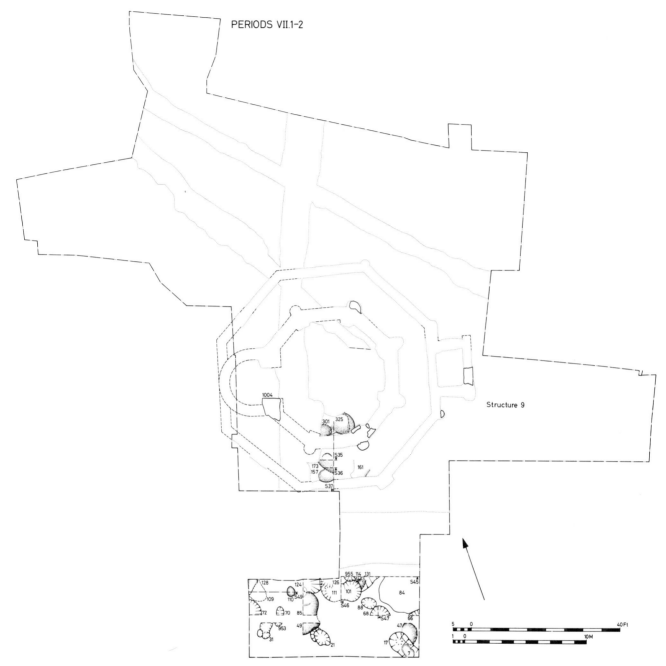

Figure 20   Site K: Period VII. Phases 1 and 2. The temple

320/5, over the earlier gravel pathway and on the same general alignment. It was octagonal in plan, c 17.70m overall with a *cella* c 11.00m overall. The *cella* walls were c 1.00m thick at foundation level, with rectangular piers internally and semi-circular piers externally at the angles. The building had been robbed, probably in two phases, with the exception of a few fragments of foundation. Where these survived, eg, 1001, 1002, they were of flint rubble, with some *septaria* and tile, in a hard lime mortar.

The floor levels had been totally eroded, and the flooring material cannot be satisfactorily identified. A lack of tesserae would seem to argue against such a floor; *opus signinum* is possible, or a raised floor

(?of timber or 'margined' floor tiles, see p 63), which would have been a wise precaution in a fairly low-lying area, probably prone to occasional flooding.

On the west side, the foundations terminated in relatively heavy pier bases, one of which survived, 1004 (Fig 18.S33), and these presumably carried an arch over an opening c 2.50m wide. The area beyond the opening was almost wholly destroyed by later disturbance, or lay outside the excavated area. However it has been reconstructed as an apsidal alcove, possibly housing a cult statue.

On the east, two additional engaged columns were provided at the outer quarter points, clearly flanking the entrance; at an unknown later date, a

Plate VI Site K: surviving masonry in the temple foundation trench, 1001, 1002 (Photo: P J Drury)

Plate VII Site K: surviving masonry pier base, 1004 (Photo: P J Drury)

rectangular porch was added, projecting forward some 3 metres. The north porch wall foundation trench was clearly misaligned, revealing the prior existence of the column foundation at that point.

Aligned on the axis of the eastern wall of this porch were two stone-and-tile packed postpits, interpreted by Drury (1972, 24) as belonging to sub-Roman lean-to structures. However, no 4th century pottery was found in them; furthermore the packing of flint and tile, including mortar bedding for *imbrices*, is no different to the rubble used to consolidate the hollows in the south-western area, prior to construction of the temple. Pit 294 (Fig 18.S41), 0.36m deep, contained packing material comprising flint, septaria, limestone and erratic quartzite pebbles; the post-pipe was c 0.25m in diameter. Pottery in the fill of the pit (packing and pipe undifferentiated) was dated c AD 250–300. Pit 586, c 0.25m deep, with a pipe c 0.27m in diameter, had been filled with flints, chalk and *septaria*. A third pit, 423, lay immediately outside the south-eastern corner of the porch. This was square, 0.45m deep, packed with tile, flint, and mortar fragments around a square post pipe c 0.30m across (pottery dated c AD 250–400). The pipe also contained tile and mortar fragments in a medium brown loam matrix. The mortar from the pit is important in that it partly comprised bedding apparently from the eaves of a building, retaining impressions of *tegulae* and *imbrices*. The *tegulae* appear to have been laid with staggered horizontal joints in each row. One tile from the packing had been purpose-made for abutment to a valley gutter or hip. This material was clearly derived from a nearby sustantial building, not necessarily the temple itself. A fourth pit may have originally existed, symmetrical with 423, on the north-east corner of the porch, lost in the sewer pipe trench.

These three pits (and the suggested fourth) are here interpreted as part of a grand symmetrical elaboration of the temple porch (*cf* Uley, Ellison 1980, and below, p 136), though it is not possible to suggest how they were incorporated (?two side arches).

For a further discussion of the temple, its reconstruction and parallels, see p 134*ff*.

The southern part of the site

The high number of 4th century rubbish pits and general debris in the upper levels of earlier features, suggests an increase of activity on the site. The area also yielded 28 4th century coins. The quantity of Oxfordshire red colour-coat and late shell-tempered pottery, dated in Chelmsford to post c 360/70 (Going 1987, 115) indicates that activity was still at a high level in the last three or four decades of the 4th century. This could of course be activity relating either to the temple's use or to the robbing of the temple's masonry. All pits contain late shell-tempered pottery unless otherwise stated.

Pit 7 was cut by 17 (Tetricus I, AD 270–3); 21 (Constantine I, AD 310–313); 31 (Gratian, 367–378); 66; 68 (denarius of Constantine I, Fig 14.S47); 70, cutting earlier pits; 72, containing the only occurrence on site of white *tesserae*; 84 (Fig 14.S45), a distinct late 4th century fill in a earlier pit (Gallienus, Constantine I, Constantinopolis, Constans, House of Constantine, Valens; copper alloy ribbon strip bracelet, Fig 40.21; nail; ornamental fixture, Fig 41.49; ferrule, Fig 40.56; lead lump); 88 (Constantine I, glass vessel fragment with blue dot, Fig 44.10); 101 (Fig 14.S46) including 111 and 126 (House of Constantine, Valentinian I, copper alloy ribbon strip bracelet); 109 (Fig 14.S49: spread of building rubble and tile lying over pit 90, denarius of Marcus Aurelius (AD 159–160, Alice Holt pottery); 114 (Fig 14.S46), relationship unknown with 101; 124 (Constantine I;

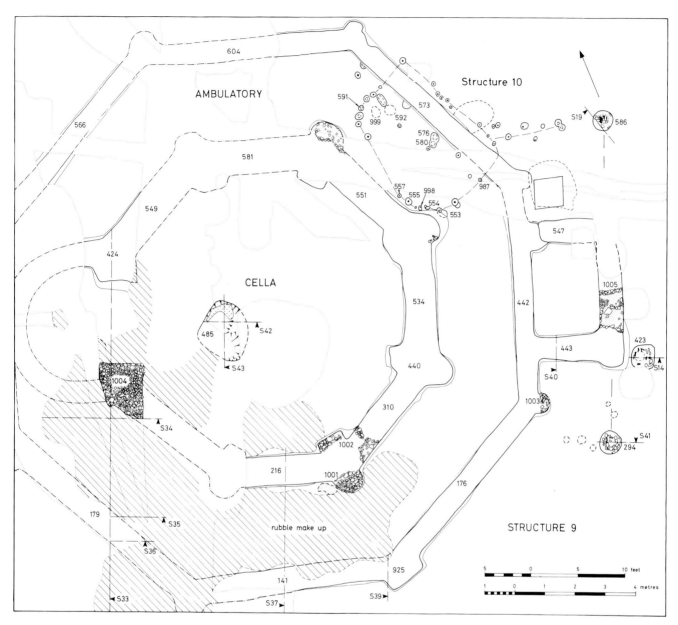

Figure 21   Site K: the octagonal Romano-Celtic temple (Structure 9)

copper alloy bracelet fragment, Fig 40.22); 127 (Fig 14.S45; Crispus, Constans, Valens, copper alloy tweezers); 953; and 955 (Fig 14.S45).

With the exception of the pit tank 90, the pits were cut down to, rather than through, the natural gravel normally underlying the brickearth subsoil. So many pits were dug that the final effect in many areas was a depth of *c* 0.75m of dark soil.

Dating evidence
7 (Pit) *Pottery* closed form (**4**), probably 4th century; melon beaker sherd (**47**), mid 4th century. *Coin* Valerian, AD 253–60 (Cat 1041)
47 (Pit) *Pottery* bead rimmed dishes x 4 (**47**), Antonine; folded beaker (**47**), *c* AD 180+
49 (Pit) *Coin* Tetricus II, AD 270–3 (Cat 1050)

85 (Pit) *Coins* Valerian, AD 253–60; Claudius II, AD 268–70; Valens, AD 364–78, all Cat 1053
110 (Pit) *Coin* Julia Domna, AD 196–211 (Cat 1059)
128 (Pit) *Pottery* Fabric **48**, post *c* AD 280
294 (Post pit) *Pottery* Late G5 (**47**), probably mid-late 3rd century.
423 (Post pit) *Pottery* ?jar sherd (**48**), probably mid-late 3rd century+

Period VIII: Temple robbing, post- c AD 390 (Fig 22, Pl VIII)

It is virtually impossible to suggest a terminal date for the use of the temple. The coin series includes Valens (x20), House of Valentinian (x16), Arcadius

Table 2: Site K: Octagonal temple component contexts and finds

Trench Location	Context	Component Cat nos	Pottery date and fabrics	Coins, other objects
Cella				
S	216 (Fig 18.S37)	232–4, 267–8, 994	360–400 **2, 3, 4, 51**	cu alloy strip
Pier (*in situ*)	1001, 1002	—	—	
SE	310	343	360–400 **3, 4, 51** Fig 59.8	Claudius I
Pier	440	—	350+, **4**, Fig 59.9	
E	534	—	60–120, **PR**	
NE	551	1029	80–140, **44, 45, 47**	
Pier (*in situ*)	—	—	—	
N	581	582	280–400, **4**	
NW	549	550	275–400, **48**	
W–N pier	424 (Fig 18.S33)	533, 1107	4th C, **4, 48**	Valens
W	432	—	360–400, **3, 4**	
W–S pier (*in situ*)	1004 (Fig 18.S33)	—	—	
SW	—	—	—	
Ambulatory				
S	141 (Fig 18.S37–8)	142, 969	—	
Pier	925 (Fig 18.S39)	—	—	
SE	176	200, 235, 348	360+, **3, 4**	
Pier (*in situ*)	1003	—	—	
E	442	529, 542, 1076	360+, **2, 3, 4, PR**	Vespasian
NE	573	574, 602–3	360+, **51**	cu alloy chain link
Pier (*in situ*)	—	—	—	
N	604	605	1st–early 2nd C, **44, 45, 47,**	
NW	566	598–9, 983	275–400; 360–400	
W	—	—	—	
SW	179	194, 262	360+, **2, 3, 4, 51,** mortarium (**4**), Fig 59.15	cu alloy pin
Porch annex				
N	547	548	200–400, **44, 45, 47**	
S	443 (Fig 18.S40)	—	350–360+ **2**, ?flagon	
E (*in situ*)	1005	—	—	

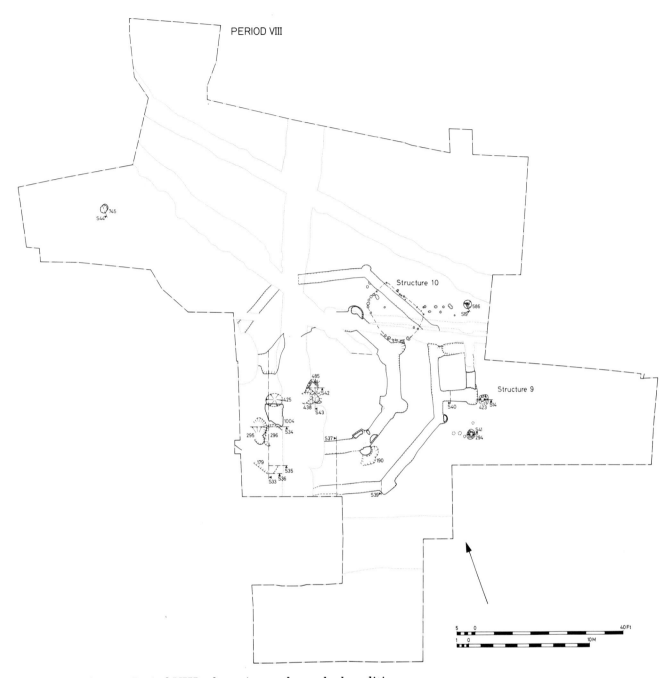

Figure 22   Site K: Period VIII, alteration and temple demolition

(x7) and House of Theodosius (x7). The majority of these were found in site clearance levels and in the many medieval ditches which cross the site. It is noticeable that only one coin of the House of Theodosius was found in the rubbish pits to the south of the drainage ditch 133. The evidence might indicate that the temple went out of use during the last decade of the 4th century (c AD 388–402), although a coin series from a Romano-British site can only rarely substantiate terminal dates after c AD 402 (Rahtz 1985, 111).

The masonry of the octagonal temple was comprehensively robbed, extending to much of the flint rubble make-up beneath the structure, which not only destroyed the outline of the foundation trenches in the south and west, but also partly

contaminated the make-up levels themselves (see above).

The robbing appears to have been carried out at the end of the 4th century, c AD 400. It is associated with much late shell-tempered pottery, but *no* hand-made, grass-tempered pottery, characteristic of the Early Saxon period (cf Drury & Wickenden 1982a). Other small finds of the same date, largely found redeposited in medieval or later contexts include a silver buckle (Fig 37.1), a copper alloy mount with ring-and-dot decoration (Fig 39.6), a polychrome glass bead (Fig 44.22) and fragments of eight glass vessels (Fig 44.16–21).

The robbing trenches were neat and flat-bottomed, where the stone-work in the foundation trenches had simply been lifted out, in a style

Plate VIII   Site K: robbed-out foundations of the Romano-Celtic temple looking north (Photo P J Drury)

similar to that noticed with the *mansio* (Drury 1988, 34, fig 16.S1). A list of component contexts and their find-dates is given above in Table 2.

The robbing trenches, as listed above, contained three medieval sherds; two sherds of Mill Green coarseware from the eastern cella trench 534, and one sherd of London ware from the eastern ambulatory trench 442 (Cat 542, *lower* fill). These cannot be attributed to any known medieval disturbances in the same area, and so it must be a strong possibility that they are contemporary within their contexts, dating the robbing of the *foundations* of the temple to the later 13th century; however, given the relative frequency of intrusive material, this must remain in doubt. The late Roman pottery was very abraded and scrappy.

The rubble make-up levels (see above) were also partly robbed; the following Cat numbers contain one or more of the late Roman pottery fabrics (Oxfordshire red colour-coat, oxidised Hadham, thick white Nene Valley, and late shell-tempered) and late coins: 147 (Valentinian I), 156, 184 (Constantine II), 227, 304, 330, and 393. In addition, the following dark loamy layers overlying the hollows contained the same late material: 158, 160, 174, 190, 213, 226, 295 (House of Theodosius), 296, 329, and 376 (House of Constantine I, Valentinian I). Hollow 425 (Valentinian I, copper alloy chain links), partly overlay the remnants of masonry pier 1004, and contained flecks of charcoal (Fig 18.S33). Also in these upper layers were three coins, Constantine I (Cats 1067, 1073), and House of Constantine (Cat 1068). Hollow 225 yielded Oxfordshire red colour-coat, but also a small, thin fragment of irridescent vessel glass, probably post-medieval and likely to be intrusive. These levels were cut (where applicable) by the medieval boundary ditch 264, and sealed or truncated by the later alluvial silts.

Feature 485 (Fig 18.S42–3) was the much disturbed remains of an oven, lined with substantial remains of a kiln structure (after Drury 1972, 25), including fired clay slabs, tiles, flint and oyster shell fragments. It was filled with a dark silty loam containing pebbles, chalk, limestone, tile, and mortar (some fragments from roof tiles). One tile had a marginal border and was covered with *opus signinum* (?floor tile, Cat 937, p 63). Finds included coins of House of Constantine and Constantinopolis, animal bone, and fragments of a late Roman bone comb, decorated with ring-and-dot (Fig 43.1). The feature was cut by a medieval ditch to the west, by a medieval pit, 371, to the east, and by pit 438, which contained a coin of Constans and a bone plaque, incised with a human bust (Fig 43.2; *cf* Wickenden 1986). Pit 438 also cut pit 427, which itself contained late shell-tempered pottery, a Barbarous Radiate and a fragment of rolled copper alloy sheeting. Hollow 516, containing late shell-tempered pottery, cut the corner of the robber trench of the pier 424. Lesser features dated to the end of the 4th century include post-hole 745 (Fig 18.S44), containing coins of Arcadius (x2) and the House of Theodosius (x2), a fragment of an iron annular brooch (Fig 42.14), and late shell-tempered pottery, together indicating a date post- *c* AD 388. To the south, a shallow pit, 191, contained late shell-tempered pottery and coins of Tetricus I, Crispus and Urbs Roma.

Dating evidence
191 (Pit) *Coins* Tetricus 1, AD 270–3 (Cat 1069); Constantine 1, AD 308–320 (Cat 202); Crispus, AD 320–4 (Cat 202); Urbs Roma, AD 330–45 (Cat 192). *Pottery* imitation f38 (**3**); flange-rimmed bowl (**51**); Fabric **2**. All very abraded, post- AD 360/70
425 (Hollow) *Coin* Valentinian 1, AD 364–375 (Cat 426). *Pottery* jar (**47**), Fig 60.50
438 (Pit) *Coin* Constans, AD 335–7.
485 (Oven) *Coins* Constantinopolis, AD 330–345 (Cat 502); House of Constantine, AD 350–60 (Cat 487)
745 (Post-hole) *Coins* Arcadius x2, House of Theodosius x2, AD 388–402 (Cats 745, 1086, 1087). *Pottery* bowl (**3**); jar (**51**). Fabric **48**

The stake-built structures (Figs 21–2)
Straddling the ambulatory wall in the north-east quarter was a possible structure *c* 4m x 3m overall, of sub-rectangular plan, though much cut by sewer trenches (Structure 10). It appears to have consisted of relatively small scantling posts penetrating the subsoil *c* 0.10–0.15m; there was evidence of internal support on the long axis, preumably in the line of the ridge. Component stake-holes are 553–5, 557, 576, 580, 591–2, 987, and 998–9; pottery in them was scrappy and residual, dated to the 1st–2nd centuries (576, 2nd–3rd centuries).

The stake-holes are absent over the ambulatory robbing trenches, probably missed in the dark loamy fill of the robber trenches. The structure appears to have been constructed against the still extant *cella* wall, but *after* the less substantial ambulatory wall had been demolished and its foundations robbed. The plan of the 'structure' appears remarkably 'Germanic', showing a resemblance to the normal form of sunken hut; indeed, it is not impossible that it was sunken, though not to any great depth.

Lines of stake-holes of a similar size and depth (less than 100mm) were also found nearby to the north and south of the temple porch, clearly related to the stone-packed post-pits, 294, 423, and 586.

Drury interpreted them as contemporary, belonging to sub-Roman lean-to structures, in use during the robbing of the temple (1972, 24). Whilst the postpits are now thought to belong to a re-construction of the temple porch (see above), the stake-holes may still belong to this 'sub-Roman' phase in the manner Drury suggested, simply utilizing the pre-existing postpits in the lean-to buildings.

IV The Other Sites

1 Site M: 1–4 The Chase. TL 710063

Introduction

In 1970, three trial trenches were dug under the direction of P J Drury. The first was later incorporated in the main excavated area dug in June 1970 (*cf* Fig 2). Trench 2 located only disturbed subsoil over brickearth. Finds included late 1st century AD to Antonine pottery, tile and fired clay. Trench 3 located a small north-south gulley with a greyish brown fill and the edge of a dark silty feature cut into, or lying over, a gravel scatter. Finds included a small amount of Roman grey ware.

The main area (Fig 23) lay some 20m to the north of the temple but was apparently wholly domestic in character, comprising a large number of intersecting pits of the 2nd to 4th centuries and three gullies. These were covered by a general level of dark loam, and this, as well as the later pits, produced an appreciable quantity of late Roman shell-tempered pottery.

The excavated features

Periods I–II Prehistoric

A number of Late Bronze Age/Early Iron Age flint-gritted sherds, and worked flints, including blades and a late Mesolithic microlith, attest sporadic prehistoric occupation — part of the same deposit as that from Site K. Details will appear in Healey *et al* forthcoming.

Period VI: 2nd Century (Fig 23)

The following features were dated to the 2nd century: two small intersecting pits, 17 and 36 (Fig 24.S50); Pit 56, sub-rectangular, with a greenish grey silty fill, is dated to post *c* AD 125. Features 32, 33, 38, 52 and 57 all contained 2nd century material, and all either cut, or are contiguous to, one another. The result of this activity of pit digging was a general hollow 54.

Continued pit cutting, and a general accumulation of rubbish introduced 3rd and 4th century finds into pits 11, 27, 45 and 49. Two intrusive medieval sherds are also present in 32 and 33.

Relevant finds include a bowl, relief-decorated with a snake (Fig 60.31 and p 128), found in Pit 54 (with a joining sherd from 45); Coins of Tiberius (Pit 52), Antoninus Pius (Pit 33), Faustina II (Pit 32), Claudius II (Pit 45); a Nauheim derivative

brooch from Pit 11 (Fig 37.2), and also from Pit 11 fragments of *opus signinum* and painted plaster. The brooch and coin of Tiberius indicate some activity in the 1st century, whilst at the other end of the scale, late shell-tempered pottery in Pits 38, 59 and in 54 indicates continued use post *c* AD 360/70.

Further east, pits 13, and 34 were probably 2nd century in origin, though again 13 contained 4th century and medieval pottery in its upper fill. Pit 68 might also be of this date, and was cut by a 4th century pit, 65.

Finally, a near complete unabraded samian bowl f18/31, stamped DIICVMINVS (Lezoux), was found in pieces lying on the brickearth, 86, and is Trajanic to Hadrianic in date. No bones or grave pit could be found in its immediate vicinity.

Dating evidence

All pits

11 *Brooch* Nauheim derivative, Fig 37.2. *Pottery* bead rim dishes (**41**, **45**); jar G5 (**47**); white-slipped Hadham ware, probably Antonine; Fabric **43**; folded beaker (**47**), and Fabric **48**, post *c* AD 280 (both Cat 14)

32 *Coin* Faustina II, AD 150-60. *Samian* f15/17R or 18R, SG, probably pre-Flavian (Cat 37, baulk). *Other pottery* Poppyhead beaker, H6 (**32**), plain-rim dish (**40**); bead rim dish (**47**), post- AD 120; Fabric **43**

33 *Coin* Antoninus Pius, AD 138–61. *Samian* f33, CG, 2nd century (Cat 43). *Other pottery* Poppyhead beaker H6 (**32**); bead rim dish (**47**, post- AD 120; plain dish (**40**)

34 *Pottery* VRW; bead rim dish (**41**), post- AD 120; folded beaker (**47**)

45 *Coin* Claudius II, AD 268–70. *Samian* f33, CG, Hadrianic or Antonine. *Other pottery* wall-sided mortarium (**24**), ?later 3rd–mid 4th century, Fig 59.24; bowl with applied snake, Fig 60.31

49 *Samian* f37, CG, *c* AD 125–50

52 *Coin* Tiberius, AD 12–20

54 *Samian* f31, EG, probably early Antonine. *Other pottery* bowl with applied snake (Fig 60.31); late shell-tempered ware, post- AD 360/70; Romano-Saxon Roberts type C38.7

59 *Samian* f18, SG, Neronian–early Flavian (Cat 63). *Other pottery*, accumulating to post AD 360/70 (**51**)

86 (brickearth) *Samian* f18/31, CG, stamped DIICVMINVS, Trajanic–Hadrianic (Table 6, No 6).

Baulks *Samian* f18, SG, Neronian–early Flavian, f27, CG, micaceous Lezoux ware, Neronian–Flavian (both Cat 62); f35/36, SG, 1st century (Cat 60); f18/31, CG, Trajanic (Cat 70); f33, CG, Antonine (Cat 61)

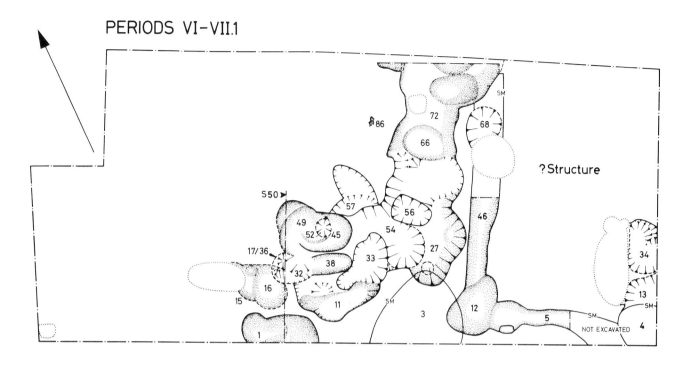

PERIODS VI–VII.1

?Structure

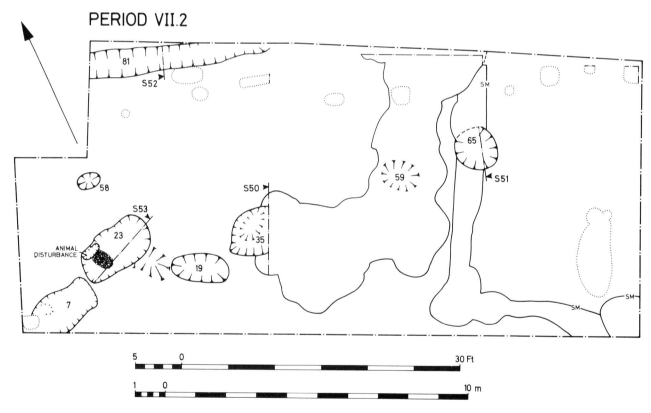

PERIOD VII.2

ANIMAL DISTURBANCE

5   0   30 Ft

1   0   10 m

Figure 23   Site M: Periods VI and VII

Period VII: 3rd–4th centuries (Figs 23, 24)

Disregarding the continued activity in the palimpsest of pits already discussed, the following features were dug: pit 1 (Fig 24.S50; post AD 280; containing much *opus signinum* and yellow painted plaster fragments); pit 3; depressions 15, 16 (Fig 24.S50; post- AD 280); quarry pit 72 (post-AD

270/80, accumulating to post- AD 360/70). This contained a deeper earlier feature, 66, and a spread of fired clay in its upper fill and part of a much weathered oven *in situ* lying over the pit.

Two gullies were dug at right angles to each other. Gulley 5 contained pottery of mid 3rd to 4th centuries and terminated in pit 4 (late 2nd to 3rd century pottery). Gulley 46 contained 4th century

Site M

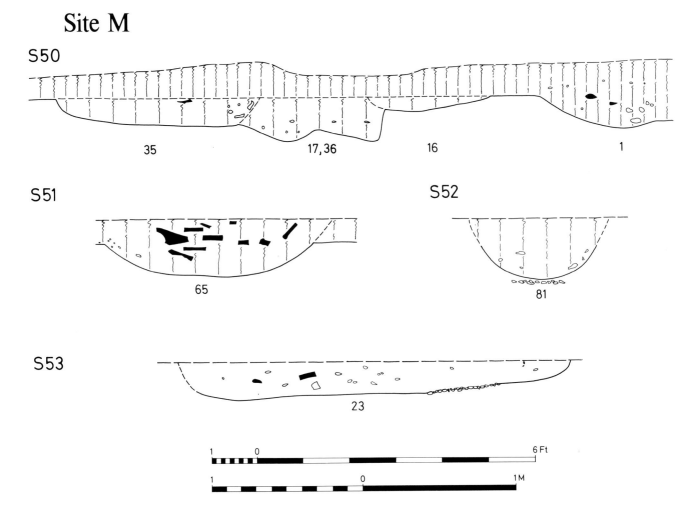

S50

35   17,36   16   1

S51

65

S52

81

S53

23

1 0   6 Ft

1   0   1M

Figure 24   Site M: Sections S50–53. For key to sections, see Fig 6

pottery. The corner junction was obscured by pit 12 (containing mid 3rd century pottery and a pin and spring from a one-piece brooch). It is possible that these form the corner of a building of timber slot construction with pit 12 acting as a corner post. The group of external rubbish pits would clearly be associated. A third gulley to the north, 81, contained late shell-tempered pottery (Fig 24.S52).

To the west two similar rectangular pits, 7 and 23, were dug. Pit 7 was disturbed by a modern pit and animal burrowing but contained 4th century pottery, a glass beaker base (Fig 44.12) and flint and greensand. Pit 23 (Fig 24.S53) contained late shell-tempered pottery and a deposit of hoggin in the bottom. Feature 58, just to the north, might be associated.

Other features which contained late shell-tempered pottery and were therefore accumulating finds later than *c* AD 360/70, were pit 19 (much building material); pit 65 (Fig 24.S51; much tile; cut Gulley 46); pit 35 (Fig 24.S50), containing coins of Gratian and Constantius II, a ribbed glass bottle handle, and part of a shale bracelet (Fig 45.35). It also yielded a late Roman copper alloy rosette attachment (Fig 41.50).

The subsoil spreads of black loam, 101/102, 0.15m deep from the cleared level, contained late shell-tempered pottery and 15 coins ranging from a copy of Claudius 1 to Gratian. In addition, half a storage jar from a hearth was found in the dark silty loam subsoil (Cat 29). Its upper half was lightly combed and decorated with a row of stab marks around the shoulder (rim not present).

Dating evidence

1 (pit) *Pottery* bowl B6 (**47**), post *c* AD 250. Fabric **48**, later 3rd century

3 (pit) *Samian* f18, SG, Claudian–Neronian. *Other pottery* bead-rimmed dish (**47**), post *c* AD 120; jar G5 (**47**). Assemblage probably 3rd century+

7 (pit) *Glass* flask (Fig 42.12). *Pottery* carinated dish (**4**), late 4th century, Fig 59.10

15 (Depression) *Pottery* Fabric **48**, post- *c* AD 280

16 (Depression) *Pottery* Late thick white ware (**2**), 4th century; **48**, post- *c* AD 280

35 (pit) *Coins* Constantius II, 350–60; Gratian, 367–375

Pottery Late shell-tempered ware (**51**), post- *c* AD 360/70. Copper alloy circular disc-rosette attachment, *c* AD 400, Fig 41.50

Figure 25   Site AB: location of trenches

12/46 (pit/gulley junction) *Samian* f36, CG, ?Hadrianic–Antonine (Cat 28)

65 (Pit) *Pottery* necked bowl-jar (**4**), later 4th century, Fig 59.13 (Cat 67); narrow-necked jar (**4**), later 4th century, Fig 59.19 (Cat 67); Fabric **51**, post-AD 360/70

101/102 (Subsoil) *Coins* Fifteen coins Claudius 1–Gratian (AD 378–383). *Samian* f31, EG, Antonine (Cat 22), Curle 15, CG, late Antonine (Cat 24); f37, EG, Antonine (Cat 25); f33, x2, EG, Antonine (Cats 25, 29). *Other pottery* handled cauldron (**47**), Fig 60.49 (Cat 22); ?pedestal jar, ?lamp chimney (**48**), Fig 60.53 (Cats 22, 29); late shell-tempered ware (**51**), post AD 360/70, Fig 60.56 (Cat 24), Fig 60.54 (Cats, 25, 87)

In addition, pits 19, 23, 72 and gulley 81 contained late shell tempered ware (**51**), indicating accumulation post *c* AD 360/70.

Medieval and later

Some medieval pits were present. Post Roman levels were truncated by alluvial action. Silt (0.60m thick, mid brown, fairly pebbly), accumulated after which, in the later Medieval period, the area was cultivated. The site was finally disturbed by 19th century pit digging.

Comment

It is possible that some of the latest pits in the sequence were dug *after* the demolition of the temple on Site K, but lack of available dating evidence for distinguishing sequences after AD 360/70 makes it difficult to prove. Most of the features, both early and late, contained tile fragments. However, the presence of *opus signinum* and painted plaster fragments in pits 1 and 11, and *opus signinum* alone in the subsoil and in pit 45, might indicate a demolition horizon, though it is also possible such material originated elsewhere in the town.

2 Site AB: 1-12 Goldlay Road

Introduction

In July 1972/February 1973, four trenches, 0.85m wide were cut by machine on the site of Mildmay Terrace in Goldlay Road (Fig 25). Trench 1 located a large quarry pit (also found in Trench 2), 0.85m deep and filled with dark grey silty loam, three intersecting pits containing fired clay and tile, and gravel metalling at the north end at 0.55m depth. Trenches 2, 3 and 4 located areas of pits filled with dark grey-black loam, some with tile fragments, ranging in depth from 0.70 to 1.00m down to natural brickearth.

An area to the west of Trench 2, and incorporating Trench 1, covering approximately 120 sq m, was later excavated by P J Drury, revealing Roman features, including a possible building (Fig 25).

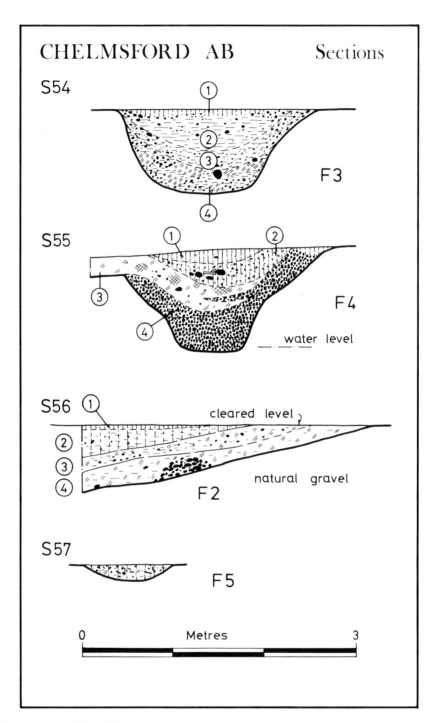

Figure 26   Site AB: Sections S54–57

The excavated features

Periods V–VI: 2nd century (Figs 25, 26)

At some stage in the 2nd century Structure 13 was constructed; it comprised two timber slots, 7 and 8, up to 0.15m deep and 4.25m apart. Slot 8 was only partly excavated but appeared to be on a slightly different alignment to 7. The eastern side of the structure consisted of post-holes 10 and possibly 9; others were probably lost in a later hollow 6, and a Victorian ash pit (1). All the features of the structure were filled with a fine brown loam with some pebbles. There were few finds. The western side lay outside the limits of excavation.

Two other features were probably associated with the building; Well 4 (Fig 26.S55) comprised a small shaft, 0.70m square, and was excavated to the water level, 1.20m below the cleared surface. There was no sign of a timber caisson which had perhaps been withdrawn. The shaft was filled with gravel (4) in a dark grey silty matrix above which was a lens of weathered brickearth (3) and packing material (flint, tile, pebble) in dark loam (2). Finds included pottery and tile, a lump of limestone and a pair of copper alloy tweezers. The upper sinkage fill (1) included pottery of the 3rd and 4th centuries.

Pit 3, 0.90m deep, was filled with a dark grey silty loam above a dirty silty clayey ballast (Fig 26.S54). Finds included tile, fired clay, 14 iron nails and two copper alloy pin fragments. The pottery from the lowest fill indicates a date in the mid to late 2nd century, and accumulating in the 3rd century, suggesting a slightly later date for this storage pit than the building and well.

The remaining area was obscured by a 2nd to 3rd century clay pit, 2, only a sample of which was excavated (Fig 26.S56); it was 0.70m deep and filled with grey loamy silt and brickearth. Finds included pottery, tile, *septaria* and fragments of a Rhenish lava quern. Cut into this was a small pit, 5 (Fig 26.S57), 0.08m deep and filled with charcoal, fired clay and 3rd–4th century pottery, possibly kiln debris, some of which joined sherds found in the clay pit.

A clean brown loamy silty subsoil accumulated over the site and contained a coin of Constantius II, and a piece of matt-glossy window glass.

Dating evidence
4 (well) *Samian* f30, SG, late Flavian; f38, EG, Antonine. *Other pottery* Dish B8.2/1 (**47**), 1st–early 2nd century, type vessel (Going 1987)
3 (pit) *Samian* **L III** f18, SG, Late Flavian
 L II f18, SG, Neronian; f18/31, CG, Hadrianic; f27, 31, CG, Antonine; f31, CG, stamped TITVRI.M, Antonine (Table 6.22); f35, SG, pre-Flavian, unusual small angular vessel (Fig 48.3)
2 (clay pit)*Samian* **L III** f18, SG, pre-Flavian
 L II f33, EG, Hadrianic–Antonine; CG fragments
 L I f29, SG, Flavian

3 Site L (Fig 2)

A machine-cut trial trench dug in 1970–1, 30m long and 1m wide, located the gravel pathway leading westwards towards the temple from the pastures by the rivers Can and Chelmer. The pathway was thus at least 75m long. Finds from this trench include pottery (Fabrics **21**, **44**, **47**, **48**; incipient flanged-rimmed bowl (**47**)), *tegulae*, combed box-flue tile and a copper alloy pin shaft.

4 Site Q: Salvation Army premises (TL 7119 0631) (Fig 27)

Five trenches, *c* 0.90m wide, were dug by JCB in April 1971 at the junction of Goldlay and Baddow roads (Figs 2, 27). 0.20–0.30m of topsoil overlay 0.20m–0.70m of greyish brown slightly pebbly alluvial silt, which overlay the natural, a compact orange gravel covered in part by a thin layer of brickearth. In some areas, especially in the south east corner, a buried medieval soil, 0.20m thick, overlay the natural. The site was much disturbed

by medieval and post-medieval features. One Romano-British 3rd century pit, 0.70m deep, with a brownish grey silty fill containing Roman pottery (Fabrics **1** or **2**, **47** plain-rimmed bowl) was discovered. The main feature, however, was a hollow-way, excavated to a depth of 1m, and filled with a grey-green pebbly silt, containing post-medieval pottery. It was *c* 12m wide. When its line is extended it joins up with the gravel surface noted on Site AS (below) and in the watching brief CR 35, which is here interpreted as a gravelled road, running east–west, forming the northern boundary of the temple complex, parallel to the road discovered on Site D. It therefore seems likely that the road in this vicinity had been heavily used in the post-Roman period, resulting in a hollow-way, in much the same way as Moulsham Street developed on the line of the main London–Colchester Roman Road (Cunningham & Drury 1985, 19).

5 Site AS: 16–18 Baddow Road (TL 709 064)

Two small area excavations, connected by a machine-cut trench, 20.5m x 2.0m overall, were carried out in May–June 1978 by R Turner for the Essex County Council Archaeology Section, and were funded by the Department of the Environment, in order to examine the development of the Baddow Road frontage, and to assess the archaeological potential of the flood plain of the River Chelmer within Chelmsford (Fig 28). A complete archive is deposited with the Sites and Monument Record.

Periods V–VI: 1st–2nd centuries (Fig 29)

On Area 1, the earliest features were a bank, 94, and a probable well, 108. Bank 94, of dark blue silty clay, was thrown up in the late 1st or early 2nd century, perhaps as part of a field boundary. Silts 105 and 112 subsequently built up around it to the level of the top of the bank. In the 2nd century, pit 108 was dug up to *c* 1.2m deep; there is little doubt that this was waterlogged in Roman times, and was thus probably a well. Two phases of this feature are apparent; the first cut may have utilised a natural hollow, though no primary fills survived. The hole appears to have been backfilled in the 2nd century with gravels 104, 106, 107, 128 and 129. Whilst these may simply represent infilling, it is feasible that they were deliberate packing for an early road surface, probably layer 106. A silt layer, 95, covered the area. In the second phase, the gravel packing was cut through by a substantial pit, possibly a second water tank or well. The lowest fill of this cut filled with slumped sandy gravel (126, Fig 30a). Above this, many alternating lenses of silts and charcoal-rich soils accumulated (124–113, Fig 30a), the bottom-most of

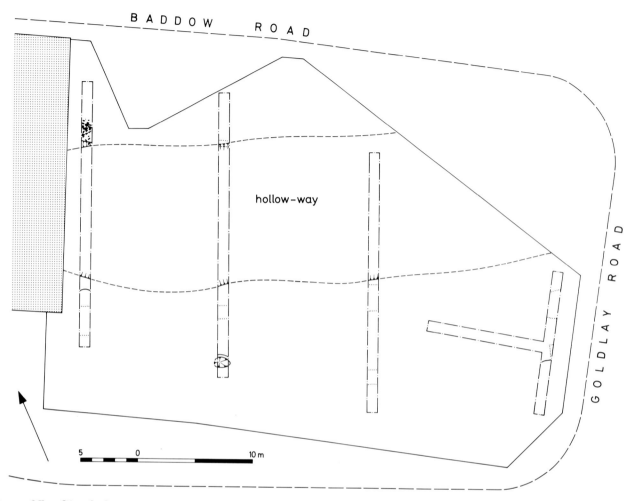

Figure 27   Site Q: location of trenches

which were deposited in anaerobic conditions — shown by the survival of fragments of leather and wood. The upper-most fills, 111 and 108 (Fig 30, S 58–9), comprised a stony loam, possibly ancient topsoil, backfilled at the end of the 2nd century in order to level the ground. After this backfilling, the land may have reverted to agricultural use since the top fills of the well seem to have been truncated by ploughing.

Dating Evidence
108 (well) *Samian* ff31, 33, 36, 37, CG, Antonine, some burnt; stamp T[. *Other pottery* 2nd–early 3rd century
LIII *Samian* f38, CG, stamped CARANTINI[M], *c* AD 150–180; f33, CG, stamped [SOSI]MIM, *c*AD 150–180; SG and CD sherds, Flavian–Antonine; *Other pottery* later 2nd–early 3rd centuries
95 (Silt) *Samian* F18/31R, SG, Flavian–Trajanic; chip ?CG. *Other pottery* 2nd–early 3rd centuries

Period VII.1: 3rd century (Fig 29)

Shortly afterwards, a metalled, cambered road, 93 (Fig 30, S 58-9), was laid down, bedded on a thin

layer of sandy gravel, 96. The road was 4.2m wide and was composed of 0.3–0.8m compacted gravel mixed with broken tiles and some occupation debris. Substantial mineralisation gave the road an extremely hard quality which would not have been so marked at the actual time of use. On the north side was a shallow ditch, 114, *c* 0.40m deep, and filled with blue-grey silt, the bottom of which was more pebbly than the top, being rainwashed gravel from the road surface (Fig 30, S 58–9).

Dating evidence
93 (Road) *Samian* f29, SG, late Flavian; ff18/31, 33, CG, 2nd century; *Other pottery* 2nd century
96 (gravel make up) *Samian* SG and CG scraps; *Other pottery* 2nd–early 3rd century
114 (Ditch) *Pottery* late 3rd century+

Period VII.2: 4th century (Fig 29)

A black silty soil, 92, accumulated over the metalled road surface, and a second road surface, 91, was laid down on a similar alignment, but was only *c* 3.5m wide (Fig 30, S 58–9).

51

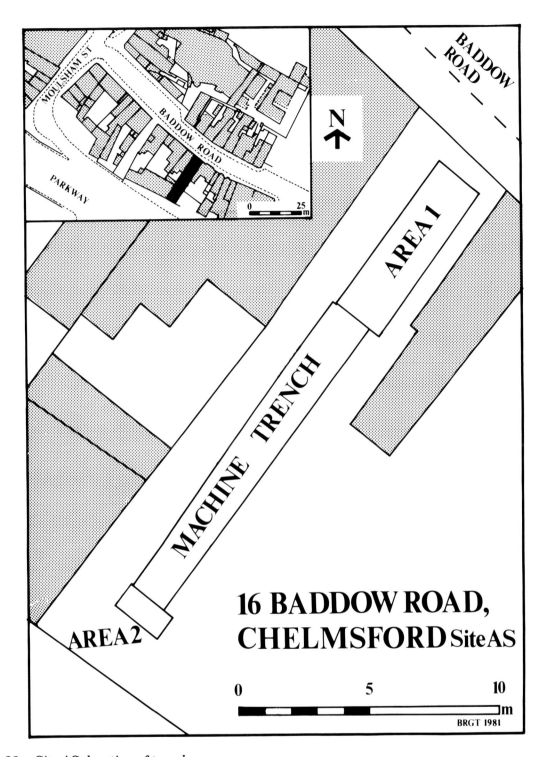

Figure 28   Site AS: location of trenches

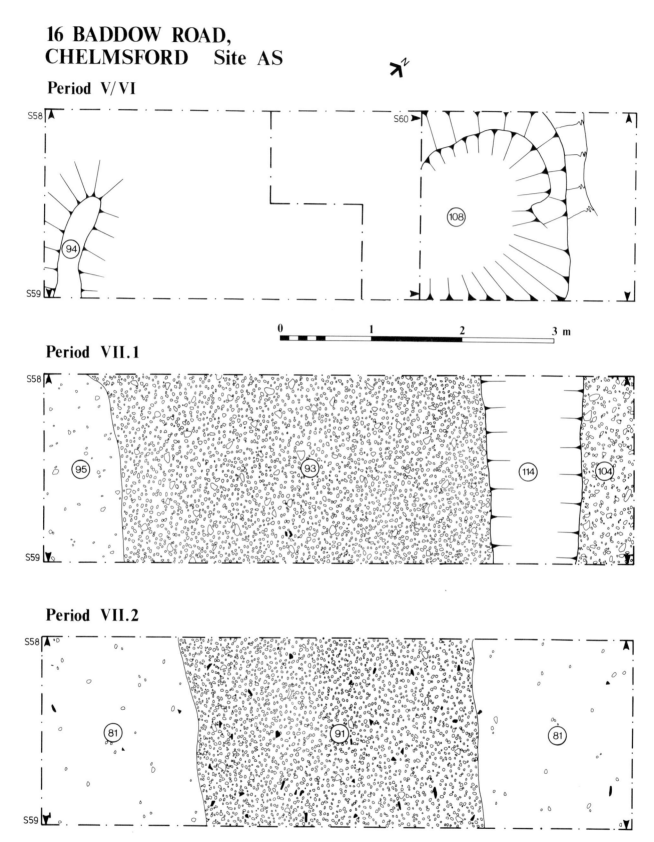

16 BADDOW ROAD, CHELMSFORD   Site AS

Period V/VI

Period VII.1

Period VII.2

Figure 29   Site AS: Periods V/VI; VII. Phases 1 and 2

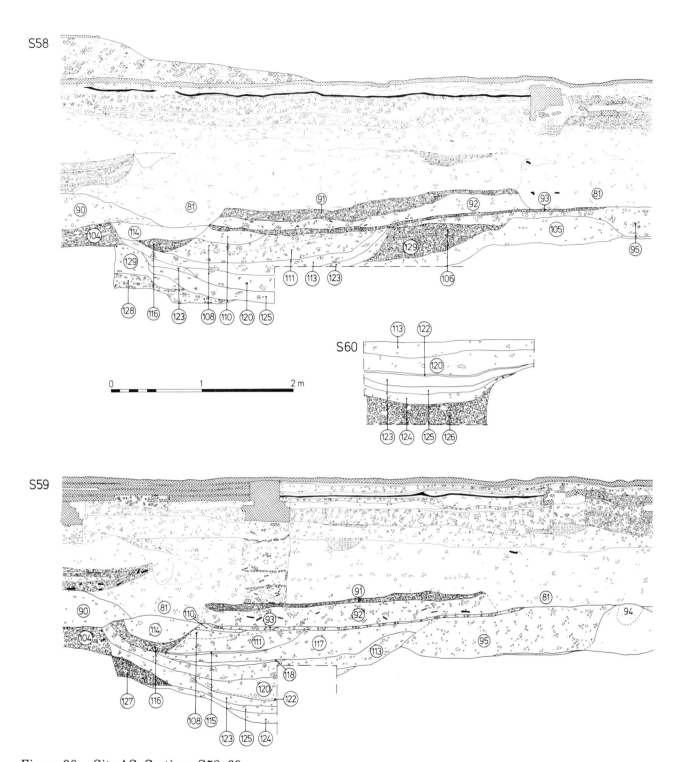

Figure 30   Site AS: Sections S58–60

Dating evidence
92 (Silt) *Pottery* AD 350+

Medieval and later

The silty soils, 90, 81, 74 and 72, which occurred immediately over the late Roman road, all contained medieval material, suggesting that the line of road 91 was at least visible, if not in use, in the 13th century. The soil layers appear to have

been deposited to a depth of 0.50m, to protect against flood (*cf* sites K, D and M). Roman finds in this soil suggest it had been taken from an area of considerable Roman activity. The medieval and post-medieval sequence, including the establishment in the 14–15th century of a major road on the line of the present Baddow Road, is described in a forthcoming report.

In Area 2 (Fig 28), a buried soil, 88, overlay the natural gravel, but no Roman features were found. Over Layer 88 a silty loam, 70, accumulated

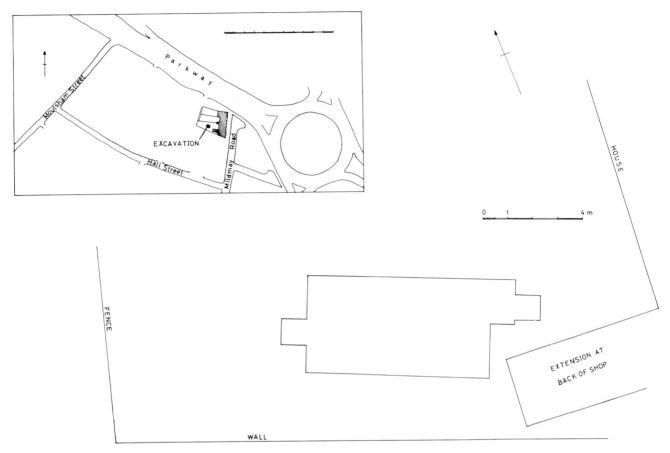

Figure 31   Site CF1: location of trenches

throughout the medieval and post-medieval periods. The machine-cut trench between Areas 1 and 2 did not reveal any features of major importance. The 13th century build-up soils were present throughout, and it was clear that the Roman silt, 95, had the effect of levelling the north part of the site to the height of the natural gravel in the south, thus filling a man-made hollow, to the south of which the original brickearth buried soil (88, Area 2) still survived above the natural gravel.

6 Site CF1: 16 Mildmay Road

A 4 x 8m trench was excavated in October-November 1983 in the garden of 16 Mildmay Road (Figs 2, 31), by Dr David Andrews of the Essex County Council Archaeology Section, prior to development. A complete level III report is deposited in the archive with the Sites and Monuments Record and only a summary of the Romano-British phases is given here.

Period IV. Phase 1. 1st century

After limited prehistoric occupation, the earliest Roman features (Fig 32A–B) comprised a number of pits, including a regular, vertical-sided ?tank,

113, containing a largely intact large carinated bowl slightly set into natural, and a small north-south slot, 99 (Fig 33). These features, combined with the large amount of household refuse found in them, suggest that the site was at this time peripheral to buildings elsewhere.

Periods IV.2–V. Later 1st — early 2nd Century

In the later 1st–early 2nd century, a series of gravel surfaces were found (Figs 32, C–D, 33). The earliest (62) survived over an area about 2m wide; this was sealed by a dark stony layer, containing some burnt material (59), in turn overlain by an orangey, sandy silt with some gravel (14, 60), below an excellently preserved gravel surface (9, 13) which was at least 4.9m wide and extended outside the excavated area to the east. A late or post-Roman boundary ditch (36/37) cut the surfaces on the west, and only a narrow strip of gravel, 115, survived to the west of the ditch. This gravel strip 115 was bounded to the west by a north-south ditch 81, approximately V-shaped, *c* 1m wide and *c* 0.7m deep (Fig 33). This may be interpreted as the western ditch of the early religious precinct, to be equated with ditches 205 and 705 on Site K (Fig 11). The gravelled surfaces 62/13 may then be seen as part of the east-west trackway found on Site K (257, Fig 2).

12-16 Mildmay Road (CF 1) 1983

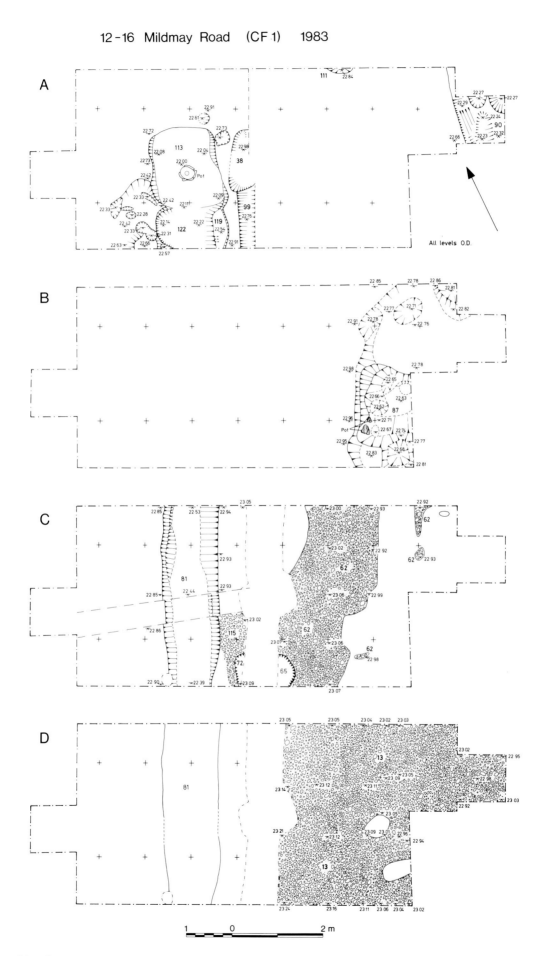

Figure 32   Site CF1: Periods IV–V

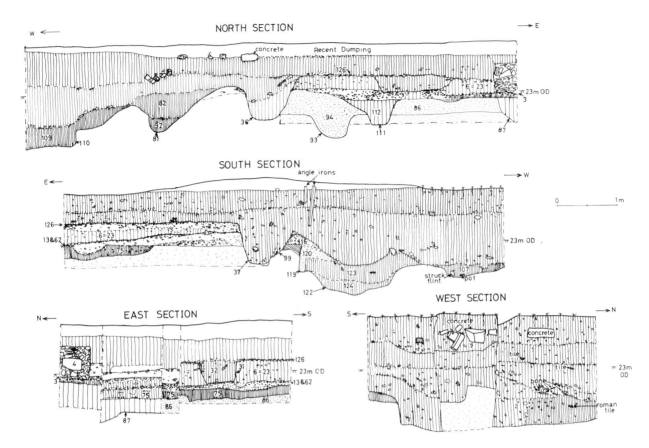

Figure 33   Site CF1: Sections

Above the second gravel surface 13 was a deposit of yellow brownish silty clay loam, overlain by a thin gravel layer 126, presumably another surface (Fig 33). The loam was thought by Peter Murphy (HBMC environmentalist) to be a levelling layer to eliminate the gradient in the surface of metalling 13. Although the latest evidence of Roman occupation, the finds from the loam are not later than the 2nd century. A little residual 3rd–4th century Roman pottery was recovered from the medieval layers. In the medieval period the site appears to have been cultivated, the boundary ditch 36/37 recalling the line of the earlier Roman trackway.

The finds

Coins, identified by D Barrett   *Context*

Constantine II	337–340	RIC 66	82
Constantius II	337–361		104
Valentinian I	364–375	RIC 7a	69

Objects of copper alloy (Fig 34)
The following is extracted from an archival report by Hilary Major.

Fig 34.1   One-piece Colchester derivative brooch with distorted 10-coil spring, *c* AD 50–70, CF1, 80 (Period IV.1, loam on eastern half of trench, west of pit 90).

Fig 34.2   Two-piece brooch of *Cam* type 14 (Hawkes & Hull 1947, 310); three coils of spring remaining. CF1, 109 (Post-Roman pit fill).

No 3   (unillustrated) Head of small Colchester brooch with plain wings, possibly moulded bow. (CF1, 114, upper fill of Period IV.1 pit 113, immediately pre-ditch 81).

Fig 34.4   Hod Hill brooch, mid 1st century. Base copper alloy contains zinc, lead and probably tin (analysis by Paul Wilthew); coated with tin, possibly with some lead. (CF1, 92, lowest filling of Period IV.2 ditch 81).

Fig 34.5   Decorated strip, possibly from finger-ring (CF1, 80, context as Fig 34.1).

Fig 34.6   Fitting, incomplete; probably originally circular with central perforation; two concentric corrugations round edge, and another around the central hole (CF1, 82; upper filling of ditch 81. The layer includes a coin of Constantine II).

No 7   (not illustrated). Corroded sheet fragment rolled into a tube, possibly originally corrugated (CF1, 114, context as No 3).

Other finds of copper alloy include a pin shaft, tapering rod, and plain strips. A fragment of sheet with a polished white metal coating may be from a mirror.

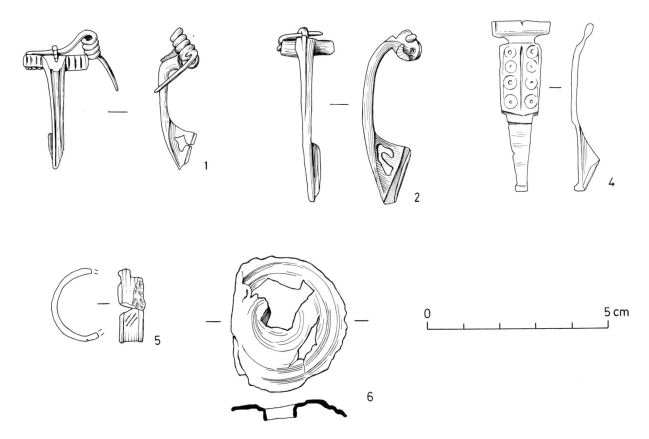

Figure 34   Site CF1: objects of copper alloy (Scale 1:1)

Discussion, by N P Wickenden

The discovery of three mid 1st century brooches in Period IV levels (and a fourth in a redeposited context), connected with ditch 81, and other pieces of copper alloy in association, can be paralleled directly on Site K (ditch 205, p 19). It is clearly part of the same general Period IV votive assemblage, and confirms the identification of ditch 81 as the western return of the enclosure found on Site K (ditches 705, 205).

The *lacuna* in subsequent stratigraphy and finds of the 2nd–early 4th centuries, followed by the group of three mid–later 4th century coins, is also strongly reminiscent of Site K, and the coins would indicate that Site CF1 was very much part of the 4th century temple complex.

7   Site CR: watching briefs (Fig 2)

Watching briefs carried out on contractors' excavations for the Inner Relief Road in 1970–1 by Messrs D Biglin, P J Drury and H E Young. Sites are numbered on Figure 2; locations of trenches etc are taken from the Borough Engineer's Inner Relief Road Stage II drawing no E.1914/1. Only those sites to the east of Mildmay Road are included here; those to the west will be included in a future report.

A continuous watch was kept during machine excavation of pipe and subway trenches, as well as of the roundabout and dual carriageway of the Inner Relief Road. Most of the subway trenches were cut to a depth of 14 feet (c 4.27) and penetrated all archaeological levels into the natural brickearth on gravel. Observation was difficult because the size of the trenches necessitated immediate shoring and/or piling.

Summary

An unsuspected area of occupation in the Baddow Road-Goldlay Road district was revealed. It was originally thought that this area would have been too wet in the Roman period to permit habitation. However the topographical evidence obtained shows that this area was composed of spurs of brickearth and gravel which would have been dry in the Roman period. The number of domestic rubbish pits, cess pits, ditches and a well noted in the Goldlay Road area, suggests an occupation site of some extent, perhaps river-side development, though the whole area seems also to have been used in Roman times as a brickearth quarry. A mortared flint wall and an area of well-laid cobbling were found in the Rochford Road subway cutting, possibly marking the eastern end of the *temenos* of the Temple. A cremation burial, probably 1st century in date, with no grave goods was dug into the gravel in the Rochford Road subway. Another burial in a Rettendon-type jar came from the Baddow Road subway, ie, post- *c* AD

260; other pots probably from burials were removed by the workmen and destroyed. The pottery recovered from the excavations spans the whole of the Roman period. Small finds include bone and bronze pins, coins, glass, tweezers, a large stone basin (Fig 35.1) and two whetstones.

All finds have been examined and catalogued as part of the archive held in Chelmsford and Essex Museum. Brief summaries (of Romano-British finds and features only) appear below. Samian identifications are by Warwick Rodwell. Pottery forms and fabrics follow Going 1987.

1A Trench S9–S10, September 1970 TL 7106037

Ditch, c 10 ft (3.05m) deep, at right angles to trench. *Finds*: pottery: Fabric **47**, jar sherds.

3 Manhole C54, after September 1970

Circular pit, 7 ft (2.13m) deep. *Finds*: Samian (late Antonine, CG, f37), much pottery (including graffito wheel, Fig 58.8), mortared bonding tile, roller-stamped box flue tile, oysters, animal bones. The pottery includes Fabrics **2** (Castor Box), **3**, **4**, **13** (mortarium), **25** (mortarium), **27**, **41**, **44**, **47** (including 4 incipient flange-rimmed bowls), **48**, **51**, and **55**, and was clearly accumulating post *c* AD 360/70.

4 Manhole R52, after September 1970 (Site P1 1970, F2–4)

F2. Part of a square cess pit? containing a hard green filling in its bottom layers. *Finds*: most of a small necked jar with a small cordon (G19) of 1st century date (Fabric **45**) and parts of several others of similar date and fabric.

F3. Part of a rectangular pit of unknown use; very little stratified material was obtained but a 2nd–3rd century date seems probable.

F4. Part of a large irregular shaped pit cutting F3. The fill was of a dark loamy material containing pottery and much building material, including 32 cubes of coarse red tile *tesserae*, some with mortar still adhering. This material seems to be the discarded waste from a building.
Small finds (unstrat) included a copper alloy needle and a bracelet fragment with notched decoration, both probably from F4. Two bronze coins of Trajan were found in spoil which appears to have come from F2.

A large amount of 1st to 4th century pottery (including Fabrics **27**, **44**, **47**) was recovered from the spoil heap the most interesting being some sherds of 'London' ware (published as Rodwell 1978, fig 7.4, no 12).

5 Trench C53-R52, after September 1970 (Site P1, F1)

Pit or ditch, and area of occupation
F1: Shallow ditch some 5ft–6ft (*c* 1.5–1.8m) wide, dug through natural brick earth and into the underlying gravel. Stratified in the bottom was a layer of oyster shells above which was black silty material, capped with a layer of gravel. *Finds*: samian, CG, f18/31, Hadrianic; f33, stamped ADVOCISIO, AD 160–190; f36 variant, LMDV, Trajanic, unusual angular form, similar to *Archaeol J*, **86**, fig 10.48 (Table 6, No 1); f37, Hadrianic–Antonine; f45, EG, late Antonine; f72, CG, Antonine with cut glass decoration; large quantities of pottery, *tegulae*, *imbrices*, bonding tile, box flue tile, abraded lava quern fragment. The pottery includes fabrics **2** (late thick Nene Valley white wares and barbotine decoration), **4**, **27** (flagon), **44**, **47**, **51**, and **55** (stamped amphora handle, Fig 57.12), and represents an accumulation beyond AD 360/70.

The subway from Rochford Road to Baddow Road

This subway was cut in sections and subsequently some sections were better recorded than others. The excavations for the two ramps, one at Baddow Road and one at Rochford Road were dug first. The excavations went through all the archaeological layers and into the gravel and sand subsoil.

6 Roundabout. North subway and ramp

Occupation, and scatter of pottery. The northern east-west Roman road appears to have been missed in this area.
Finds: heavily burnt samian (f31, Antonine), pottery, fragment lava quern, large stone basin (Fig 35.1). The pottery includes Fabrics **24** (mortarium, black trituration grits), **44**, **45** (large pieces of a 1st century jar), **47** and **55**. The mortarium was current in Chelmsford *c* AD 260–360 (Going 1987, 21).

Fig 35.1 Large portion of basin, 724mm in diameter, 158mm high at rim and 84mm thick at base. The undersurface is roughly dressed with pick marks in evidence. The edge, rim and shallow convex working surface are smoothed, and there are some lightly incised parallel grooves running around the

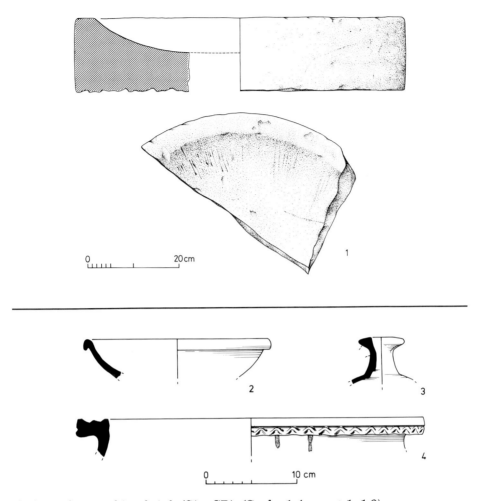

0   20cm

0   10 cm

Figure 35   Finds from the watching briefs (Site CR). (Scale 1:4 except 1, 1:8)

inside curve below the rim. Light grey, fine granular limestone.

7 (also 18)   *Roundabout. Southern subway area (Site RR 3 1970, F1–6)*

This cutting was some 16ft in depth and revealed the following stratification.

A.   Top soil and silty loam, 3 ft thick (0.91m)
B.   Brickearth tapering from 4 ft 6 ins thick at the south end to 2 ft 4 ins thick at the north end.
C.   Gravel with layers of sand to 16 ft (4.88m).
F1.   Cremation burial, interred in a pit dug into the natural gravel, and exposed when the mechanical excavator sliced through the top of it. The pit was covered with a mass of fragments of burnt wood, which appear to have been planks. Beneath the wood was a mass of burnt bones, but no grave goods or dating evidence whatsoever. It seems probable that it was of 1st century date as the gravel metalling must at one

F2.

F3.

time have covered it. A probable second cremation burial was recovered in July 1971 during a partial collapse of the subway cutting.

A 12 ins (0.30m) wide mortared flint wall was exposed in section, its alignment suggests that it ran at right angles to the known Roman road. The wall was built of fragments of roofing tile and flints bonded with a white mortar. It may mark the eastern boundary of the *temenos* of the Temple. Overlaying a floor or metalling (F4 below) was a layer of oyster shells, in places some 12 ins (0.30m) thick. Later observations showed that this deposit covers a large area, and that it was deposited in the 4th century. Boon (1974, 291) describes a similar deposit and recalls Hope's belief that the shells were being burnt to produce a fine lime plaster. It is possible that it was being used here for the same purpose when the temple was being built. However Boon suggests that the deposit may be connected with producing a solution of slaked lime for tanning. Other deposits

F4.
Metalling, well preserved and consisting of fairly large cobbles which had been firmly compacted. Lying directly on the surface and sealed by the oyster midden was a copper alloy pin and half a pair of tweezers; associated pottery included samian (Antonine, f18, 18/31R, 33, ? 31R; ? f72 with external vertical ribbing, cut glass decoration, probable EG, late 2nd century); miscellaneous pottery including Fabrics **2, 27, 44, 47** and **55**, all worn and undiagnostic, though Nene Valley wares do not reach Chelmsford in any quantity before well into the 3rd century.

are also known in temple contexts, eg, at Chanctonbury Ring, West Sussex, and believed to be connected with festivals or ritual practices (Bedwin 1980, 188–9) and Hayling Island (Downey, King & Soffe 1978).

When constructing this part of the subway a ramp was dug to enable the mechanical excavator to gain access to it, and this was part sectioned. This showed that at this point the layer of oysters overlay a strata of black silty loam and disclosed two underlying features:

F5.
Small gulley or pit with a filling of dirty brickearth and charcoal; stratified in it were several sherds of a small grey ware pot tempered with black grog, of 1st century date.

F6.
Small ditch with a dense black fill and which cut all the layers exposed in the cutting. In its lowest fill were pieces of Roman tile and brick, otherwise it was undateable.

It is perhaps significant that at this point the cobbled surface ceased to exist, and the layer of oysters became much thicker suggesting an area outside the *temenos*.

Further work in July 1971 revealed a late 4th century pit or ditch. Pottery included Fabrics **3, 4, 25** (mortarium), **47** including a colander base (Type M2), and **48**. A bowl with convex side and hooked rim, similar to Going 1987, type C1.1, is in a Nene Valley red-painted parchment fabric (Fig 35.2).

Finally two machine-cut trenches across the subway ramp (Site E) located a small 4th century gulley.

Unprovenanced CR7 finds include Fabrics **2, 4, 24** (mortarium), **47** and **51**, indicating occupation beyond AD 360/70.

8   *Manhole C39 and trench C39–R46*

Gravel surface, 10cm (4 inches) thick. No Roman finds, but presumably the gravel paving of the *temenos*.

10B   *Trench S8–S9 (east of Mildmay Road), September 1970*

Occupation, scatter of pottery in silt at a depth of *c* 6 ft (1.83m). Also found in a pipe trench along the line of the pavement on the eastern side of Mildmay Road (CR12). *Finds*: samian (SG, pre-Flavian, f35; ?EG, Antonine, f38 or Curle 11); much pottery of the 1st–2nd centuries (Fabrics **44, 45** and **47**, including jars G5 and cordoned bowl-jars); *tegula*.

19A   *Northern end of roundabout subway*

Cremation, and ?3rd century gulley. *Finds*: a little cremated bone in cremation urn; an abraded lump of lava quern appears to have been used as a lid.

Jar, G20, with undercut rim, sandy grey ware (**47**). Some sherds missing (broken in antiquity) but a circular hole in the base may be deliberate 'killing' of the vessel. 1st–early 2nd century.

Central area of roundabout

21   *Unstratified*

Finds: samian (SG chips; CG, LMDV, f37, Trajanic–Hadrianic).

Pottery Fabrics **2** (late thick white ware), **3** (mortarium), **27, 44, 47** (incipient flanged bowls) and **48**, representing accumulation post- AD 360/70.

21A   *Site RR 3B 1971, F1–7*

F1.
Post-hole.

F2.
Post-hole.

F3.
Small pit which cut F4; sealed with a layer of midden material; fill of dark silty loam. Nothing datable was found.

F4.
Small gulley.

F5 (Pit 2).
Pit which cut F6; its fill was dense black with much domestic refuse, including much 4th century pottery. Fabrics include **2, 3** (white paint decoration), **4** (flagon neck J7), **24** (mortarium), **47**.

F6 (Pit 3).
An irregular shaped pit cut through the brickearth and into the natural gravel. It was sealed by the midden deposit below which lay a quantity of worn brick and tile. The rest of the fill was a grey black loamy mixture including some domestic debris, and pottery. *Finds*: a small fragment probably from the base of a pipe clay statuette; samian (SG, Flavian, f30; CG, Antonine, f31, stamped] M; ?f36, 2nd century). Other pottery includes

Fabrics **2** (bifid rim jar), **3, 4, 24** (reeded-rim mortarium), **25** (mortarium), **41** (incipient flanged bowl), **47, 48**, indicating accumulation post-AD 350.

F7. Large shallow pit, probably dug to obtain brick earth. It covered an area 13 ft x 10 ft with a dark fill containing much tile. A coin of Victorinus (AD 268–270) in good condition was found as well as pottery of 3rd century date.

A sherd marked RR3 B 1971, D, is an unusual late 1st century disc-mouthed flagon (**27**), with a single handle scar (Fig 35.3).

21B *Site RR 4 1971, F1–4*

A small sloping ramp dug to allow the contractors machinery to gain access to the subway.

F1. Small pit dug into a larger pit (F2) with a fill of dark silt and at its base brown silt and oysters from which came part of a bone pin and a few sherds of probable 3rd century date. Samian (SG, Flavian, f33, trace of graffito). Other pottery Fabrics **2, 16, 21, 27, 39, 47.**

F2. Large shallow pit or ditch one side of which was sectioned, showing a sloping profile cutting through the natural brickearth. The lowest fill was of green material perhaps from a cess pit. Above this were layers of stones (?deliberate capping) and oyster shells with an upper filling of brown loam. Slag, charcoal and large flints were scattered throughout the filling. Samian (SG, Flavian, f36). Other pottery Fabrics **27** (Type J3), **44, 47.**

F3. Opposite F1, a similar sequence of stratification was noted; although it was badly mutilated by late foundations, a fragment of 1st century glass and a sherd of 1st century pottery (Fabric **47**) was recovered from its bottom layers.

F4. The lowest silt layers *in situ*. The silt was dense black and contained much pottery and animal bone (sheep/goat, pig, cow, bird; oyster). *General finds*: Samian (SG, ?pre-Flavian, f18; SG, Flavian, f30 or 37) pottery; *tegulae*, *imbrex*, bonding tile, combed box-flue tile, 3 mortared tile *tesserae*. The pottery included Fabrics **?1, 21, 44, 47** and **55** (amphora handle). A large thick tazza rim in a ?sandy Colchester buff fabric had brown painted stripes on the shoulder (Fig 35.4).

22 *Trench C53–C54*

Silt. *Finds*: 1 sherd Fabric **47**.

29 *Site P F5, September 1970 (PJD)*

Sporadic occupation on gravel below alluvial silt. *Finds*: Pottery (Fabrics **44, 47**, undiagnostic).

30 *Site P, F6, October 1970*

Pottery scatter in silt under gravel paving. *Finds*: Iron Age pottery, fired clay, Roman pottery (1 sherd jar with hooked rim, **45**; 1 sherd **47**).

31 *Trench R51–R52 (Site P2)*

Pottery scatter, 4th century in date, lying on the old ground surface. The rest of the trench was devoid of any features except two modern burials in a brick vault, from the Congregational Church. *Finds*: pottery (Fabrics **3, 27** (mortarium), **45, 47**), indicating occupation post AD 350.

32 *Trench R48–C13*

Scatter of worn Roman tiles.

33 *Trench C12–C13 (Site P, F8)*

Area of higher gravel. ?Roman road on ridge (see below for postscript).

34 *Goldlay Road — Lynmouth Avenue, May/June 1971*

A trench cut on the south side of the new road between Lynmouth Avenue and Goldlay Road disclosed a vertical-sided Roman feature, probably a well. The feature was not bottomed but pottery from its top fill was of 3rd–4th century date. In June a trench disclosed a stream bed with worn Roman pottery in its lowest levels.

35 *Sewer trench (Site P, F1), July 1970 (PJD)*

Shallow U-shaped ditch, lying under gravel of northern east–west Roman road. *Finds*: tegula, imbrex.

36 *Watermain trench (Site P, F2) (PJD)*

Area producing much pottery, and domestic refuse in a dense black silt. Large pit or ditch cutting into natural gravel. *Finds*: much pottery, samian (SG,

Flavian, f27; Antonine, CG, f31, 31R, 33, 37), sherd of bottle glass, *opus signinum*, illegible ?3rd century coin, charcoal, animal bone. The pottery includes Fabrics **2, 4** and large quantities of **39, 44** and **47**, including bead rimmed dishes, folded beakers, beakers with tall vertical necks, cavetto-rimmed jars and a lid.

37 *Sewer trench (Site P, F3), July 1970 (PJD)*

Roman well with timber-framed caisson (*c* 1.10m wide). Three planks surviving, *in situ*, dovetailed at corners with corner rungs, similar to wells from Wickford (Wickenden in prep) and one from Site K (above, p 20). Truncated severely by sheet piling. Upper frame found on spoil heap. Filled with a light grey sludge, bottoming on gravel at 2.70m (the cleared level being at 2.10m), where a complete jar was found. Date suggested in 2nd half of 3rd century, with signs of a replaced upper framing. *Finds*: samian (Flavian SG; Trajanic CG, f18/31), pottery including Fabrics **41, 44** and **47** (folded beaker); organic remains; fragments of leather offcut (now delaminated); animal bone; *tegula*. For a narrow-necked jar with a beaded rim and a cordon dividing the neck from the body, see Going 1987, Type G36.1/1 (**47**, 3rd–?4th centuries).

38 *Site P. F4, July 1970 (PJD)*

Pottery from alluvial silt, over gravel, adjacent to CR 37; section slipped into trench and stratigraphy lost. *Finds*: samian (CG, late Antonine, f31, 31R, 33, 45, 46, 79R; EG, f37, stamped ATTILLVSF, retrograde, Table 6; No 2); pottery including Fabrics **2, 3, 44, 47** and **51** (thick storage jar), indicating accumulation post AD 360/70; leather.

39 *Site C, January 1970 (PJD)*

Three trenches dug on the site of 66 Goldlay Road failed to produce any ancient finds.

40 *Site A (PJD)*

Several trenches were excavated. No ancient finds were recovered.

41 *M & S Motors, March 1970 (PJD)*

In excavating for a garage inspection pit, half a pottery bowl was found in a pit, *c* 5ft (1.5m) below ground level.

CR Unstratified

Samian, SG, ?Ritt 9, Neronian–Flavian.

Postscript (March 1991). During the installation of a rainwater soakaway in the front garden of 31 Goldlay Road, at a depth of 4ft 6in (1.26m) under about 2ft (0.60m) of 'clay' (?alluvial silt), an area of at least 1 square metre of a cobbled surface was found. The cobbles were 'apple-sized', and well-set into a firm hoggin and shingle base, itself over 18in (*c* 0.50m) thick. This may well be the same surface as that of number **33**, and *could* indicate a road at right angles to the main side road as excavated on Site D.

V The Building Materials

The Stone

All that survived of the temple masonry were a few small sections of flint rubble foundation, with some *septaria* and tile, in a hard lime mortar; the section of portico foundation contained some possibly reused lumps of greensand. It is probable that the walls were constructed of similar materials. Though totally robbed, no architectural fragments were found, and the only stone building materials found in excavation were *septaria* nodules, flint, chalk, limestone, greensand, some red sandstone and iron conglomerate, and some local erratics.

The Tile

Fabric

The normal range of Roman tile fabrics, hard, red and variably sandy, accounts for the bulk of the material. A softer micaceous fabric, thought to be early and possibly connected with military rather than civilian production, was also noted; so too were nine fragments of gault tile from sites D, K and AB. Both these latter types are discussed in the *mansio* volume (Drury 1988). The gault fabric, however, is very similar to the DUA fabric 2454 now believed to have been manufactured near Eccles, Kent, *c* AD 50–65 (Ian Betts, pers comm). There were many overfired or wasted 'blown' building tiles.

Types

Fragments of building tile, *tegulae*, *imbrices*, box flue tile and 'margin' floor tiles were present. Bonding tile fragments were small, and probably mainly derived from the *mansio*. No dimensions were recorded, but thicknesses indicated the presence of the *lydium*, *bessalis* and *pedalis*. The *tegulae* were fairly unremarkable; one large fragment from D 124 (Structure 1, VI.2) was 280mm wide and 30mm thick. Semi-circular finger-wiped 'signatures' were common. It is probable that some fragments came in hardcore from the *mansio*, but much came from the roofing of the temple. The same is true of the *imbrices*; two from K 423 (pit, VII) measured 160mm wide x 70mm high and 170mm x 70mm. The box flue tiles all came from K and M, and comprised six cross-hatched examples, 59 combed and six abraded roller-stamped pieces (Die 4: K 551 (temple robbing trench); Die 16: D Cat 277 (x2), D Cat 284, K Cat 98, Subsoil; *cf* Lowther 1948 for publication of dies). All probably originated from the *mansio* construction, and a discussion appears in Drury 1988.

The 'margined' ?floor tiles were not recorded in the *mansio*, and probably were used in a structure in the vicinity of the temple. The earliest occurrence was in Structure 1 on Site D (Period VI.2). Nine fragments are known from sites D, K and AB (AB 2, VII.1; D 124, Structure 1, VI.2; K 142 (VIII), 161 (VII), 231 (PR), 238 (subsoil), 239 (gravel 237, VI+), 323 (subsoil), 937 (oven 485, VIII) with *opus signinum* covering). They are 34–40mm thick and have an impressed margin of differing width and depth along each edge, possibly where another tile or mould has stood when wet (see Fig 36.1).

Impressions, decorations, traces of use

Four pawprints were recorded (D 257, subsoil; 283, unstrat; K 497, 935, both ditch 205, IV) and one ungulate (K Cat 202, hollow 191, VIII). One flat fragment, 20mm thick and combed with a simple square chessboard pattern, was pierced by a hole, *c* 21mm in diameter narrowing to *c* 10mm (M Cat 41, pit 23, VII.2). Another flat fragment, 20mm thick, had a hole gouged in it, but this did not quite pierce the underside (D Cat 226, unstrat). Finally one probable *tegula* fragment had been neatly chipped into a circle, 70mm in diameter, for use as a ?counter (D Cat 180, ditch 173, VI.1; see Fig 46.5).

Mortar

A lump of lime came from AB 4 (well). Site M yielded white mortar fragments from Cat 53 (pit 54, VI+; very gritty) and Cat 87 (unstrat; chalky). One lump came from D Cat 263 (hollow 261, VII.2). The largest assemblage was from K where 26 contexts produced white gritty mortar with crushed brick inclusions, one with building flint embedded in (K961). Pit K 423 (VII, Cats 423, 433) contained large pieces of roofing mortar, in a white powdery fabric with flint pebble and grit inclusions, and bearing *imbrex* impressions. *Opus signinum* was also found on site K (six contexts) and M (eight contexts) including a piece of flooring from M11 (VII), and a large amount from pit M1 (VII).

Wall plaster

Site M produced a plain white fragment (pit 35, Cat 51, VII.2), a red painted piece (pit 1, Cat 2, VII), and a small group from Cat 11 (VII) of six red fragments, one white, two yellow, and one white fragment with a black stripe at least 12mm thick.

The largest assemblage came from K where odd red and black painted fragments were found in Cats 330, 342 (both pre-temple make-up) and 918 (unstrat), but two contexts in particular produced

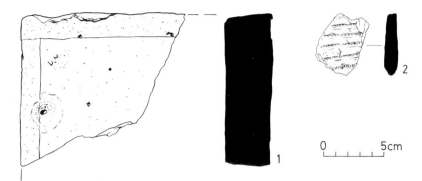

Figure 36   1, 'margined' tile; 2, roller-stamped daub (Scale 1:3)

substantial amounts. Pit 392 (PR) contained five red pieces; two grey; one with black brush marks on grey; a faint dark stripe; an orange-brown stripe, 20mm wide, on grey; and a red stripe, 27mm wide, bordered by thin yellow lines, on a red background. Feature 195 (pre-temple make-up; Fig 18.S35) produced many smaller fragments with yellow, red, green, yellow/red, red/green, red stripe, and white with yellow and red colours.

Some of the fragments are grittier and more weathered than others. Since several of the contexts are from pre-temple make-up, it is clear that the plaster was derived from an earlier building, possibly the temple's predecessor.

Tesserae

A fragment of flooring from K 72 (pit, VII.2) consisted of eight irregular cubes of hard white chalk set in *opus signinum*. Their surfaces were quite worn. It is odd that this should be the only occurrence of *tesserae* on the site, if one were to imagine a tessellated floor in the temple. Perhaps it is more likely that the piece is hardcore, reused from the *mansio*. For a possible glass paste *tessera*,

see Fig 44.32. Tile *tesserae* were found in CR 4, F4; 21B, F4 (Section IV).

Burnt clay and daub

Small fragments of abraded, shapeless burnt clay were ubiquitous. Pieces of daub with wattle impressions were recorded from D 241 (pit, VI.1), 247 (ditch 244, VII.2). Much of the assemblage appeared to have white-washed faces; one large piece from K 937 (oven 485, VIII) was 60mm thick. Many fragments appeared to be veneers, c 10mm thick, probably as a final finish for unplastered walls. One such piece (M 29, topsoil; Fig 36.2) had a pattern of parallel grooves, probably keying for a coat of plaster, and possibly applied with a roller (see Drury 1988, 86).

Other fragments, largely vegetable-tempered, have been interpreted as objects (loomweights, etc) or briquetage, see below.

Pigment

A lump of Egyptian blue frit came from D 253 (subsoil).

VI The Loose Finds

The Roman coins, by Richard Reece

Site D (bronze)

—	1st–2nd century	Dupondius	Ditch 23 (VI.1)
?Domitian	1st–2nd century	Dupondius	Ditch 244 (VII.2)
Gallienus	260–268	?as RIC 157	Pit 241 (Cat 243; VII.1)
Claudius II	268–270	as RIC 79	in road surface 259 (V–VII)
Claudius II	268–270	RIC 261	subsoil over slot 212 (VII)
Antoninus Pius	138–161	Dupondius, rev uncertain	on gravel surface 220 (V–VII; Cat 314)
Constans	348–350	CK 43 (excellent condition)	rubble 258 over road (VII.2)
House of Constantine	330–345	obv as HK 51, rev as HK 52	subsoil over slot 212 (VII)
House of Constantine	345–348	as HK 137	Posthole 320 (VII.2)
Valens	364–378	CK 309	clearing
Arcadius	388–402	as CK 164	subsoil (Cat 55)
House of Theodosius	388–402	as CK 162	subsoil (Cat 159)
House of Theodosius	388–402	as CK 796	subsoil (Cat 35)
illegible	3rd–4th century	—	clearing
illegible	—	—	subsoil clearance
illegible	—	—	subsoil (Cat 79)

Site AB (bronze)

Constantius I	294–305	as RIC 6 Lon 14a	subsoil over 2 (Cat 12)

Site M (silver)

Severus Alexander	222–235	RIC 91	Pit 54 (VI–VII.2)

(Bronze)

Tiberius	AD 12–20	RIC 1, rev Augustus 245	Pit 52 (VI)
Claudius I	43–64	Copy as RIC 1, rev 100	subsoil (Cat 71)
Vespasian	69–79	As, rev uncertain	on brick-earth sub-soil (Cat 102)
?Trajan	98–117	Dupondius, rev illegible	topsoil (Cat 22)
?Antoninus Pius	138–161	Dupondius, rev illegible	Pit 33 (VI)
Faustina II	150–161	as RIC (Ant Pius) 1402	Pit 32 (VI)
Marcus Aurelius	161–180	RIC 992	topsoil (Cat 24)
Gordian III	238–244	RIC 230, rev Philip I, II (white metal wash)	subsoil (Cat 25)
Claudius II	268–270	RIC 34	Pit 45 (VII)
Constantine II	330–340	Copy as HK 49	topsoil (Cat 24)
House of Constantine	330–345	Copy as HK 48	topsoil (Cat 24)
Helena	337–340	as HK 112	post-Roman (Pit 92)
Constans	337–341	HK 133	topsoil (Cat 24
Constantius II	350–360	Copy as CK 25	Pit 35 (VII.2)
House of Constantine	350–360	Copy as CK 25	subsoil (Cat 26)
Valens	364–378	as CK 97	subsoil (Cat 61)
Valens	364–378	as CK 97	topsoil (Cat 22)
Valens	364–378	CK 319	topsoil (Cat 22)
Valentinian I	364–375	as CK 96	subsoil (Cat 74
Valentinian I	364–375	CK 501	topsoil (Cat 69)
Gratian	367–375	as CK 503	Pit 59 (Cat 63; VII.2)
Gratian	367–375	CK 529	topsoil (Cat 24)

Gratian	367–375	CK 529	Pit 35 (Cat 51; VII.2)
Gratian	367–378	CK 1411	Pit 27 (VII)
Gratian	378–383	CK 378	subsoil (Cat 71
House of Valentinian	364–378	as CK 275	post-Roman (Posthole 43)
illegible	3rd–4th century	—	subsoil (Cat 26)

Site K *(silver)*

Marcus Aurelius	159–160	RIC 483 (Ant Pius)	Cat 1047 (subsoil)
Julia Domna	196–211	RIC 575	Cat 1059 (Pit 110; VII.1)
Elagabalus	218–222	RIC 153	Cat 1040 (on brick-earth sub-soil)
Valerian I	253–260	as RIC 106	Cat 1053 (Pit 85, VII.1–2)
Valerian I	253–260	RIC 126	Cat 1041 (Pit 7, VII.1–2)

(bronze)

Claudius I	43–64	Copy as RIC 1, rev 95	Cat 918 (trial trenching)
2 x Claudius I	43–64	Copy as RIC 1, rev 100	Cats 1058 (Pit 90, VI), 479 (early gravel 257, IV.3)
2 x Claudius I	43–64	Copy, rev illegible	Cats 851 (Ditch 705, IV.2), 440 (temple robbing trench)
Vespasian	69–79	as RIC 500	Cat 151 (PR)
Vespasian	69–79	RIC 528	Cat 476 (silt layer 465, IV–V)
Vespasian	69–79	RIC 764	Cat 476 (silt layer 465, IV–V)
Domitian	81–96	RIC 353	Cat 476 (silt layer 465, IV–V)

Domitian	81–96	RIC 423	Cat 1076 (temple robbing trench)
Trajan	98–99	RIC 392	Cat 167 (PR)
?Trajan	98–117	*As*, rev illegible	Cat 1085 (site clearing)
Antoninus Pius	138–161	RIC 656	Cat 354 (gravel over Ditch 205)
Faustina I	141–160	RIC (Ant Pius) 1155	Cat 259 (subsoil)
Marcus Aurelius	161–180	Sestertius, rev ?Vesta. Good copy on proper flan	Cat 1060 (rubble 109, over Pit 90)
Lucius Verus	161–168	RIC 1397	Cat 1048 (Pit 50, IV.2)
—	1st–2nd century	*As*, illegible	Cat 253 (silt 240, V)
Septimius Severus	193–211	Corroded denarius, rev illegible	Cat 916 (unstrat)
Gallienus	253–260	joint, rev illegible	Cat 83 (Pit 84, VI+)
Claudius II	268–270	RIC 62	Cat 1053 (Pit 85, VII.1–2)
Claudius II	268–270	as RIC 261	Cat 1084 (PR)
Victorinus	268–270	RIC 61	Cat 105 (subsoil)
Tetricus I	270–273	?as RIC 79	Cat 6 (Pit 17, VII.2)
Tetricus I	270–273	as RIC 136	Cat 1069 (Pit 191, VIII)
Tetricus II	270–273	Copy as ?RIC 254	Cat 1050 (Pit 49, VII.1)
Tetricus II	270–273	RIC 272	Cat 525 (PR)
Maximian I	286–294	as RIC 5 Lyons 397	Cat 546 (subsoil)
Barbarous Radiate	270–290	Rev ?Fortuna	Cat 397 (PR)
Barbarous Radiate	270–290	Rev Pax	Cat 427 (Pit, VIII)
Barbarous Radiate	270–290	Rev uncertain	Cat 915 (unstrat)

2 x Barbarous Radiate	270–290	Rev illegible	Cat 1078 (PR), 1090 (PR)
Constantine I	310–317	as RIC 7 Trier 132	Cat 1067 (?make-up 147)
Constantine I	312–313	RIC 6 London as 265, but bust G	Cat 1056 (Pit 88, VII.1–2)
Constantine I	310–313	RIC 6 Lyons 308	Cat 1042 (Pit 21, VII.2)
Constantine I	318–319	RIC 7 Trier 208A	Cat 68 (Pit, VII.2)
Constantine I	318–319	RIC 7 Trier 213	Cat 169 (unstrat)
Constantine I	318–320	Copy as RIC 7 Trier 213	Cat 202 (Pit 191, VIII)
Constantine I	320–330	Copy as RIC 7 Trier 341	Cat 124 (Pit, VII.2)
Constantine I	320–324	RIC 7 Trier 370	Cat 242 (baulk)
Constantine I	320–324	RIC 7 Lyons 115	Cat 1073 (?disturbed make-up)
Constantine I	324–330	RIC 7 Arles 309	Cat 680 (subsoil)
Constantine I	324–330	RIC 7 as London 293	Cat 106 (Pit 84, VI+)
Constantine I	335–337	HK 92	Cat 239 (Gravel 237, VI+)
Crispus	320–324	RIC 7 London 247	Cat 127 (Pit, VII.2)
Crispus	320–324	RIC 7 Trier 307	Cat 202 (Pit 191, VIII)
Constantine II	330–340	Copy as HK 49	Cat 525 (PR)
Constantine II	330–335	HK 56	Cat 1044 (subsoil)
Constantine II	330–335	HK 353	Cat 184 (robbed make-up)
Urbs Roma	330–345	Copy as HK 51	Cat 146 (subsoil)
Urbs Roma	330–335	HK 65	Cat 259 (subsoil)
2 x Urbs Roma	330–345	Copy of HK 184	Cats 192 (Pit 191, VIII), 252 (Gravel 237, VI+)
Urbs Roma	330–335	HK 200	Cat 239 (Gravel 237, VI+)
Constantinopolis	330–345	as HK 52	Cat 265 (PR)
Constantinopolis	330–335	HK 59	Cat 154 (PR)
Constantinopolis	330–345	Copy of HK 66	Cat 502 (Oven 485, VIII)
Constantinopolis	330–345	as HK 201	Cat 81 (Pit 84, VI+)
Theodora	337–340	as HK 113	Cat 137 (PR)
Constans	335–337	HK 95	Cat 438 (Pit, VIII)
Constans	337–341	HK 110	Cat 1054 (Pit 84, VI+)
Constans	337–341	Copy of HK 123	Cat 1049 (subsoil)
Constans	337–341	HK 133	Cat 1051 (baulk)
Constans	345–348	as HK 138	Cat 1045 (subsoil)
Constans	345–348	HK 142	Cat 915 (unstrat)
3 x Constans	345–348	HK 150	Cats 1065 (Pit 127, VII.2), 1082 (subsoil), 1088 (clearing)
Constans	345–348	HK 155	Cat 1070 (medieval disturbance)
Constans	345–348	as HK 261	Cat 1066 (subsoil)
Constantius II	356–360	as CK 77	Cat 1072 (Roman subsoil 260, IV–V)
3 x Magnentius	350–360	Copy as CK 8	Cats 889 (subsoil), 918 (trial trench), 1093 (sewer trench)
House of Constantine	310–317	rev uncertain	Cat 183 (subsoil)
House of Constantine	320–324	as RIC 7 London 250	Cat 259 (subsoil)
3 x House of Constantine	330–345	Copy as HK 48	Cats 265 (PR), 1052 (subsoil), 1063 (Pit 84, VI+)

Identification	Date	Reference	Catalogue
House of Constantine	330–345	Copy as HK 49	Cat 1081 (subsoil)
House of Constantine	335–348	Copy as HK 87	Cat 429 (PR)
House of Constantine	337–341	as HK 133	Cat 1092 (PR)
2x House of Constantine	345–348	as HK 137	Cats 1068 (?robbing disturbance), 1066 (subsoil)
6x House of Constantine	350–360	Copy as CK 25	Cats 230 (subsoil), 239 (Gravel 237, VI+), 376 (PR), 487 (Oven 485, VIII), 865 (PR), 1061 (Pit 101, VII.2)
House of Constantine	350–360	Copy as CK 256	Cat 481 (subsoil)
3 x Valens	364–378	as CK 97	Cats 1057 (Pit 84, VI+), 1083 (site clearing), 1089 (PR)
Valens	364–378	as CK 282	Cat 395 (PR)
2 x Valens	364–378	CK 309	Cats 418 (PR), 381 (PR)
Valens	364–378	CK 319	Cat 1066 (subsoil)
2 x Valens	364–378	as CK 319	Cats 920 (subsoil), 436 (cleaning)
Valens	364–378	CK 336	Cat 230 (subsoil)
2 x Valens	364–378	CK 480	Cats 432 (temple robber trench), 1055 (Pit 78, IV.2, intrusive)
Valens	364–378	CK 483	Cat 901 (trial trench)
Valens	364–378	as CK 492	Cat 1066 (subsoil)
Valens	367–375	CK 510	Cat 265 (PR)
Valens	364–378	CK 523	Cat 178 (PR)
Valens	364–378	CK 968	Cat 1053 (Pit 85, VII.1–2)
Valens	364–378	CK 1031	Cat 87 (Pit)
Valens	364–378	CK 1330	Cat 1079 (clearing topsoil)
Valens	364–378	CK 1416	Cat 1064 (Pit 127, VII.2)
Valentinian I	367–375	CK 338	Cat 265 (PR)
Valentinian I	364–375	CK 984	Cat 147 (robbed temple make-up)
Valentinian I	364–375	CK 1014	Cat 1062 (Pit 101, VII.2)
Valentinian I	364–375	CK 1409	Cat 43 (non-feature)
Valentinian I	364–375	CK 1419	Cat 426 (Pit 425, VIII)
Gratian	367–375	CK 310	Cat 376 (PR)
Gratian	367–378	CK 341	Cat 1043 (Pit 31, VII.2)
Gratian	367–375	CK 517	Cat 1075 (PR)
Gratian	367–375	CK 529	Cat 340 (PR)
Gratian	375–378	CK 540	Cat 236 (clearing)
2x House of Valentinian	364–378	as CK 96	Cats 165 (PR), 1072 (Roman subsoil)
House of Valentinian	364–378	as CK 317	Cat 481 (subsoil)
House of Valentinian	364–378	as CK 481	Cat 1077 (on brick-earth sub-soil)
Valentinian II	383	CK 2158	Cat 167 (PR)
Flavius Victor	387–388	CK 561	Cat 918 (trial trench)

2x Arcadius	388–402	as CK 164	Cats 1046 (subsoil), 1066 (subsoil)
Arcadius	388–402	CK 167	Cat 307 (PR)
Arcadius	388–402	CK 392	Cat 229 (subsoil)
Arcadius	388–402	CK 566	Cat 899 (PR silt)
Arcadius	388–402	as CK 798	Cat 1086 (Posthole 745, VIII)
Arcadius	388–402	CK 1107	Cat 745 (Posthole, VIII)
5x House of Theodosius	388–402	as CK 162	Cats 295 (PR), 1071 (sewer trench), 1087 (x2) (Posthole 745, VIII), 1091 (PR)
House of Theodosius	388–402	as CK 796	Cat 144 (subsoil)
House of Theodosius	388–402	rev uncertain	Cat 154 (PR)
House of Theodosius	4th century	uncertain	Cat 1074 (PR)

Total 147

For three coins from Site CF1, see p 56

Summary, by R Reece, N Wickenden and R Kenyon

Mid 1st century activity and supply to the site is shown by the coin of Tiberius (Site M) and by the six copies of Claudius (Site M, 5 x Site K), which should indicate some form of contact with officialdom. Claudian copies have been found elsewhere in Chelmsford (five from Site S (Drury 1988), six from Site AG, one from Site V72, two from V75, one from the Orchard Site and one from the Prince of Orange) and in other Roman settlements in Essex (Kelvedon (4); Rivenhall (2); Wickford (5); Heybridge (1)). The Claudian coinage also suggests that the issues of Vespasian and Domitian are 1st century, rather than later, losses. Mr Robert Kenyon has examined the Claudian issues; their smaller size and lighter weight indicate a late Claudian date of manufacture. A post-Boudican date is quite likely for their loss (circulation likely late 50s/early 60s to early 70s when Vespasian's massive supplies of bronzes in Britain saw an end to the circulation of Claudian coins). The coin from Site M is die-related to one from Lincoln.

The list from Sites D and M are unremarkable, save for noting that coins of the House of Theodosius are present on Site D. On Site K there are enough coins of the 2nd–3rd centuries to indicate continued occupation; if anything the five silver issues are more than might be usually expected. The lack of bronzes in the first half of the 3rd century is totally consistent with other Roman sites. However, there is an apparent hiatus in the ceramic sequence in the 3rd century (see p 129); taken together, this could be evidence for a hiatus in the occupation of the site from c AD 220 to 250, which would fit in with the lack of 3rd century features on the site. The group of Gallienus coins

Table 3 Coins from Site K

	Roman feature	Roman layer	Roman/post-Roman subsoil	Post-Roman features, unstrat	Disturbed temple make-up, Robber trenches	Total	%
1st–mid 3rd	4	8	2	5	2	21	14
Mid 3rd, Barbarous Radiates	8	—	2	6	—	16	11
Constantinian	17	5	19	14	4	59	40
Valentinian	10	2	5	16	2	35	24
Theodosian	4	—	4	8	—	16	11
Total	43	15	32	49	8	147	100
% of total	29	10	22	33	5	99	

Breakdown of Constantinian coins by date:

AD 310–320 :	7	345–348:	9
320–330 :	8	350–360:	11
330–345:	24		59

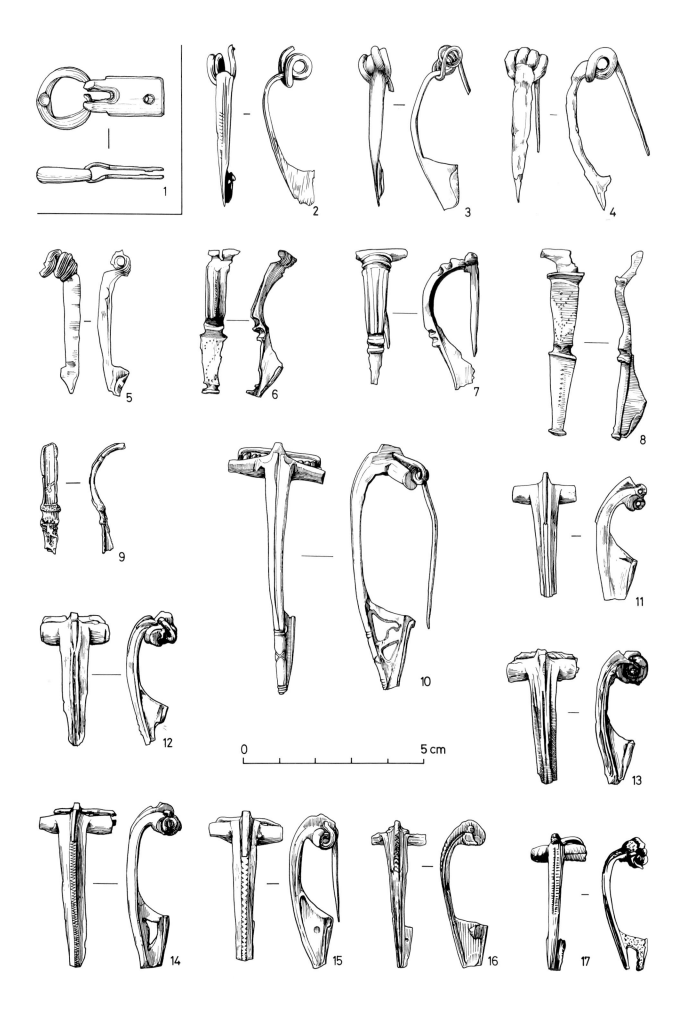

0   5 cm

could be taken as a slightly later addition to the Julia Domna/Elagabalus group, or they can be put in the later radiates sequence, all of which could be in circulation until *c* AD 315, with the exception of Maximian which suggests activity pre-300.

There is clearly a high number of 4th century coins from Site K, which is always to be expected on Roman 'small town' sites. Of the 147 coins from K, 59 are Constantinian (40%), and of these, 15 can be dated 310–330 — an unusually high figure, indicating definitely increased activity *c* AD 320–330. This clearly coincides exactly with the estimated construction date of the Romano-Celtic temple. As on Site M, the area in the south of Site K was full of intercutting rubbish pits of all dates, near to roadside frontage structures, but totally different in nature to the main temple area further north. Forty-one coins (out of the total 147) were found here, ranging from Claudius I consistently through to Arcadius, but including all five silver coins. It is possible that the contents of these pits were liturgical rubbish (see p 140), representing periodic cleansing of the temple precinct, though the pits contain very little else in the way of possible *ex votos*.

Silver buckle, by V I Evison

Fig 37.1   Small buckle; penannular loop with a groove for the tongue point. The ends of the loop are covered by the tabs of the small double rectangular plate, fastened by one rivet hole. Length 35 mm. K 183, VIII.

The buckle is of simple type, but distinctive as the loop is circular and the material is often silver. It sometimes occurs in late Roman contexts, bronze at Richborough in the topsoil (Bushe-Fox 1926, pl XXV, 78), in silver at Traprain Law (Curle 1923, pl 32, 33), Mainz Kastel and Lorch (Böhme 1974, 66). Sometimes the silver loop was attached to a circular plate, as at Kingsholm (Brown 1975, fig 8), and the well-furnished grave 43 at Krefeld-Gellep (Pirling 1966, taf 10.3). One with rectangular plate was in the Germanic warrior's grave at Vieuxville, coin-dated to the beginning of the fifth century (Böhme 1974, taf 110.14). According to M Kazanski this is a Germanic type of buckle found among Goths south of the Baltic and the Huns north of the Black Sea, with some in western Europe (Piton 1985, 269). One occurs in grave 54 at Nouvion-en-Ponthieu, associated with a knife, a Gothic brooch and a bead similar to one from Chelmsford (Fig 44.22; Piton 1985, pl 10). The buckle type occurs mostly in contexts of the first half of the 5th century.

The brooches, by S A Butcher

The full descriptive catalogue with references is available in the site archive. Here only the more significant points are mentioned. The metal alloy of most of the brooches has been established by X-ray fluorescence (Justine Bayley, Ancient Monuments Lab Rep No 4845). Those marked * were from the votive deposit (see p 19).

One-piece brooches (Fig 37.2-5).
These are all of the type usually called the 'Nauheim derivative' or 'poor man's brooch'; *Camulodunum* Type VII (Hawkes & Hull 1947, 312).

Fig 37.2	Bronze	M	Pit 11	
*Fig 37.3	Bronze	K	Early Roman soil 260	(Cat 293)
*Fig 37.4	Gunmetal	K	Ditch 205 IV	(Cat 290)
*Fig 37.5	Bronze	K	Ditch 205 IV	(Cat 284)

The type is common in deposits of the mid 1st century AD in Britain and on the continent, but is frequently found in later contexts.

Hod Hill brooches (Fig 37.6-9)

*Fig 37.6	Brass	K	Silt 465	(Cat 1105)
*Fig 37.7	Brass	K	Gravel 258	(Cat 532)
Fig 37.8	Brass	K	Subsoil	(Cat 1145)
Fig 37.9	Brass	D	Subsoil	(Cat 55)

This sub-type of the Hod Hill brooch, with bow divided into two panels, occurs both in Britain and on the continent; it can be dated to the mid-1st century AD.

Colchester B or two-piece Colchester brooches (Figs 37.10–17; 38.18–21)

*Fig 37.10	Leaded bronze	K	Early Roman soil 260	(Cat 1072)
*Fig 37.11	Gunmetal	K	Roman subsoil 258	(Cat 518)
*Fig 37.12	Gunmetal	K	Ditch 205 V	(Cat 496)
Fig 37.13	Gunmetal	K	Loamy silt	(Cat 1132)
Fig 37.14	Gunmetal	K	Clearing	(Cat 236)
*Fig 37.15	Brass	K	Early Roman soil 260	(Cat 1106)
Fig 37.16	Leaded bronze	K	Clearing medieval silt	(Cat 1148)
Fig 37.17	Leaded bronze	M	Upper subsoil	(Cat 22)
Fig 38.18	—	D	Early Roman subsoil	(Cat 78)
Fig 38.19	Bronze	K	Sinkage over ditch 205	(Cat 403)

Fig 37 (opposite) 1, silver buckle; 2–17, copper alloy brooches (Scale 1:1)

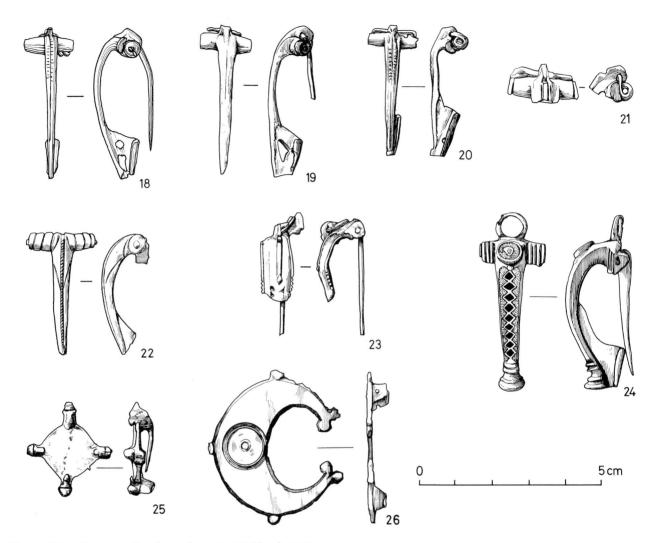

Figure 38 Copper alloy brooches, 18–26 (Scale 1:1)

*Fig 38.20 Leaded   K Silt 240   (Cat 219)
     bronze

Fig 38.21 Gunmetal K Gravel   (Cat 1131)
Several sub-types can be distinguished amongst the above and in the case of Fig 37.11–13 the identity of the alloy suggests that they are a genuine group. The absence of the general type from the King Harry Lane cemetery at St Albans (in use until the Roman conquest; seen by courtesy of Dr I M Stead) supports the *Camulodunum* dating of AD 50–65 (Hawkes & Hull 1947, type IV, 311). The type appears from its distribution to be native to south eastern Britain and is particularly common in Essex.

Hinged T-shaped brooch (Fig 38.22)

Fig 38.22 Leaded   K Disturbed (Cat 1169)
     bronze   subsoil
This belongs to the varied developments from the Colchester type which had begun before the mid 1st century AD and seem to have continued until after *c* AD 100. Although the pin is hinged, the crossbar has grooves which appear to imitate a spring. The closest parallels for the general design are sprung

brooches from *Camulodunum* (Hawkes & Hull 1947, nos 48 and 49, pl xcii).

Sprung brooch with toothed bow (Fig 38.23)

*Fig 38.23 Bronze   K Early   (Cat 293)
     enamelled   Roman
             soil 60
This clearly defined type with toothed edges and 'Polden Hill' construction is commonest in western Britain. Several, but not all, of the parallels come from religious sites. It probably dates to the later part of the 1st century AD.

Hinged head-stud brooch (Fig 38.24)

*Fig 38.24 Brass,   K Ditch 205 (Cat 222)
     enamelled   III

The type is common throughout Britain but this is the earliest well-dated example; the deposit is dated before AD 100.

Early plate brooches (Figs 38.25-6)

*Fig 38.25 Gunmetal K Silt 465   (Cat 1105)

This probably had an applied metal plate holding a glass 'stone'; the type is datable to the mid 1st century.

    Fig 38.26 Brass   K Ditch 705   (Cat 851)
The type is well-known in Britain and the continent and is dated to the mid 1st century.

Although too small for detailed analysis this group of brooches is interesting for its date: nothing which need be later than AD 100 and most a good deal earlier. The brooches from the votive deposit are on the whole rather earlier in date than their context, suggesting that 'old' (but possibly valued) objects were offered. The types are those in general use, only Fig 38.23 having other religious associations, and that not exclusively so. It appears therefore that offering was made of personal possessions rather than objects specifically bought for the purpose.

    For one-and two-piece Colchester derivatives, and a Hod Hill brooch, from Site CF1, see p 56 and Fig 34.

Objects of copper alloy
incorporating metal analyses by Paul Wilthew (formerly Ancient Monuments Laboratory)

This report is designed to accompany and supplement that published in Volume 3.1 (Wickenden in Drury 1988). Thus objects identical to ones from the *mansio*, such as tweezers, *ligulae*, nails, needles, and studs, are not illustrated again here. Other objects, whilst similar to some from the *mansio*, are different enough to warrant full publication. However, use has been made of Nina Crummy's typology of Roman small finds from Colchester wherever possible (1983). Only those objects with some interest or diagnostic feature are published. A full list of the copper alloy is deposited with the archive. A selection of the finds have been conserved under various Area Museums Services schemes. The assemblage is typical of a Roman small town, and similar in many ways to that from the *mansio*. Of particular interest are the two distinctly military items (Fig 39.2–3), the ?votive bar (Fig 39.5), and the late ring-and-dot decorated mount (Fig 39.6) and rosette attachment (Fig 41.50). The assemblage is slightly biased by a group of votive objects of copper alloy from Site K, mainly brooches and other jewellery, in exactly the same way as with the late 4th century shrine at Great Dunmow (Wickenden 1988b). For a discussion of these votive objects, see p 127. For a number of copper alloy objects from Site CF1, see p 56 and Fig 34).

The analyses, by Paul Wilthew

Nine objects (AML 852625–33) were analysed elementally using qualitative energy dispersive

X-ray fluorescence analysis (Ancient Monuments Lab Rep No 4872). The aim was to determine alloy types used, and to identify any inlays or platings. All the objects contained small amounts of lead. Where the level was high enough to suggest that lead was probably added deliberately, the object is described as leaded. Where an object is described as containing a small amount of an element, it implies that, although that element was detected, the alloy almost certainly contained only a few percent or less. The three copper alloys identified are bronze, brass and gunmetal. Bronze contains significant amounts of tin, but only relatively low levels of zinc (if any); brass contains significant amounts of zinc, but at most relatively low levels of tin; and gunmetal contains significant amounts of both tin and zinc. The following items have been analysed: Fig 39. Nos 2, 3, 4, 12; 40. No 16; 41. Nos 60–63.

Fig 39.1   Enamelled belt slide. No parallels have been found for this object, which comes from a medieval context. However, the slightly olive-green, overall patina and the method of casting the decoration seem distinctly early Roman. The central hole possibly held a 'stone' or glass pellet; it could not have held a stud as might be expected, since this would have obscured the enamels in the roundel. Justine Bayley has examined the enamels: the fields in the central roundel are alternately blue and 'green'; the leaf-shaped fields are 'green', and their shape paralleled for instance in Bateson 1981, fig 9, C.I. The 'green' colour referred to was probably originally red or possibly orange. Pit 679 (PR).

Military (Fig 39.2–3). See also Fig 39.60–62, 64
Fig 39.2   Abraded legionary apron terminal or strap end, with remains of a dome-headed stud attachment. For a range of similar terminals from Colchester, see Hawkes & Hull 1947, plate C11.24–7. Bronze, with a small amount of zinc. 1st century AD. D 261, VII.2, silt over road.
Fig 39.3   Stud with quatrefoil decoration, which is typically military. Brass, with a small amount of lead. The inlay appears to be niello (unconfirmed). See, for instance, Hawkes & Hull 1947, plate C11.30; Brailsford 1962, fig 5.A 125–6; Ritterling 1913, taf xii. K 479 (early Roman gravel 257, IV.3). The same context also yielded a coin of Claudius I.
Fig 39.4   Plated box hasp with transverse mouldings and a 'scallop' terminal. For a parallel, see Down & Rule 1971, fig 5.16, 171K. The same motif appears on a hasp from Richborough (Wilson 1968,

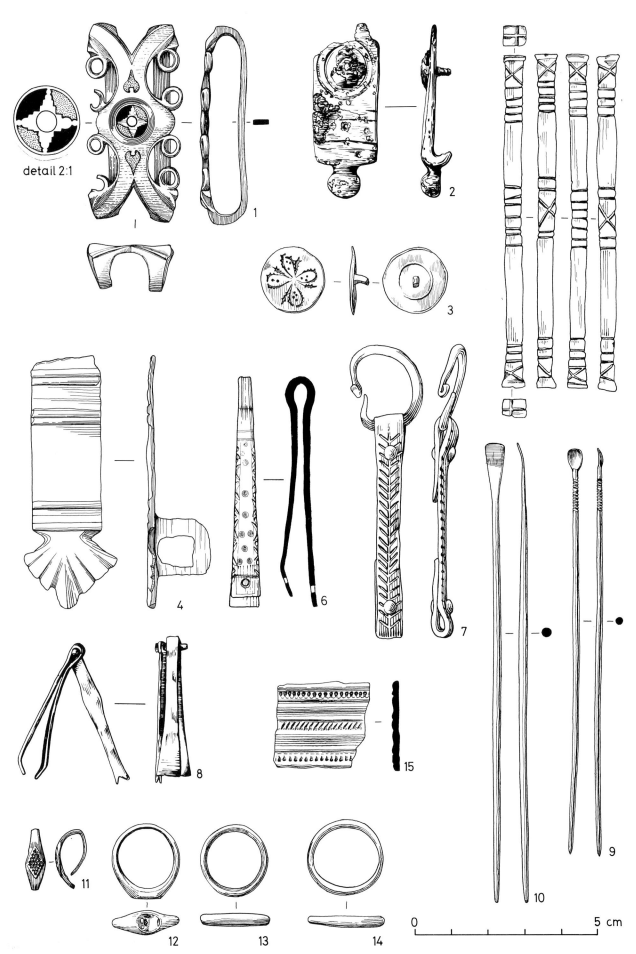

detail 2:1

0　　　　　　　　　　　5 cm

Figure 39　Objects of copper alloy, 1–15 (Scale 1:1)

Plate IX   a) Copper alloy votive bar, Fig 39.5; b) bone plaque, Fig 43.2 (Photo: H Ferguson)

plate XLV, 193) and a military harness pendant from Kelvedon, Essex (Rodwell 1988, fig 46.34). Very high levels of both tin and lead were detected. It was, almost certainly, white metal plated on both the back and front which made it difficult to determine the composition of either the base metal or the plating. However the levels of tin and lead detected strongly suggest that the plating was a tin-lead alloy. The base metal was probably bronze (?leaded), but could have been copper, and also contained a small amount of zinc. D 71, IV–V, subsoil under ovens.

Fig 39.5   ?Votive bar, of wrought brass, bearing zones of incised lines and crosses (Pl IX). Note that similar crosses and grooves are often found on 'cult' objects. Published in full (Wickenden 1986, 348–51, fig 8, pl xxviic) in response to which David Gurney had kindly drawn my attention to a worked bone object of similar shape and decoration from a salt production site at Denver, Norfolk (N Crummy in Gurney 1986, fig 70.29). Perhaps more relevant are two copper alloy bars from Springhead, Kent. One, from ploughed topsoil over the temple complex, has faint criss-cross markings around each terminal (*Archaeol Cantiana* (1959), **73**, 50); the other (unstratified) has criss-cross markings along its length, created by four spiralling lines (in different directions). Both objects are round-sectioned with squared ends. I am grateful to the curator, J Vale, for this information (Gravesham Museum, Accn no G1109). K 454 (primary fill of ditch 205, IV.2).

Fig 39.6   *by V.I. Evison*
Mount consisting of a band bent double as though for tweezers, narrow at the looped end and widening towards the terminals. One side only is decorated with transverse lines at top and bottom, ring-and-dot stamps in the middle and arc stamps at the edges giving a serrated effect. The decorated band is bent at one end but a perforation which matches a perforation on the opposite band shows that the two were originally flat and riveted together.
Two similar mounts were found in a late 3rd or 4th century context at Shakenoak (Brodribb *et al* 1973, 110, nos 211–2). No 211 was similarly decorated, though the two ends were bent away from each other; the other was undecorated. A pair were

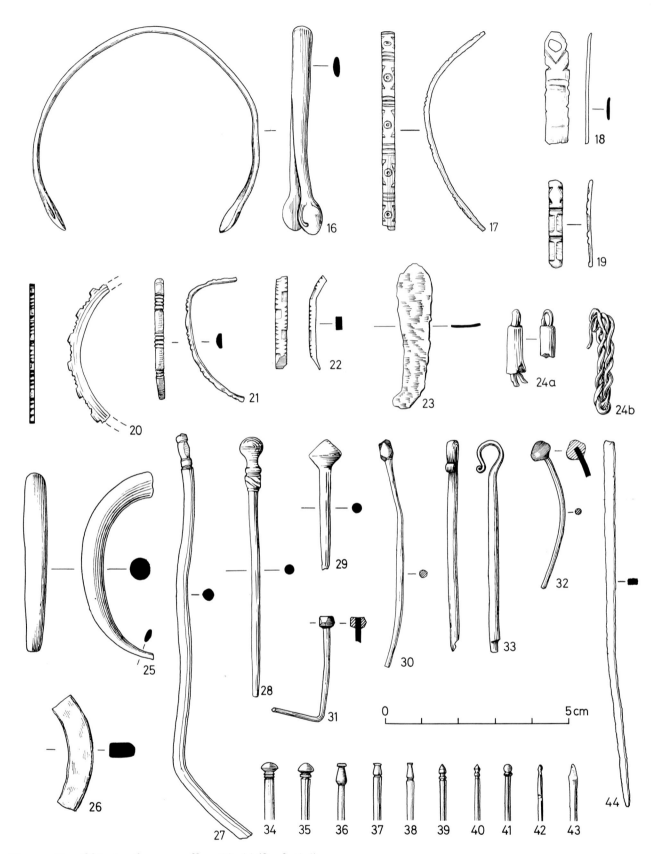

Figure 40   Objects of copper alloy, 16–44 (Scale 1:1)

found in a grave in the Germanic cemetery at Kempston, Beds (Fitch 1864). Both were 80 mm long, one fitted with a loose ring at the looped end and decoration was by small ring-and-dot stamps and transverse lines. The rivet remains in position at the end, showing that the material held there (?leather, cloth) was about 2 mm thick. These were in a woman's grave richly furnished with Saxon objects of the 5th or 6th centuries such as disc brooches and beads, and which contained also a Roman bracelet and Roman coins. As the bronze mounts are not recognisably Saxon objects, as the ornamentation is of late Roman type, and as in the Kempston grave they are accompanied by other Roman objects, they can only be regarded as heirlooms there and of late 4th century manufacture. K 509 (subsoil).

Fig 39.7   Chatelaine belt fitting comprising a strip with incised herringbone decoration folded over at each end to form a loop and riveted (the rivets are missing). A copper alloy split ring is attached to one terminal. K 121 (pit 90, VI).

Cosmetic Implements

Fig 39.8   Cosmetic set of nail cleaner and tweezers, on a copper alloy spindle; undecorated, *cf* Wedlake 1958, fig 59.3T. M 25, subsoil.

Unillus   Tweezers, Crummy type 1879 (AB 4); Crummy type 1883 (K 1130); Crummy type 1884 (K 1128, subsoil). Very corroded nailcleaner or earscoop, (D 263, silt 261, VII.2). Complete nail cleaner, Chelmsford type B (Wickenden in Drury 1988, fig 64.43), with marginal grooves parallel to each edge (K 1144, subsoil).

Fig 39.9   *Ligula* with cup-shaped scoop and twisted zone on shank, *cf* Goodburn 1984, fig 14.105, K 90 (pit, VI).

Fig 39.10   *Ligula* with flat, triangular scoop. K 968 (pit 90, VI).

Unillus   *Ligulae*, identical to Wickenden in Drury 1988, fig 64.50-1 from the Chelmsford *mansio*; also Crummy types 1899, 1901 (K 259, subsoil; K 760, Hollow 719, VI; K 918, unstrat). Swollen probe end of *Spathomela*, *cf* Crummy 1983, fig 65; Wheeler 1930, pl 37 (K 528, gravel 237, VI+).

Jewellery

Fig 39.11   Bent and incomplete finger ring with raised lozenge-shaped bezel, decorated with small dots. For identical examples, see Wheeler & Wheeler 1936, fig 47 (Flavian deposit); Stead 1976, 205.52; Partridge 1977, 35, fig 7.3. K 356 (sinkage fill over ditch 205, V).

Fig 39.12   Finger-ring with oval bezel. Bronze also containing small amounts of zinc. No visual or analytical evidence for an inlay in the bezel was found. The material in the bezel appeared to be entirely corrosion products. K 414 (early Roman soil 260, IV.2).

Fig 39.13   Plain finger-ring. K 1105 (early silt 465, V). A second identical ring came from K 1129 (cleaning).

Fig 39.14   Plain finger-ring. K 793 (PR).

Fig 39.15   Piece of broad strip bracelet decorated with alternating zones of peck marks and ribs. The type is characteristically early Roman in date, *cf* Hawkes & Hull 1947, pl C.30; Crummy types 1586-7; Frere 1972, fig 32.30-1. (pit K 87, IV.2).

Fig 40.16   Complete bracelet with expanded, cupped, and plated terminals. Gunmetal; slightly higher levels of tin were detected in the plated areas at the terminals, and the plating was probably tin, although it is possible that it also contained lead. K 1072 (early Roman subsoil 260, IV–V).

Fig 40.17   Fragment of ribbon-strip bracelet; the decoration is identical to Crummy type 1728 (D 254, subsoil).

Fig 40.18   Small fragment of bracelet with pierced terminal. K 8 (pit 2, VI).

Fig 40.19   Small fragment of bracelet with decoration. D 179, (ditch 173, VI.1).

Fig 40.20   Part of toothed and crenellated bracelet, *cf* Kenyon 1948, fig 83.3; Crummy type 1659; Wickenden 1988b, fig 28.15. M 25 (subsoil). A similar fragment came from K 252 (gravel 237, VI+).

Fig 40.21   Length of bracelet with zones of grooves, identical to an example from the late 4th century shrine at Dunmow, Wickenden 1988b, fig 28.16; *cf* also Crummy type 1721. K 83 (pit 84, VI+). Other similar pieces came from K 1095 (pit 101, VII.2), and K 259 (subsoil).

Fig 40.22   Short fragment of bracelet with zones of nicks along each edge. K 1096 (pit 124, VII.2).

Unillus   Short fragment of ribbon strip bracelet with two grooves (K 265, PR); fragments of bracelet made from twisting two wires of oval or sub-circular section, *cf* Drury 1976, fig 11.4; Crummy types 1610–1613. (K 28, pit 17, VII.2; 952, subsoil; 1061, pit 101, VII.2).

Fig 40.23   Flat strip bracelet terminal, undecorated but similar to one from the *mansio* with two eyes, indicating a snake's head (Wickenden in Drury 1988, fig 63.28; *cf* also Allason-Jones & Miket 1984, 132. 3.243. D 146, unstrat.

Fig 40.24   Terminal and short length of double loop-in-loop bracelet, *cf* Crummy type 4441. D 262 (silt 261, VII.2).

Fig 40.25   Plain bracelet of tapering round section, similar to Crummy types 1650-1, 1710. K 1141 (ditch 705, IV.2).

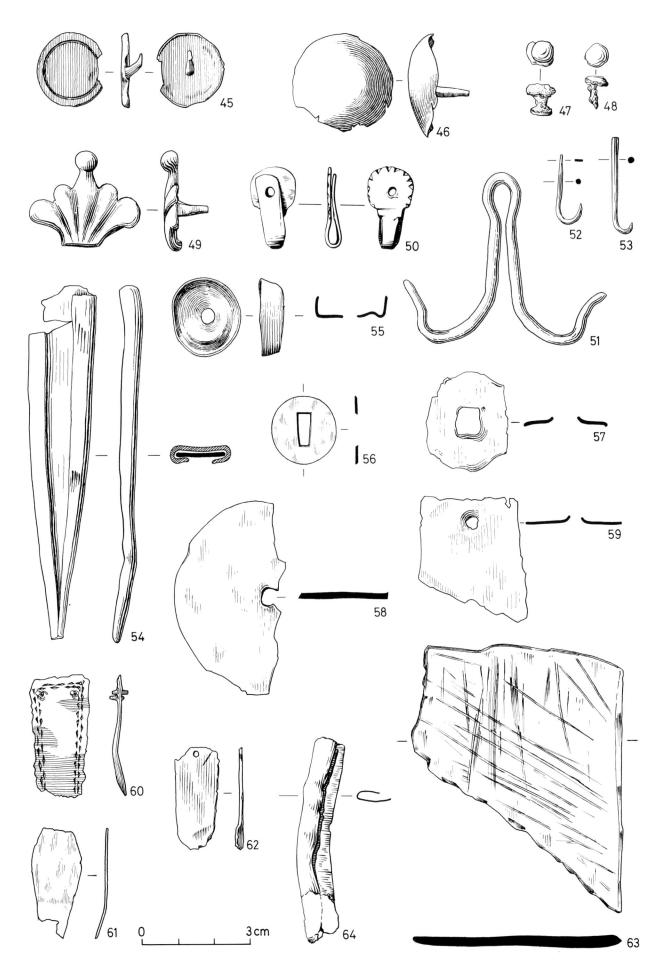

Figure 41   Objects of copper alloy, 45–64 (Scale 1:1)

Fig 40.26   Section of plain, heavy bracelet. K 336 (PR).

Needles

Unillus   Four examples of Crummy type 1991 from: D 56 (ditch 23, VI.1), 117mm long; K 60, subsoil, 60mm long and possibly resharpened; K 1163, subsoil, 90mm long; K 1164, subsoil, 121mm long. One example of Crummy type 1993 from K 441, unstrat, 45mm long. One example similar to Wickenden in Drury 1988, fig 65.54, from K 918, unstrat, 61mm long. Fragments also were recorded from D 139 (ditch 23, VI.1), K 239 (gravel 237, VI.1+), K 715 (?hollow 713) and K 1100 (pit 84, VI+).

Pins

Fig 40.27   Pin with moulded, baluster head, similar to Allason-Jones & Miket 1984, 178, 3.510. D 314 (road 259, V–VII).

Fig 40.28   Pin with a head combining several motifs, *cf* Crummy 1983, fig 27; Allason-Jones & Miket 1984, 180,3. 540. M 25 (subsoil).

Fig 40.29   Biconical-headed pin, cf Crummy type 480. K 698 (subsoil).

Fig 40.30   Pin with an elongated, multi-faceted head, cf Crummy 1983, fig 29 (post-AD 250). K 1161 (subsoil).

Fig 40.31   Pin with multi-faceted head (incomplete), made separately and wrapped around the top of the shaft to give the impression of ring-and-dot decoration.An exact parallel comes from *Verulamium* (Goodburn 1984, fig 16.131) from a context dated AD 360–370.K 218 (gravel 237, VI.1+).

Fig 40.32   Pin with applied head of black and green glass, cf Wickenden 1988b, fig 28.4, from the late 4th century shrine at Dunmow. K 1162 (pit 47, VII.1).

Fig 40.33   Pin with 'shepherd's crook' head, possibly from a penannular brooch (cf Boon 1974, 69, fig 9.2). K 7 (pit 17, VII.2).

Figs 40.34–43   Selection of pins with various types of common moulded heads (shafts not shown): 34, K 481 (subsoil); 35, K 354 (sinkage over ditch 205); 36, K 121 (pit 90, VI); 37, K 92 (pit 90, VI); 38, K 251 (subsoil); 39, K 481 (subsoil); 40, K 259 (subsoil); 41, K 1072 (early Roman subsoil 260, IV– V); 42, M 25 (subsoil); 43, K 121 (pit 90, VI).

Unillus   Five ?pin shafts, or wire fragments, from D, L and AB, and 15 fragments from K.

Fig 40.44   Rod with a pointed end and a rectangular section; ?stylus. D 253, (subsoil).

Nails, studs and rivets

Unillus   Square-sectioned nail with spherical head, Crummy type 2992 (K 471, silt 465, V); round-sectioned nail with spherical head, cf Wickenden in Drury 1988, fig 65. 62 (AB 3); square-sectioned nail with flat head, Crummy type 3057. K 82 (pit 84, VI+).

Fig 41.45   Stud with concentric groove on upper surface; the rim is slightly turned down. K 92 (pit 90, VI).

Fig 41.46   Stud with convex head. K 118 (pit 90, VI).

Unillus   Stud with large flat head, and short, square-sectioned shank, cf Wickenden in Drury 1988, fig 65.67. K 481 (subsoil).

Fig 41.47   Small rivet. D 114 (subsoil).

Fig 41.48   Small corroded tack. D 26 (subsoil).

Miscellanea

Fig 41.49   Mount, similar to one from *Verulamium* (Frere 1972, fig 33.50); but possibly post-Roman. K 81 (pit 84, VI+).

Fig 41. 50   Circular disc (rosette) attachment, folded over and riveted through the centre with nicked decoration around the circumference. For the type, see Hawkes & Dunning 1961, 67; Evison 1968, 240 and fig 1, where three such mounts form part of the Dorchester belt. The Chelmsford piece is quite crude by comparison, but must belong to the same *genre*, and should be dated to *c* AD 400. M 35 (pit, VII.2).

Fig 41.51   Double hook, similar to those used on steelyards for holding the scale pan(s), *cf* Wheeler 1930, fig 22.2; Gibson 1970, 109, fig 1. A similar hook comes from Wickford (in prep). K 1143 (well 813, V.2–VI).

Fig 41.52–3   Two fish-hooks. D 244 (ditch, VII.2), 261 (silt, VII.2).

Unillus   Hook-and-eye similar to one from the *mansio* (Wickenden in Drury 1988, fig 65.73), K 160 (pre-temple make up); single round chain link, K 573 (robbing trench); two joined figure-of-eight links, K 426 (hollow 425, VIII); three joined oval split links (Crummy type 4427), K 1146 (?gravel 608, ?VII).

Fig 41.54   Thin sheet tapering to a point, with a second sheet wrapped around it, forming a sheath. K 936 (earliest Roman gravel 257, IV.3).

Fig 41.55   Ferrule for tool, *cf* Brailsford 1962, fig 1.A16. K 1053 (pit 85, VII.1–2).

Fig 41.56   Ferrule; a simple disc with cut out slot. K 83 (pit 84, VI+).

Fig 41.57–9   Sheeting pierced by nail or rivet holes. 57, K 418 (PR); 58, K 1135 (subsoil); 59, K 230 (subsoil).

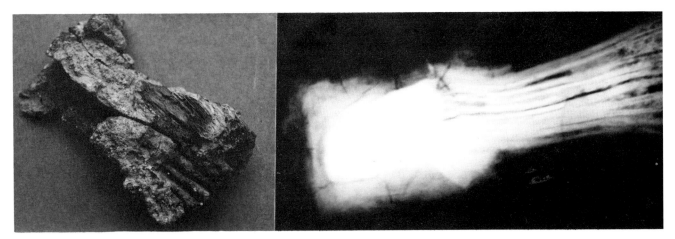

Plate X   Iron woolcomb, Fig 42.1 (record photograph during conservation, Verulamium Museum)

Fig 41.60   Sheet with a small hole at each top corner with copper alloy wire passing through, tapering slightly towards the bottom (incomplete); the edges are decorated with two rows of peck-marks. Possibly a fragment of *lorica squamata* (*cf* Robinson 1975, fig 159, pl 436–41), though the object appears to be soldered on its under-side. Gunmetal; the white metal plated area contained higher levels of lead and tin than the base metal; hence the plating was a tin-lead (?solder) alloy. K 748 (non-feature).

Fig 41.61   Cut sheet fragment, or possibly inlay for furniture (*cf* Neal 1974, fig 59.110–11). Gunmetal; the white metal plated area on the underside contained higher levels of lead and tin than the base metal and was almost certainly solder. K 108 (pit 84, VI+).

Fig 41.62   Sheet fragment with a small drilled hole top centre. Gunmetal; the white metal area on the underside contained higher levels of tin and lead than the base metal and was almost certainly a tin-lead solder. K 1139 (clearance).

Fig 41.63   Heavy piece of sheeting, substantially worn, with criss-cross ?keying on the reverse and a 10mm band of white metal plating along the inside edge. Leaded bronze; rather higher tin levels were detected in the plated area, but the presence of lead in the base metal made it impossible to be certain whether the plating was tin or a tin-lead alloy. From its position, it seems likely that the plating was a solder, in which case it would probably

have contained some lead. K 593 (post-hole, VI).

Fig 41.64   Folded sheet binding, with a slightly curved edge and small hole pierced for attachment to wood or leather, ??shield binding (*cf* Brailsford 1962, fig 1.A9–11). K (trial trench).

Unillus   Many small corroded pieces of sheeting and binding, including pieces from M 53 (pit 54, VI+), K 674 (Roman subsoil, VI), K 1135 (subsoil), and strips from K 231 (PR), K 267 (robber trench 216), K 915 (unstrat) and M 44 (pit intersection).

The Lead

Molten lumps came from D 256 (unstrat), and 257 (subsoil), and a D-sectioned strip from D 258 (rubble, VII). From K a fragment with a flat edge (?window came, guttering, or repair) came from Cat 313 (sinkage over ditch 205), a bun or furnace bottom came from 229 (subsoil), and molten lumps came from pit 49 (VII.1). Cat 83 (pit 84, VI+) and Cat 673 (subsoil).

Objects of Iron

The assemblage comprises, for the most part, nail fragments, sheeting fragments (some with nail holes), bars and unidentifiable scrap. Those objects which were clearly not nails were X-rayed through the Area Museum Service at *Verulamium* Museum in 1980, and a small proportion cleaned and conserved. The condition of the ironwork leaves much to be desired. Only those objects with some form or interest to them are illustrated here.

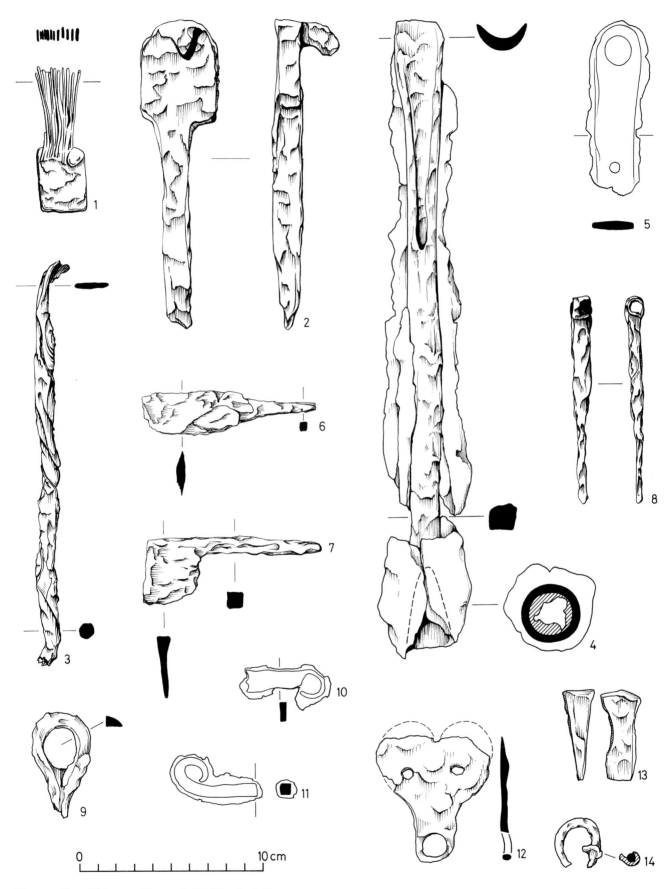

Figure 42   Objects of iron, 1–14 (Scale 1:2)

Objects which are *not* illustrated include hobnails, knife blades, wire, a small split loop (K 90, VI), a possible wall hook (K 80, subsoil), a T-headed nail (D 15, subsoil), Manning Type II nails and a small perforated loop terminal (K 745, pit, VIII). Full lists are deposited in the archive. The lack of quantity and variety in the assemblage, when compared to that of the *mansio* emphasises the general non-domestic nature of the temple sites.

Fig 42.1 (Pl X)	Woolcomb with thirteen teeth surviving, splaying out symmetrically from the plate which holds them, in the same manner as one found at Dunmow (Wickenden 1988b, fig 40.14). For recent discussions of woolcombs, though of an apparently different type, see Manning (1966, 1972) and Wild (1982). The Essex group (Chelmsford, Dunmow and Harlow) seem to be complete miniatures. D 131 (pit 123, V.1).
Fig 42.2	Spatulate-headed linch pin, with part of the turned over loop surviving (*cf* Manning 1976, fig 9.2b). D 259 (road, V.2–VII).
Fig 42.3	Twisted shaft with both terminals broken; possibly from a ladle (*cf* Manning 1972, fig 60.6), fire shovel (*cf* Manning 1976, fig 23.149) or flesh-hook. K 451 (primary fill, ditch 205, IV.2).
Fig 42.4	Corroded square-sectioned shaft with broken socket at one end, and scoop-shaped open socket at other end. ?Carpenters tool, possibly a gauge. M 67 (pit 65, VII.2).
Fig 42.5	Bucket handle mount with loop terminal (*cf* Manning 1972, fig 66.53–4). K 866 (clearance).

Knives

Fig 42.6	Knife with central tang. K 828 (subsoil).
Fig 42.7	Fragment of blade and straight backed tang of knife. D 246 (slot 244, VII.2).

Bars with loop terminals

Fig 42.8–11	8, With spike for driving into a wall, D 235 (pit, VI.2); 9, ?Key terminal (*cf* Manning 1976, fig 23.147), D 246 (slot 244, VII.2); 10, K 253 (silt 240); 11, simple folded round terminal. K 121 (pit 90, VI).
Fig 42.12	Flat object with perforated terminal; the other end splays out into a bilobate terminal with a central hole in each side. ?Hinge plate. D 68 (pit 51, V.1).
Fig 42.13	Small wedge. D 315 (silt 261, VII).
Fig 42.14	Fragment of annular brooch with stub of pin surviving, folded around the wire; corroded. K 745 (pit, VIII).

No 15	(Unillustrated) Folded strip with applied thin sheet of silver, totally corroded. Possible knife handle? K 914 (clearance).

The Metalworking Debris
by J G McDonnell

Table 4 lists the total quantity in grammes of slag from each site reported here. A full report is deposited with the archive.

All the debris derived from the smithing process and in such insignificant quantities that it must be considered background level. On site D, period V.1 pits 123 and especially 273 produced 955 gms (36.1% total). On Site K, Period IV ditches 205 and 705 together produced 635 gms of smithing slag, 180 gms hearth bottom and 475 gms hearth lining. Associated with the Period V.2 structure K41 were 480 gms of smithing slag and 530 gms of hearth lining. Otherwise the slag was scattered both temporally and spatially.

Table 4 The slags (weight in gms)

Site	Smithing	Hearth bottom	Cinder	Hearth lining
D	2215	430	0	0
K	4635	3830	100	730
M	530	0	0	75

Objects of Bone

Fig 43.1	Fragment of double-sided composite comb. For the terminology used, see Galloway 1976, 154–6. Two of the *tooth segments* which make up the body of the comb survive with a number of finely sawn teeth. Part of one *end* of the comb is also present, decorated with a semi-circular nick (see figure), and a small drilled hole, which should not be confused with the rivet holes. The tooth segments were held together between two *connecting plates* with iron rivets, two of which survive. One end only of one of these plates is present, decorated with five incised ring-and-dot motifs. Its edges are chamfered, and the two long sides incised with a row of short parallel nicks, caused by the sawing of the teeth once the comb had been assembled. The fact that both sides are incised proves that the comb was originally double-sided, though nothing of the other side survives. From the spacing of the nicks, however, it is clear that the teeth on the missing side were finer still.

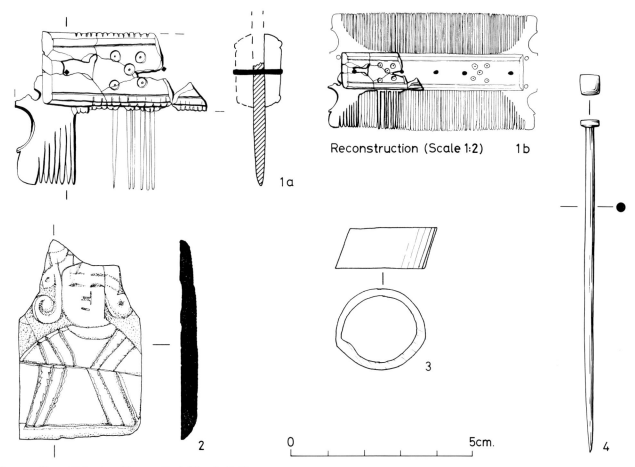

Figure 43   Objects of bone, 1–4 (Scale 1:1)

The type is characteristically late Roman; see for example, Bushe Fox 1932, pl 13.42 (Richborough); Brodribb *et al* 1972, 118–23, figs 56–9 (Shakenoak). An unpublished parallel from Great Chesterford is in the Cambridge Museum of Archaeology and Ethnography (Acc no 48.865; Dr Stephen Greep, pers comm). K 1137 (oven 485,VIII).

Fig 43.2   Flat plaque carved from a split rib with human figure; posibly from a box inlay (Pl IX, b). Published in Wickenden 1986 (p 351, fig 9, pl xxviic). Subsequent to its publication, I am grateful to P J Drury for the suggestion that the person may be wearing some form of elaborate head dress, rather than a rather exotic hairstyle. If this is true, it may well have had a liturgical use. K 438 (pit, VIII).

Fig 43.3   Sawn ring fragment of a long bone. D 36 (subsoil, V–VI).

Pins
Fig 43.4   Square flat head, 88 mm long. M 45 (pit, VII).

Unillus (incomplete)
No 5   Crummy Type 2 D 68 (pit 51, V.1), *cf* Drury 1988, fig 71.9–10 (98 mm).
No 6   Crummy Type 2 D 79 (subsoil), *cf* Crummy 1979, no 197 (63 mm).

No 7   Crummy Type 2 K 90 (pit, VI), *cf* Crummy 1979, no 197 (74 mm).
Pinshafts: K 6 (pit 17, VII.2), 121 (pit 90, VI).
Needle: Fragment of shaft & part of eye, 92 mm long. D 60 (oven 47, V.2).

The Glass

The assemblage for the most part comprised small 'natural' blue-green or transparent body sherds of Roman vessels of the 1st–4th centuries, including mould-blown prismatic bottles, and blown flasks, jugs, bowls and beakers. The more diagnostic pieces are illustrated here. Nothing is out of the ordinary; even the interesting group of olive-green, flame-rounded everted rimmed beakers, dated to *c* AD 400, have parallels in other Essex towns, including Heybridge (Wickenden 1987, fig 12.51–2), Dunmow (Wickenden 1988b, fig 34.19–23), Wickford and Witham.

Bowls, Jars

Fig 44.1   Rim, 'natural' blue green colour, of Airlie bowl, so called after a complete example from Airlie, Angus (Thorpe 1935, 39, pl 66). For a full discussion of the type see Harden 1971, 102, 107 nos 112–5, fig 44.55–6; Isings 1957, 102

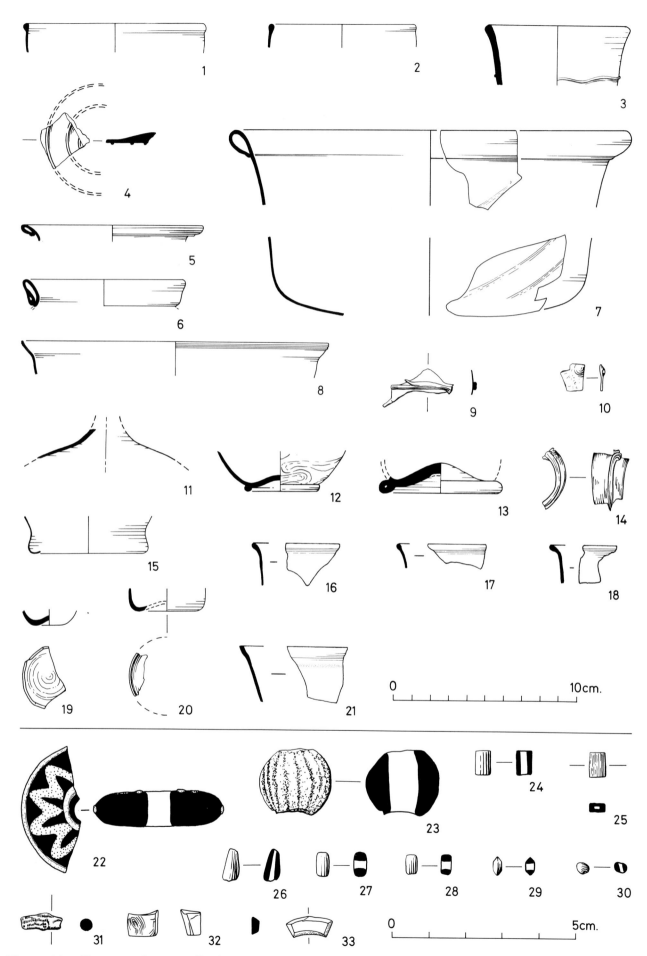

Figure 44   *Glass vessels, 1–21 (Scale 1:2); beads and paste objects, 22–33 (Scale 1:1)*

form 856; Harden & Price 1971, 352, fig 141.74). The type was common in the later 2nd and 3rd centuries. K 70 (pit, VII.2).

Fig 44.2   As Fig 44.1. K 273 (temple make-up).

Fig 44.3   Thick colourless cylindrical bowl rim (or ?beaker), flame-rounded and thickened, some small horizontal bubbles near rim, and applied, self-coloured trail, diam *c* 85mm. D 48 (subsoil).

Fig 44.4   Fragment of base with three concentric raised ridges on underside, 'natural' blue-green. K 952 (subsoil).

Fig 44.5   Rim, of bowl or jar folded outwards, light green. K 395 (PR).

Fig 44.6   Rim of jar, folded outwards and inwards, light blue. D 7 (pit 3, VI.2).

Fig 44.7   Many fragments of rim and body, including the carination, of a bowl with tubular folded rim, and some very light ribbing on body, green, many large bubbles. These bowls first appear in the second half of the 1st century AD and are quite common throughout the 2nd century. *cf* Charlesworth 1972, 199–200, fig 74.10–11; 1978, fig 10.22, no 14 & p 267. Site D, cats 11, 20, 36, 57, 68, 74, 93, 119, 132, 133, 160, 161, 229, 337, 338 (Period V.1).

Fig 44.8   Colourless rim of bowl, everted, knocked off and ground smooth; two wheel-incised grooves below rim; diam 170 mm. K 753 (ditch 705, IV.2). For a similar bowl, see Charlesworth 1972, fig 78.56, p 210.

Fig 44.9   Sherd from body of ?cylindrical bowl, pale green colour, decorated with applied, self-coloured trail, with part of a second trail. K 436 (clearance).

Fig 44.10   Small sherds from ?bowl, colourless, pinhead bubbles, with applied blue glass blob. K 1151 (pit 88, VII.2).

Flasks

Fig 44.11   Neck and shoulder of flask, 'natural' blue-green, probably 1st–2nd century. D 178 (ditch 173, VI.1).

Fig 44.12   Folded ring base with low *omphalos* and sides of ?flask, light green with milky swirling marks. M 7 (pit, VII.2).

Fig 44.13   Base of flask or beaker, with folded tubular foot, *omphalos* base with pontil mark, light green, 2nd–3rd century. D 339 (subsoil). See, for instance, Charlesworth 1981, fig 15.2, no 17.

Fig 44.14   Handle with central ridge, very pale blue. K 450 (ditch 205, IV.2).

Fig 44.15   Part of base and side of flask or *olla*, very pale blue. K 454 (primary fill, ditch 205, IV.2). Probably same vessel as Fig 44.14.

Unillus   Angle of ribbed handle of mould-blown prismatic bottle. M 51 (pit 35, VII.2).

Late 4th century glass

Rim, base and body sherds of eight original vessels, showing little sign of abrasion by wear, come from Site K. All are in an olive green metal with many pinhead bubbles. Fig 44.16–20 are from cone-beakers (Isings 1957, form 106b), produced in France and the Rhineland in the later 4th century. Other examples with flame-rounded rims in Essex have been dated to *c* AD 400; eg, from the Shrine at Great Dunmow (Wickenden 1988b, fig 34.19–23). The classic group from Burgh Castle is now believed to have been deposited in the first quarter of the 5th century (Harden 1983, 81–8, fig 37, pl xii). Fig 44.21 is from a type also manufactured in the decades just before and after AD 400 (Isings 1957, form 96; Vanderhoeven 1958, pls i–iii). A bowl which matches very closely in colour, size, rim and decoration was found in a child's stone coffin at Glaston, Rutland, with bronze bracelets and a conical glass beaker (Webster 1950, 72–3, fig 1.4). A number were found at Mayen in Germany, where they occurred in coin-dated graves of the end of the 4th century. Most are plain, but one is decorated with zones of wheel incisions (Haberey 1942, 249–84, Abb 2, a). The form, and even the unfinished rim, continue into the 5th century, but decoration by abrasion does not seem to have survived the 4th century.

I am grateful to Professor V Evison for her comments on this group, written in 1975.

Fig 44.16   Everted, smoothed rim; light olive green metal with bubbles and striations, and a black impurity in the rim; diam *c* 80 mm. K Cat 1136 (PR).

Fig 44.17   Everted, finished rim; bubbly, light greenish-yellow; diam *c* 90mm. K Cat 341 (PR).

Fig 44.18   Everted, finished rim; light olive green metal with bubbles and striations; diam *c* 90 mm. K Cat 152 (PR).

Fig 44.19   Fragment of a base with pointed kick and pontil mark; light olive green with very small bubbles and a good gloss; wall 2 mm thick. K Cat 417 (PR).

Fig 44.20   Fragment of a kicked base; light green, small bubbles, worn outer surface. K 418 (PR).

Fig 44.21   Rim of an hemispherical bowl, cupped, broken off and left unfinished; a faint wheel-abraded horizontal band below the rim; light greenish-yellow, good quality glass with good sheen; diam *c* 85 mm. K Cat 417 (PR).

Window Glass

Matt/glossy fragments came from AB 2 over F2 (*possibly* mould-blown prismatic bottle fragment); M 32 (pit, VI+, flame-rounded edge); D 64 (unstrat), 109 (ditch 23, VI.1), 170 (?Roman subsoil 13, IV–VI; again, *possibly* from mould-blown prismatic

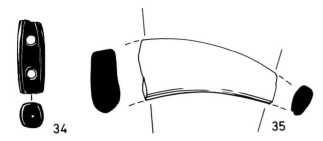 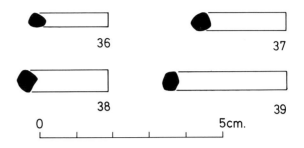

Figure 45   Objects of jet and shale, 34–39 (Scale 1:1)

bottles); K 369 (subsoil, flame rounded edge). Possible double-sided glossy fragments came from K 17 (pit, VII.2), 418 (PR), both with flame-rounded edges.

The glass beads, and other objects

I am grateful to Marjorie Hutchinson of the Ancient Monuments Laboratory for her comments on Figs 44.22, 25, 31–3.

Fig 44.22   Bead *by Vera I Evison* (July 1989)
Fragment of a large disc bead, very dark green, trail decoration on one face, an unmarvered yellow ring round the perforation and yellow circumference trail, a marvered red zigzag trail between. Diam *c* 35mm. K 230 (subsoil).
This bead is one of a series of large, disc-shaped which occur with slight variations in shape, some being flatter on one side than the other. Some are decorated on both sides, but most, like this one, on one side only. The design is generally by trails, circumference and central, with a zigzag or flower shape between. As they have often been found in association with a sword, one use is certainly as a sword-bead, presumably thought to have magical properties (Menghin 1983, 142–3, Karte 19, 355–6; Meaney 1981, 195–6). The custom of carrying a sword bead in glass or other materials travelled westwards with the Huns between the 1st century BC and the 5th century AD, and occurs both west and east of the Rhine (Werner 1956, 26–37, Karte II; Raddatz 1957/8; Evison 1967, 64–6; Tempelmann-Maczynska 1985, 62–3, 145–6, taf 13.380a–c, Taf 56). When occurring in women's graves, the large disc beads have been interpreted as spindle whorls or necklace beads. This particular pattern of glass bead occurs in England in contexts from the late 4th century to the 6th century (Guido 1978, 64, pl ii, 10f), eg, grave 44, Little Wilbraham, Cambridgeshire (Evison 1967, fig 2c–g, pl viiic) and grave 2,

Alton, Hampshire (Evison 1988, 5, fig 22).

Fig 44.23   Half turquoise frit melon bead, K 1155 (primary fill, ditch 205, IV.2).

Fig 44.24   Cylindrical green glass bead, D 239 (post-hole, VII.2).

Fig 44.25   Flattened cylindrical transparent green glass bead, K 309 (PR).

Fig 44.26   Tapering green glass bead, K 1149 (pit, IV.2).

Fig 44.27   Short barrel bead, green paste, K 1158 (PR).

Fig 44.28   As Fig 44.27, but smaller, K 683 (PR).

Fig 44.29   Small biconical bead, green paste, K 382 (subsoil).

Fig 44.30   Minute blue glass bead, opaque, K 244 (clearance).

Unillus   Post-medieval multi-faceted, black glass bead, diam 15 mm with tapering hole, 4.0–1.5 mm, K 259 (Road, V–VII).

For a glass head on a copper alloy pin, see Fig 40.32.

Fig 44.31   Small section of burnt blue and black opaque glass bangle; diameter varies between 3.4 and 4.3mm. K 265 (PR).

Fig 44.32   Irregular opaque green glass ?*tessera*, measurements 8.1 mm length, 7.4 mm max width, 3.3 mm max thickness. K 272 (post-hole, IV.1).

Gems

Fig 44.33   Flat-bottomed curving fragment of jewellery or inlay, opaque dark green, bevelled edges, Malachite. Possibly comparatively modern jewellery. K 1156 (sewer trench).

Objects of Jet and Shale

Fig 45.34   Plain bead of jet, 19mm long and subsquare in section (6 mm), pierced by two holes, 3 m across, with traces of wearing. D 79 (subsoil).

Fig 45.35   Fragment of tapering shale bangle, similar to an example from the *mansio* at Chelmsford (Drury 1988, fig 73.3). M 51 (pit 35, VII.2).

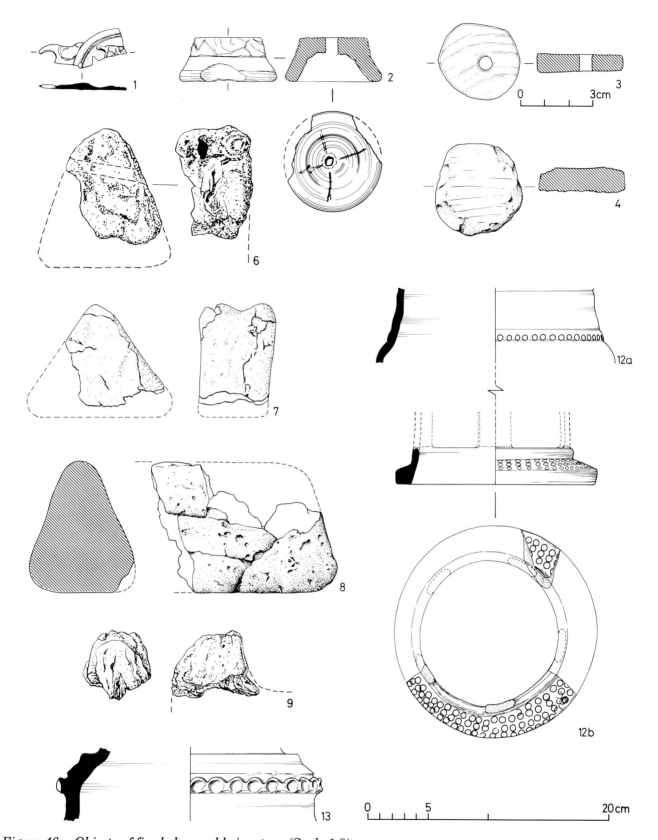

Figure 46   Objects of fired clay and briquetage (Scale 1:3)

Fig 45.36–9 Fragments of plain shale bracelets. Internal diameters 35, 40, 40, 60mm (K 1159 (subsoil), 98 (subsoil), 239 (gravel 237,VI+) and 1149 (pit, IV.2)).

Objects of Fired Clay and Briquetage

Fig 46.1 Lamp fragment in buffware. An example of Type II, see Wheeler 1930, 62–3, fig 15, based on Walters 1914: *Lamp with nozzle ending in a rounded termination, flanked on either side by a double volute; decorated in relief on the Discus.* This latter decoration is unfortunately too fragmentary for identification. K, Cat 495 (ditch 205, IV.2). A second, smaller rim fragment with the same double groove, came from K, hollow 483 (IV.2).
The type first appeared at the end of the 1st century BC, and became the normal type from about 40 AD until the last decade of the century, when it seems to have vanished in N Western Europe.

Fig 46.2 Samian base, f33, EG, Antonine. Drilled through centre of base for use as a spindle whorl. Unstamped, but with graffito 'X' on underside. D258 (VII.2).

Fig 46.3 Spindle whorl, 36mm x 32mm, made out of a base, 9mm thick, of a greyware pottery vessel with flint inclusions. The hole, 7mm across, shows some wear traces. D 253 (subsoil).

No 4 (Unillustrated) half sandy greyware base, 90mm in diameter, edges not particularly abraded; pierced in centre by hole, c 7mm across; too large for a spindle whorl, and Crummy suggests they may be counters, pierced so they could be strung together in sets (1983, 94 and fig 99). K 34 (pit 21,VII.2).

Fig 46.5 Fragment of *tegula* in the normal hard orange tile fabric, 18mm thick and 70mm in diameter, chipped into the shape of a circle. Similar examples, made from Roman tile, were found in 16th century contexts in Chelmsford (Cunningham & Drury 1985,81); possibly used as a gaming piece. D 180 (ditch 173, VI.1).

Fig 46.6 Fragment of Iron Age-type triangular loom weight with part of one diagonal piercing, 10mm across; fabric as below. K unstrat (Cat 918).

Fig 46.7 Fragment of Iron Age-type triangular loom weight, 60mm wide. Though unpierced, there is a groove 8mm deep and 35mm across in the centre of the apex of the triangle, and several ?string impressions on one surface (see drawing). The clay is compact, without voids, with large flint inclusions (burnt and shattered pebbles) 20mm long. The type is common and widespread; for a recent gazetteer of finds from Essex, which does not include Chelmsford, see H Major in Priddy 1982, 117–22. K, Cat 817 (well 813, V.2–VI).

Fig 46.8 Large incomplete object, triangular in section. The fabric is similar to that of the loomweights (Fig 46.5–6). The use is unknown though a similar object from Danbury, (*cf* Colchester Museum Report 1947), is thought to be a pottery fire dog. Alternatively, it might belong to a massive form of fire bar. K Cat 760 (hollow 719, V.2).
Small fragments from K 672, 675, 812, 817, 822 and M 7 might belong to this, or possibly loomweights as above. That from Cat 812 bears the impression of a nut or shell, c 10mm across, in its clay matrix. The 'nut' has a flattened conical end, similar to an almond, but is ribbed rather like a cockle shell. Further attempts to identify it have not met with any success.

Fig 46.9 Possible fragment of the expanded terminal of a pedestal, well known from Essex Red Hills (Rodwell 1979, fig 5); or a 'horned stand' similar to an object found at Canewdon and thought to be Bronze Age or early Iron Age (Colchester Museum Rep 1937, 8, pl II). It is in a crumbly light purplish-brown fabric, tempered with abundant, coarse vegetable matter, and reminiscent of briquetage. Well K 813, V.2–VI (Cat 819).

No 10 (Unillustrated) Two joining fragments from Cats 816 (well 813, V.2–VI) and 822 (slump 820), in an identical fabric to No 9, form part of a plate, c 43mm thick and c 115mm wide, and at least 130mm long. A small part of one side survives, absolutely flat; the opposing side is more rounded and worn. Possibly part of a hearth wall, or a fire bar grid (see Rodwell 1979, fig 7.G).

No 11 (Unillustrated) Wall fragments of thin, straight sided pans connected with salt production, and in a classic soft, soapy, vegetable-tempered 'briquetage' fabric with cream-light, purple-orange surfaces, were found on Sites K and AB. Pieces from K Cats 185 (ditch 177, IV.2), 672 (clearing), 819 (well 813, V.2–V1) and 927 (ditch 205, IV.2) range from 8–19mm thick. Site AB produced nine pieces, 10–15mm thick but more irregular and without the typical cream-purple colouring. This identification must remain in doubt.
For this type of vessel, see Rodwell 1979, fig 8. Rodwell also discusses the

evidence in general for the salt industry in Essex, and includes an appendix of finds of briquetage (nearly always pan fragments) from inland sites (*ibid*, 172). Chelmsford itself has also produced fragments from the *mansio* (Drury 1988) and Site V (in prep).

No 12   (Unillustrated) A small fragment of pipe clay, possibly from the base of a statuette, came from CR 21A, F3.

Fig 46.13 The pottery 'lamp chimney'

Flanged base-ring ('rim' as thrown), in a relatively soft, buff fabric with pinkish core and some find sand, chalk and reddish ferruginous inclusions; decorated on the upper surface, (as used) with circular punch-marks mainly in three rows, though some of the impressions are irregularly placed. Traces of a white slip survive, largely in the punch-marks. External diameter of base flange *c* 170mm, but the surviving fragments vary by up to 10mm, and the vessel was clearly not perfectly circular. The bottom of the sides of the flange have been knife trimmed. The wall survives enough to show that there were wide openings probably five in all, in between five narrow panels. The shape of the openings is unknown, though since the bottoms are flat, a square or triangle is likely. Other fragments, with a slightly larger diameter, decorated with a single row of punch-marks, must come from an upper portion of the vessel (Fig 46.13a).

There are no traces of any sooting. The fine decoration clearly indicates that the vessel was intended to be seen from close quarters, at or below eye-level. Further, the relatively soft fabric and thin walls suggest it was not intended for external use.

The vessel is undoubtedly in the same class (and fabric) as the complete example from *Verulamium* (Wheeler & Wheeler 1936, 190 fig 32 & pl 58), found in the enclosure of the 'triangular' temple, and dated to the early 2nd century. Wheeler suggested it was presumably intended to shelter a light, or for burning incense. Since then, other similar vessels in a pottery fabric and side openings have been listed posthumously by Lowther (1976, 48). They include Braintree (Drury 1976, 23–4), Godmanchester, from the 'Temple of Abandinus' (HJM Green unpub), Eccles, Kent (Detsicas 1974, 305f, fig 8) and London. Thus three are known from temple sites, where they may have had a ritual function; the secular examples may have been housed in a domestic shrine or *lararium*. Detsicas has suggested that the Eccles examples may have been candle-covers, and this is accepted by Drury for the whole group (1976, 23). What is absolutely clear is that the group has a totally different function from Lowther's Type B (1976), which are always in a sandy tile fabric, and intended for external use as chimney pots or other similar

roof-furniture. An example of one was found on Site M (below).

The fragments of lamp chimney were found in contexts alongside other ritually deposited material (copper alloy brooches, finger rings and an incised rod, Fig 39.5). Two fragments came from the primary fill of the early enclosure ditch 205; thus a date of *c* AD 60–75 is suggested for the vessel's breakage. A discussion of this significance of this 1st century votive deposit is on p 127–8. K, Cats 408, 415, 422, 467 and 495.

Fig 46.14 The 'chimney pot'

Two fragments in a hard, sandy grey 'tile' fabric, partly orange on the lower exterior, bearing an external flange decorated with continuous thumb impressions. Above the flange, the wall slopes sharply inward as if to a conical point; the surviving fragment is decorated with a series of probably three ridges.

Unlike Fig 46.13, this is an example of Lowther's Group B (1976). These are cylindrical, tower-shaped objects with a tapering profile with zones of side-openings, separated by flanges. A middle Roman date is suggested for them. Their function seems either to be that of chimney pot/ventilator, or an an ornamental roof finial (*ibid*, 39). No cut-outs are visible on the Chelmsford fragments; it seems likely that they come from the conical apex of the object above the highest tier of side openings. (eg, *ibid*, fig 1.1, from Ashstead, Surrey). M 22 (subsoil), 32 (pit, VI).

Objects of Stone (Fig 47)

The Querns

Lava

As on the *mansio* sites, there were many more fragments of Rhenish lava quern than any other type, and mostly in small abraded pieces. It has been assumed that all pieces are Roman and from querns, though other possibilities are equally feasible. Fragments included an edge of an upper stone with the normal raised collar (Fig 47.1, 45mm thick and wide) and traces of original grooving from K Cat 914 (clearance), a piece with radial tooling from D 318, part of a lower stone from D 92 (oven, VI.1), and part of a lower stone with the central fixture hole (Fig 47.2, D 159,

Table 5 The querns (numbers of fragments)

	K	D	M	AB	Total
Millstone Grit	10	8	2	—	20
Lava	40	31	1	1	73
Puddingstone	7	—	—	—	7
Total	57	39	3	1	100

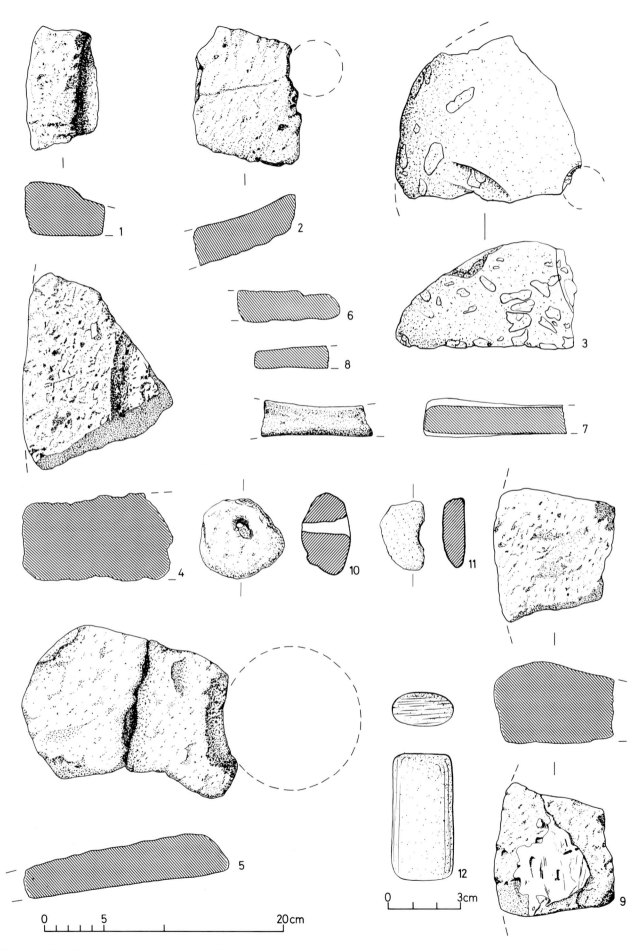

Figure 47 Objects of stone (Scale 1:3)

subsoil). For good examples of the standard forms of querns found in Essex, see Buckley & Major 1983, 73–6, fig 78.

Puddingstone

Diagnostic pieces of bun-shaped stones come from K 47 (pit, VII.1; upper stone with part of hopper hole; Fig 47.3), K 753 (baulk) and K 914 (clearance). The grinding surface of Fig 47.3 is slightly concave; its height at the centre is 82mm (see *ibid*, fig 78.2071, 2075).

Millstone Grit

Whilst not as common as lava, Millstone Grit is well represented in Chelmsford, as well as Wickford, Heybridge, Braintree, Witham and Great Dunmow. Strangely, it was totally absent from the sites recently published at Colchester (*ibid*, 75).

Fragments include part of a ?lower stone (Fig 47.4), with an edge, 60mm thick, an irregular lower surface, and a worn grinding surface with traces of deep radial grooving, (D 121, oven 92, VI.1); part of an upper (?) stone (Fig 47.5) with grinding surface worn smooth, ?re-used, upper surface smooth but irregular and part of the hopper hole; broken in two (K 241, clearance); part of a ?upper stone, 20mm thick, with hopper hole. The grinding surface has worn radial grooving, and the upper surface has a deep concentric groove (Fig 47.6; M 60, baulk); a reused quern (Fig 47.7), 25–8mm thick, concave on both faces, with edge surviving and surfaces worn smooth (D 188, ?subsoil); a small thin fragment of ?upper stone (Fig 47.8), 15–22mm thick, convex shape with edge, smooth upper surface, and grinding surface with traces of radial grooving (M 22, subsoil); finally a fragment (Fig 47.9) 60mm thick -at its edge (45mm where broken in middle) and reused as a smoothing stone on a *broken* edge, so that there is a smooth surface perpendicular to the original edge. The underside is smooth, with an area of fired clay attached to it (D 89, oven 92, VI.1).

Other objects

Fig 47.10 Lump of sandstone, fine cream to orange-red fabric, pierced by a hole and with some signs of wear. ?Loomweight (D 124, Structure 1, VI.2).

Fig 47.11 Small fragment of grey ?Millstone Grit, re-used and highly worn to a smooth finish, and with part of a central hole (K 199, PR).

Fig 47.12 Whetstone of very regular shape and rounded sub-rectangular section, silvery grey, micaceous fine sandstone (K 215, PR).

See also Fig 35.1 for a stone basin from CR 6.

Leather

An offcut in dark brown-black ?cattle hide came from K (well 558, IV.2–V), and bears the cut-out shape of the heel and back quarters of a one-piece *carbatina*.

VII The Roman Pottery

The Samian, by W J Rodwell

Site K

The assemblage comprised about 500 sherds, mostly very small. About 75% is 1st century material; one f30 is Claudio–Neronian, a few pieces are Neronian, but the bulk is Neronian–Flavian and Flavian (AD 60/65–80/85). The plain ware is mostly common forms, f18, f27 and f15/17. The small amount of decorated ware includes some good (but small) pieces of Neronian–Flavian f29. There is not much f37 present. The shortage of 2nd century materal is striking, and there is a clear lack of distinctively late Antonine forms, making this an entirely uncharacteristic collection for a small town site. One sherd of f33 is probably Antonine Colchester ware, with a curious chocolate brown gloss.

Table 6 The stamps, by W J Rodwell
Details of the dies and date of manufacture have kindly been supplied by Mr B R Hartley. The superscript 'a' attached to a factory name indicates a die attested at the named factory

	Potter	Die	Stamp	Form	Factory	Date	Context
1	**Advocisus**	IIa	ADVOCISIO	33	Lezoux	160–190	CR5
2	**Attillus**	VIIIf	ꟼꙅVꞀꞀITT[Λ]	37	Rheinzabern		CR38/PF4
3	**Av**	AV[		18/31–31			D26
4	**Balbinus**	IIb	[BA]LBINV[S.I:]	18/31	LMDV		K121
5	**Carantinus**		CARANTINI[M]	38	Lezoux	150–180	AS111
6	**Decuminus**	IVa	DIICVMINVS	18/31			M86
7	**Gippus**	Ia	GIPPI.M	31	Lezoux	150/180	D330
8	**Immunus**	Ia	IMꟿИI	18/31 R–31R			D133
9	**?Maccalus**		]ΛLIM	31R			K123
10	**Mettus**	IIa	METTI.ꟲ	18.31 R–31R			D15
11	**?Mettus**		]I.ꟲ	31			CR RR3B Pit 3
12	**Niger ii**	IVa	ΘFNIGR	15/17–18	La Grauf[a]	55–65	D119
13	**Pater**	XIXa	PATER.F	18/31	LMDV		K90 (Fig 54.49)
14	**?Paterclus**		]IERCLV	27			K752
15	**Roppus**	VIIa	ROPPVSFE	18/31	LMDV		D140
16	**Roppus**	VIIa	[ROPPV]SFE	18/31	LMDV		D58
17	**Scoplus**	Ia	SCOPLI.M	31R	Lezoux[a]	165–195	D331
18	**Senilis**	IIIb	:SENILI.M:	18/31	Lezoux		K968 (Fig 54.50)
19	**Sen**		SEN[	33	?Lezoux	150–180	AS96
20	**Soiellus**	IIa	SOIILLVM	33	?Lezoux	150–180	AS96
21	**Sosimus**	IIa	[SOSI]MIN	33	Lezoux	155–190	AS111
22	**Titurus**	IIa	TITVRI.M	31	Lezoux		AB3
23	**Viducos ii**	IVa	VIDVCOS.Γ	33a	LMDV[a]	100–120	D140
24	**?Vitalis**		VI[	27	SG		K822
25	**?Vitalis**		IFVIΛ [	24/25	SG		K914
26	**?**		ΛIIIVꙅ[	18/31–31			CR5
27	**?**		]CR\\\[	15/17–18	SG		K899
28	**P**		P[	18/31	CG		K695

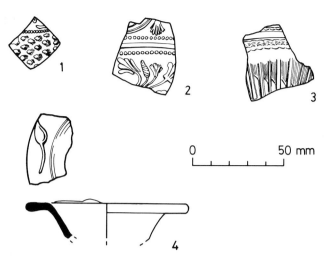

Figure 48   The samian

Site D

The material totals about 150 sherds, mostly small, but not unduly abraded. Little if anything is pre-Flavian, but there is a high percentage of Flavian plain ware, much of which is badly burnt. There is also an unusually high proportion of early 2nd century Central Gaulish ware, of which little if any is burnt. The fire damage is therefore a specific phenomenon somewhere near AD 100, presumably connected with oven 47. Apart from a few strays, apparently in upper levels, there is very little Antonine samian. Again an atypical collection for a small town, but different in composition to Site K. Of note is a *graffito* from Cat 15, a spindle whorl from Cat 258 (Fig 46.2), and a repair with a lead dovetail rivet on a late Antonine f37 (Cat 282, ditch 280, trial trench 1).

Catalogue

Fig 48.1   Upper zone f29, SG, Neronian. Ditch K177 (Cat 186), IV.2.

Fig 48.2–3 f29, SG, early Flavian. Well K 813 (Cat 819), V.2–V1.

Fig 48.4   f35, SG, small angular unusual vessel. AB Pit 3 II,VI–VII.1.

The other pottery, by C J Going

Introduction

The sites referred to in this report produced *c* 1 tonne of pottery — a substantially greater quantity than was found in the south-eastern sector of the town (Going 1987). However constraints of space and time made it impossible to envisage the full quantification of the site assemblages. A two tier system was thus adopted. Firstly, the pottery from each context was examined in order to produce a site chronology. This entailed re-uniting extracted material (colour-coated wares, mortaria, etc) with their parent contexts to assemble a card index containing notes on fabrics and forms of chronological significance, intrinsically interesting material (published here, below), and the quantity of pottery recovered, context by context.

Secondly, a small number of contexts, or group of contexts which together form a substantial assemblage, either closely dated or of special interest, have been fully quantified. These are presented below. They comprise ditch K205, an assemblage of Flavian date; pit D123, a group of probable production waste, and pit K90.2 (2nd century).

Dating evidence sections are presented with the site reports at the end of each phase. The fabric and form references are those used in Going 1987. For ease of reference, a brief list of fabrics can be found on p 3.

The conditions under which many of the sites were excavated, mainly in the early 1970s, were not ideal. It has, therefore, not always been possible to separate material from, eg, primary, main fills and later consolidation. The general lack of deep stratigraphy, and the truncation by post-Roman flooding and robbing has also led to severe problems with residuality and contamination.

Quantified data from selected contexts

1. The pottery from ditch K 205 (primary and main fills only) (Figs 49–51, 56a; Table 7)

The assemblage of pottery retrieved from ditch K 205 was of roughly the same date and of a size approaching the mid Flavian assemblage from Site S pit 205, which has already been published (Going 1987, figs 22.73–25.140 and p 56). It was therefore decided to quantify fully and publish it in some detail in order to make available as much data on the Flavian ceramics from the town as possible.

Perhaps unsurprisingly, the similarities of the two groups are quite striking, both in terms of the proportions of fabrics represented, and in the proportions of vessel classes present. But until more quantified data on other contemporary assemblages is available, particularly from a variety of sites, the significance of these resemblances is uncertain.

Lead glazed wares (**10**) 10g (Fig 49.1–1a)
A single sherd only was recovered. This came from the base of an open form, probably a bowl imitating samian f30 (for its probable appearance, see Fig 49.1a, after Arthur 1978, fig 8.2, no 5.3). The fabric is Arthur's 'South East English Group' (*ibid*, 298–308). Production waste suggests the fabric was manufactured in the Staines region. Probably Flavian.

Verulamium Region Wares (**26**) 30g (not illustrated)
The group produced a few sherds of closed forms in the characteristic *Verulamium* Region fabric (Going

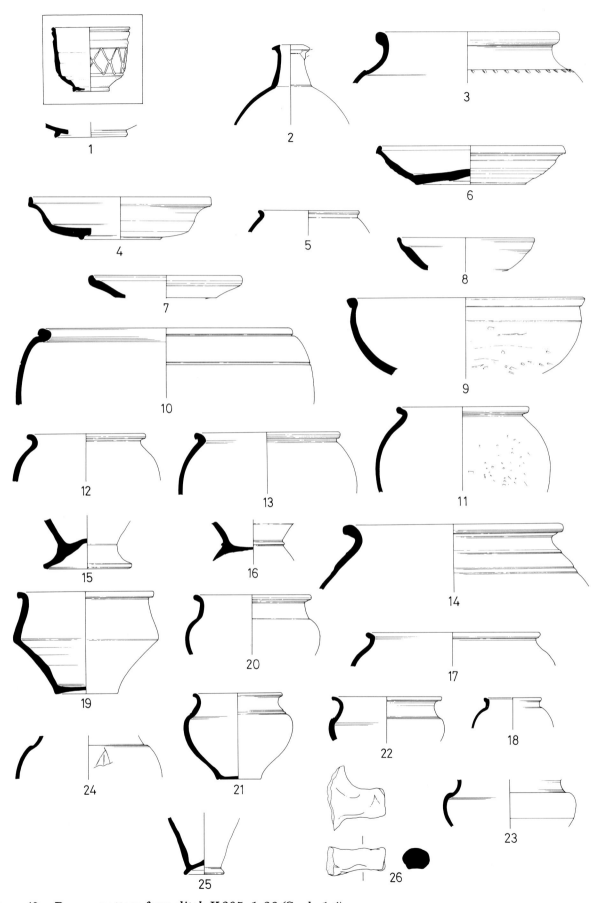

Figure 49 Roman pottery from ditch K 205, 1–26 (Scale 1:4)

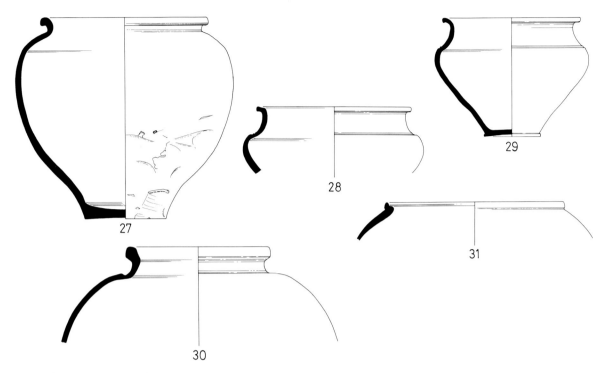

Figure 50   Roman pottery from ditch K205, 27–31 (Scale 1:4)

1987, 6–7). The sherds probably derive from ring-necked flagons of type J3, a substantial number of which were found in Flavian–early Antonine levels in the town. After segmental bowls (C16), the type was the most common VRW product imported into Roman Chelmsford.

Colchester Buff Wares (**27**) 3.96% Eves. (Fig 49.2)
The group produced a variety of oxidised wares, most of which probably came from early kilns in the Colchester region. With one exception, few identifiable forms were present, but most of the sherds were from closed forms, probably flagons. The example illustrated, the only rim, is from a one-handled, disc-mouthed vessel resembling flagon type J6, or more closely *Camulodunum* (*Cam*) ff148 or 150 (Hawkes & Hull 1947, Pl LXII and P 245). These latter forms are not common, but appear to persist at Colchester into the Flavian period.

Miscellaneous oxidised wares (**21**) 3.57% Eves. (not illustrated)
A small assemblage, mostly comprising body sherds of closed forms, like the Colchester buff wares, probably flagon types. There are, however, two fragmentary rim sherds from ?high-shouldered jars. The origins of this fabric group are probably varied. Some of the vessels are quite likely to derive from the Colchester area, but the discovery of oxidised jar waste on site D (see below) confirms that there was local pottery production in the Flavian–Trajanic period. While the wares in this group are generally finer, some of these sherds may have come from quite local kilns.

Fine grey ware (**39**) 3.30% Eves. (not illustrated)
A few sherds only were found, mostly from closed forms, probably beakers. No fragments of early 'Poppyhead' types were noted (as they were in contemporary deposits from site S; Going 1987, fig 22.62–3). The group was notable, despite its size, for the general lack of 'drinking' vessels, which suggests that the deposit may not be a straightforward 'domestic' assemblage. It is, however, of some interest to note that the sudden fall-off of 'beaker' types after Chelmsford Ceramic phase 2 (*ibid*, table 10, p 109), is matched by a corresponding increase in the proportion of the jar class — which makes it clear that whatever these vessels (mainly type H1) were actually used for, they should not have been classified as beakers.

Storage jar fabrics (**44**) 2.42% Eves. (Fig 49.3)
A variety of sherds from large, crudely-finished containers — 'storage jars', were found in the group. Most were body or base sherds, save one rim (illustrated). It resembles type G44. It is probably a local product.

Romanising grey wares (**45**) 73.37% Eves. (Fig 49.4–26)
This is by far the commonest fabric group represented in the deposit. Almost all vessel classes are present. Open forms include a number of platters, variants of types A1–4 (Going 1987, fig 1), and these are closely matched in contemporary contexts on site S (eg, *ibid*, S245, fig 20.4–8; S205, fig 22.73–78). Other open forms present included bowls of types C28–9 (*ibid*, fig 4) and also a fragment from a handle, probably from a

Table 7 The quantification details of the Roman pottery from ditch K205

	Eve	% Eves	Weight (kg)	% weight
South-east English lead-glazed wares (**10**)	0.00	—	0.010	0.038
Verulamium Region wares (**26**)	0.00	—	0.030	0.116
Colchester buff wares (**27**)	0.72	3.96	0.105	0.407
Miscellaneous fine buff/oxidised wares (**21**)	0.65	3.57	1.970	7.637
Fine grey wares (**39**)	0.60	3.30	0.060	0.232
Storage jar fabrics (**44**)	0.44	2.42	7.310	28.338
Romanising grey wares (**45**)	13.34	73.37	12.600	48.846
Sandy grey wares (**47**)	1.73	9.51	3.305	12.812
South Essex shell-tempered wares (**50**)	0.26	1.43	0.305	1.182
Samian (**60**)	0.44	2.42	0.100	0.387
Total	18.18	99.98	25.795	99.94

skillet-like vessel (Fig 49.26). It is comparable to a handle from excavations at Colchester (Symonds 1983, fig 55, no P659). Jar forms include a variety of globular vessels resembling types G3–4 (*cf* Fig 49.11–13 with *ibid*, fig 20.12–22), the G5, (Fig 49.10; *cf* especially the ?residual specimen in Site S context 182, *ibid*, fig 27.210). The bulk of the remaining jar forms are high-shouldered variants of types G16–20 (and include a graffito of a cross within a circle (Fig 58.7, Cat 411)). In the first Chelmsford report (Going 1987), it was suggested that a Colchester/Ardleigh origin for the bulk of these wares was possible, but it now seems that a more local origin is at least as likely.

Grey wares (**47**) 9.51% Eves. (Fig 50.27–30)
The commonest fabric after Romanising grey wares, and present, like that fabric group, in a wide variety of classes including platters, jars, including the G5 and types G16–20 (Fig 50.28–9). For a graffito 'X' on a G20 (Cat 409), see p 108. While this fabric group only came to dominate Chelmsford pottery assemblages from the 2nd century AD onwards, none of the vessel types represented here need be later than Flavian. Bead-rimmed dishes, for example (a form characteristic of the Hadrianic and later periods: *cf* Going 1987, type B2/4), are conspicuously absent.

South Essex shell-tempered wares (**50**) 1.43% Eves. (Fig 50.31)
A number of sherds, all from closed forms, were present. Most if not all are from the G5 jar type (illustrated). Recent examination of the crushed shell fragments in sherds of this ware recovered from 1st century AD contexts in London suggest two production sources in Essex, one utilising clays characteristic of the Orsett-Ockenden districts, the other, shell from deposits of more recent origin, from the Thames estuary (see below, p 97–8).

Discussion of pottery from ditch K205

Fabrics and trade (Table 7; Fig 51)
In terms of its origins, the assemblage is broadly comparable with the contemporary assemblages from the south-east sector of the town (Ceramic phases 1–2; Going 1987, 106–8). The great majority of the pottery belongs to fabric groups **45** or **47**, for which a local origin is likely. Comparatively little material was imported into the town from a distance — recognisable provincial imports are restricted to a few sherds of *Verulamium* Region wares, and a single vessel from the ?Staines region. Continental importation is extremely scant also, and restricted to samian, which comprised only 2.59% of the assemblage.

Assemblage composition (Fig 56a)
In terms of the range of vessel classes represented, the group, again, resembles those of Chelmsford Ceramic Phases 1–2 (Going 1987). While most of the major divisions are represented, the bulk is present only in very small quantities, By far the most common was the jar, and the total, curiously, was significantly higher than in the contexts examined from the south-east sector of the town. The significance of this is not certain, but if the vessels classed as H1 beakers in those groups are reconsidered as jars, as evidence set out elsewhere suggests they should be (p 95), the totals are much more closely comparable (one then is required to explain the virtually complete absence of this form in ditch 205, which is, after all, contemporary). The next most common vessel classes after jars were platters and dishes (as in Ceramic phases 1–2).

While there is woefully little data with which to compare this material at present, this assemblage seems to be more characteristic of a 'small town' than, say, with London, where quantified data suggests that there is generally substantially lower proportion of jars in comparison with eg, dishes and bowls at this time (see Tyers 1984 for a discussion

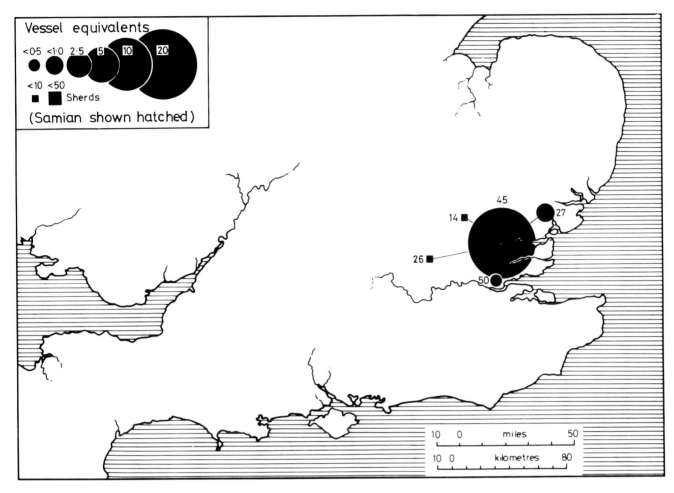

Figure 51   Pottery supply to Chelmsford as evidenced by ditch K205

of the material from London, and Millett 1979 for a brief examination of the change over time of the vessel composition of several assemblages drawn from a wide variety of sites).

2. The Roman pottery from pit D123 (Figs 52, 56b)

Pit D123 is dated to the Trajanic period. It contained a substantial assemblage of Roman pottery (14.41 EVE), of which some 83% comprised jar fragments of various types (see Fig 56b). But some two-thirds of the jar class (almost 50% of the total assemblage) comprised large fragments of a single type (the G5), in a highly characteristic sandy, oxidised fabric. While no associated kiln debris was found in this feature, or in others nearby, it is probable that this pottery represents the waste of one or more firings from a close, but undiscovered kiln.

The ?production waste

The fabric

The jars were in a distinctive, sandy oxidised ware, with abundant inclusions of milky, roseate and transparent sub-rounded quartz grains up to 0.5mm in diameter, and sparse to moderate

inclusions of crushed flint up to 1mm in diameter. The fabric is highly distinctive when compared with other 1st and 2nd century fabrics in the town, and quite recognisable away from the presumed kiln site. It has been retrospectively identified on site AR (originally published in Going 1987).

The forms (Fig 52.1–8)

The bulk of the assemblage (7.20 EVE) comprised jars of type G5.2. Their diameter range varies between 70–120mm, but peaks at 90–95mm (75% of the total Eves). The interiors of the pots are reduced but the exterior is an even, bright orange colour. The surfaces are friable to the touch, and all the pottery is slightly underfired, although usable (as the occurrence of a few sherds elsewhere in the town makes plain). The G5 jar type is a fairly common 1st century one, and was produed over a wide area occurring in grog- and sand-tempered fabrics in the Hertfordshire, and south-east Midlands regions as Thompson's (1982) type C5–1 ('lid-seated jars, plain'). But it is most commonly found in Essex in ?South Essex shell-tempered fabrics (**50**), and production evidence has been found at Mucking, and Gun Hill (Jones & Rodwell 1973; Drury & Rodwell 1973).

Examination of the preserved shell inclusions suggest two certain sources for the London

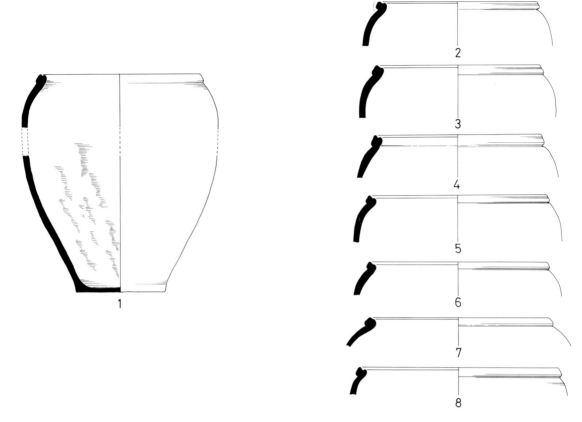

Figure 52   The production waste from pit D123 (Scale 1:4)

examples of the fabric, one characteristic of the shell inclusions in drift deposits in the Orsett region, while the other contained material more akin to shell deposits from the Thames estuary (B Richardson, pers comm). It has been suggested that the Chelmsford shell-tempered material was imported into Chelmsford from south Essex (Going 1987, 10), and perhaps the Mucking–Gun Hill area. There is some evidence (apart from the similarity of the forms), that the potters who produced the site D material were familiar with pottery production in the Thames-side kilns, for a sherd of the same form from the subsoil under the ovens (D70), and in the same distinctive fabric, was inscribed with a pre-firing graffito of the same type as those found in the Mucking and Gun Hill kiln assemblages (see Fig 58.1 and p 106, with refs). While it is possible that this feature simply imitated, it seems more probable that some south Essex potters should seek to take advantage of an expanding market for their wares by setting up a small workshop industry on the outskirts of Flavian–Trajanic Chelmsford. Precisely how long the enterprise lasted, however, is unknown, but it seems to have been brief: as noted above, there is no identifiable kiln debris known in site levels post-dating c AD 120–130, when the 'ovens' were built — unless, of course, these structures were themselves used as kilns in which case activity persisted into the Hadrianic–early Antonine era.

Pottery production in Chelmsford

In his discussion of pottery and tile production in the *territorium* of the Trinovantes, Dr W J Rodwell has located five possible kilns at Chelmsford (1982, 62). His kilns I and II are fully published elsewhere (Going 1987, section V). With the publication of the material from D123 (which Rodwell advanced as evidence for his kiln III, and dated to the period c 50–100 AD), the best-attested evidence for pottery production in Roman Chelmsford is now available.

The two additional postulated kilns (Rodwell's IV–V) are only indirectly evidenced, and based on ill-recorded discoveries to the south-west and north-west of the town respectively. Kiln IV is attested by the discovery, in 1839, 'of a mass of Roman pottery amounting to 1–2 cubic yards' during the removal of a hedge by Cherry Garden Lane (Rodwell 1982, 65). Such a volume of pottery is likely to have weighed at least 50–75 kg, a rather greater total than that recovered from the Moulsham Street kilns (c 58 kg, Going 1987, 73). The material was then thought to be kiln waste, and, it was noted, included rims of 'seventeen different sorts and sizes' — clearly a catholic assemblage, and perhaps of later Roman date. It is now lost.

In 1956 the late Mr M J Campen, a local amateur, appears to have excavated a kiln on the Melbourne Farm Estate (Rodwell's kiln V). Roman material has certainly been found in the area (Mr

M Cuddeford, pers comm), but no record of what Mr Campen found survives.

Postscript (August 1990):. A small group of grey-ware pottery, including flanged bowl rims, undercut everted jar rims and storage jars rims from Mr Campen's discoveries on the site have recently been shown to NPW by Mr Tony Rawlings, though they are hardly suggestive of kiln material. With the pottery was a piece of mosaic, comprising 37 hard chalk *tesserae* on an *opus signinum* backing.

3. The Roman pottery from pit K90.2 (Table 8, Figs 53–56c)

The lower levels of pit K90 (ie, 90.2) contained a substantial assemblage of Roman pottery. The group contained fragments of bead-rimmed dishes in BB2 (**41**), and other material which suggested a depositional date in the Hadrianic–early Antonine period. There was no obviously later material in the lower pit levels, but the pottery from the upper levels, while broadly contemporary, included a few sherds of pottery of a substantially later date. While this material was also quantified, it has not been otherwise examined in detail.

Lower Rhineland Fabric 1 (**6**) 10g (not illustrated)
Three sherds, from at least two bag shaped beakers, were found. One of the sherds was decorated with rough casting. For the form, see Going 1987, fig 15, type H20. These vessels are the only continental fine ware import represented in the group with the exception of samian.

White-slipped ?Hadham wares (**14**) 65g (not illustrated)
A few sherds only, all body or base sherds from closed forms, probably flagons, Although no certain examples have been found in Chelmsford to date, the most common flagon forms found in the fabric in the Flavian–Antonine periods from elsewhere in Essex are variants of type J3, examples of which have been found in Essex at Great Dunmow (Grave 3, Going & Ford 1988, fig 16.26), and Harlow (Felmongers Pit, unpubl). The most comprehensive published selection is that from the Flavian–Antonine and later cemetery at Skeleton Green, Hertfordshire (Partridge 1981, 252, and figs 94–5.20–1, 27–32, 34). While these vessels are stated to have been 'certainly produced in some quantities' in the St Albans region, the fabric description (there classified as 'D', *ibid*, 249), suggests they do not derive from that area, but from the Hadham region.

Verulamium Region wares (**26**) 70g (Fig 53.1, 1a)
Sherds from two vessels were noted; three were from a closed form, almost certainly a flagon of type J3, but of rather greater interest, most uncommon in Chelmsford in any fabric, were sherds from a *tazza*. The form did reach in Essex in limited quantities from the *Verulamium* region, however; a number were found in contexts associated — perhaps significantly — with the Harlow temple (Wilkinson & Clarke 1985, fig 57.77, 79; 60.192 — there described as 'Hertfordshire' fabric). Most of the Essex examples of the form, however, are in miscellaneous buff fabrics. I am indebted to my colleague, Mr Colin Wallace, for showing me further examples from excavations conducted by the Essex County Council Archaeology Section (Sites CC 81, CF 16).

Colchester buff wares (**27**) 1.44% Eves (Figs 53.2.2a; 54.45)
The small assemblage of Colchester buff wares recovered was almost wholly restricted to fragments of at least two mortaria, although sherds of one or more flagons were also noted. The mortarium (Fig 53.2) resembles the *Cam* f496 rather than the earlier *Cam* f195. M R Hull originally dated the 'uncommon' f496 to the Trajanic–Hadrianic period in Roman Colchester (Hull 1958,292), but was subsequently of the opinion that it should be dated 'to much later' (Hull 1963, 190). This group does not seem to be datable to later than the early Antonine period, with some later material probably coming from consolidation levels. While Colchester mortarium production appears to have had a *floruit*, with colour-coated wares, between c AD 160 and 210, the absence of the latter fabric in these levels suggests this deposit is earlier, and therefore that the dating evidence originally advanced by Hull was perhaps the more accurate.
The flagon neck (Fig 54.45) is a trefoil-rimmed type, a fairly unusual from in this fabric group. It is probably of Trajanic–Hadrianic date.

Miscellaneous oxidised wares (**21**) 7.71% Eves (Fig 53.3–6).
A small group, of disparate origins, comprising sherds from a variety of closed forms including a high-shouldered jar, two small, neckless ?beakers (Nos 3, 5), and a lid. All are probably derived from local industries.

?North Kent Grey wares (**32**) 3.39% Eves (Fig 53.7–8)
A few sherds only were found, mostly from closed forms, presumably beaker types. Of the few rim sherds present all appeared to be from a variety of poppyhead beakers (see Fig 53.7–8). The rim forms suggest a 2nd century date.

White-slipped grey ware (**37**) 0.59% Eves (not illustrated)
A number of sherds in a fine reduced ware with a translucent thin white slip were found. Most were from closed forms, and the few fragmentary rim sherds recovered suggest the vessels present were high-shouldered jars with a neck cordon or cordons. The fabric group (**37**: Going 1987, 8), is rare in central Essex (very few sherds were found in the south-east sector of the Roman town), but

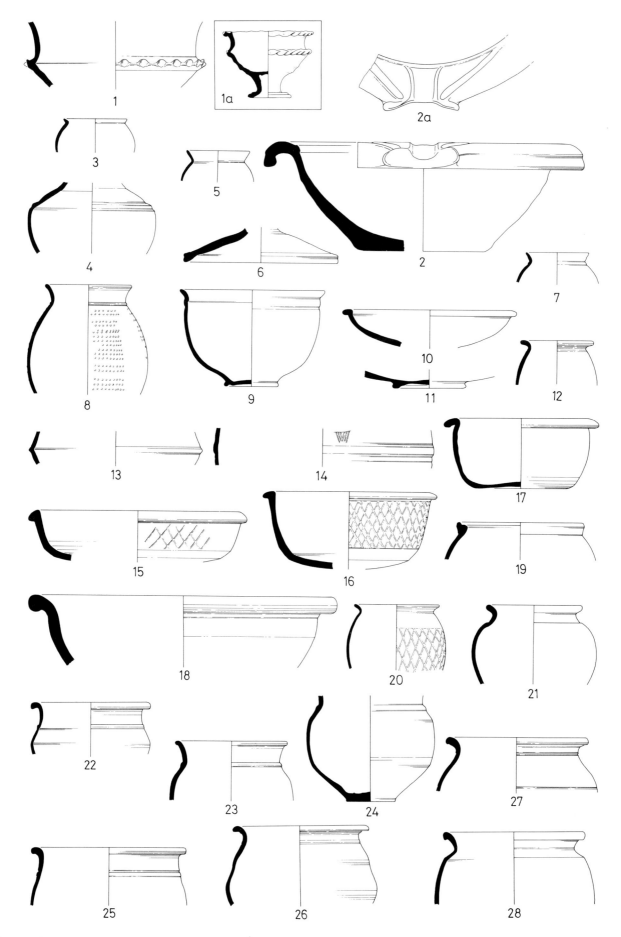

Figure 53   Roman pottery from pit K 90.2, 1–28 (Scale 1:4)

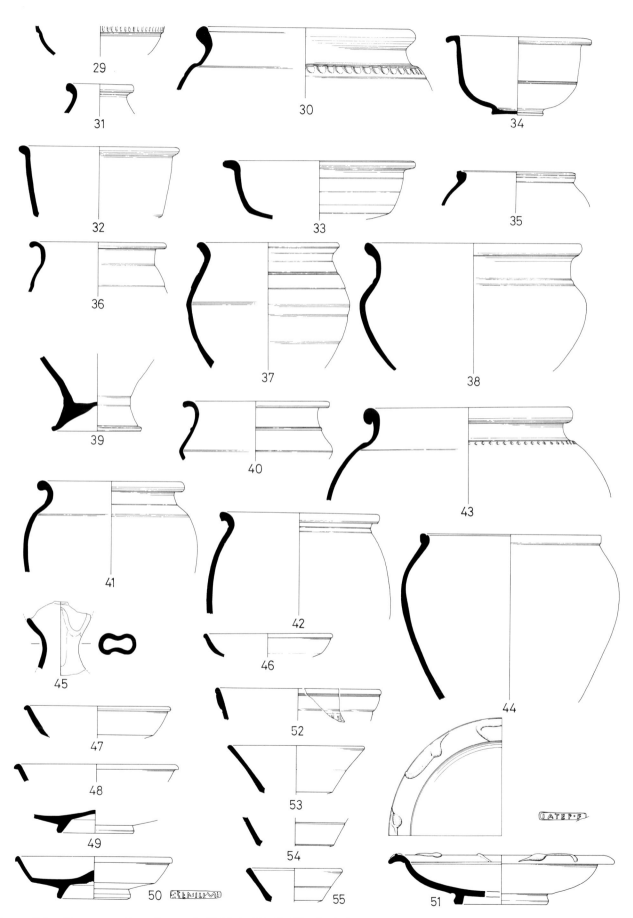

Figure 54   Roman pottery from pit K 90.2, 29–55 (Scale 1:4)

appreciably commoner in the western part of the county.

The possibility that they might be products of the Highgate industry cannot be excluded, but it is more probable that they derive from another, more local, industry. In view of the manufacture, in the Flavian to Antonine periods, of a variety of oxidised and reduced, white- or cream-slipped wares in the Hadham region, a source in the east Hertfordshire region seems likely. Recent air photographic evidence and surface collection of pottery suggest that there was substantial pottery production in the Hunsdon region, 8–10 km west of Harlow (C Partridge, pers comm). Clearly a wide variety of origins is possible.

Fine grey wares (**39**) 6.44% Eves (Fig 53.9–14)
A small group of vessels, mainly open forms (9–11), although a number of sherds of closed forms were also present (12–13). Their exact origin is not certain, but was presumably fairly local. Figure 53.9 is a version of the bowls which were produced, in a variety of fine wares, in imitation of samian forms in the later 1st and early 2nd centuries. It closely resembles Chelmsford form C15.1 (Going 1987, fig 3), which was dated to the 1st century AD, but perhaps persisted into the second quarter of the 2nd century. Nos 10–11 are perhaps variants of the C2, which is probably contemporary.

Black-Burnished 2 (**41**) 2.20% Eves (Fig 53.15–16)
The fabric is represented by sherds from at least two bead-rimmed dishes (illustrated). The form first appears to have been imported into the town in the Hadrianic-early Antonine periods (Going 1987, 8, 14–15). The precise origins of these vessels are uncertain. Pollard has noted the apparent rarity of the lattice-decorated form on attested BB2 production sites on the Essex bank of the Thames (although some of the Mucking kilns produced them). It is possible that some of these early examples came from Kent.

Storage jar fabrics (**44**) 1.96 kg (not illustrated)
The assemblage produced a number of body sherds of large containers (storage jars). While no illustrable fragments were found in the character-istically crudely-finished fabrics, rims of two vessels identified as storage jars, in Romanising grey ware (**45**), and sandy grey ware (**47**), are illustrated (Fig 54.30, 43)

Romanising grey wares (**45**) 49.38% Eves (Fig 53.17–54.31)
Romanising grey wares comprised the largest fabric group in the assemblage. A wide variety of forms were represented, including a dish-bowl — a variant of a deep, bead-rimmed form (53.17), and also a bowl resembling type C28 (Fig 53.18). The commonest vessel class, however, was the jar (Fig 53.19–54.29), the types present mostly comprising variants of types G18–20, some of which are characteristically 2nd century (Fig 53.27–8). There was also a rim fragment of a storage-jar like vessel

(30). Beakers were not well evident, but Nos 29 and 31 may be beakers, as 54.29 resembles type H30.1, while 54.31 is possible an example of type H7.

Sandy grey wares (**47**) 22.23% Eves (Fig 54.32–43)
The second most common fabric group after group **45**. Again, the range of vessel classes represented is wide, but mostly comprises bowls (Fig 54.32–4), and jars (Fig 54.35–43). The latter mostly consist of variants of G18–20 (Fig 54.36–40). There was also a pedestal base, probably from a similar type. The forms of jars 41–2 are characteristic of the 2nd century.

South Essex shell tempered wares (**50**) 1.06% Eves (Fig 54.44)
Most sherds in the fabric come from a single jar of type G5. Evidence from the south-east sector of the town suggests that the use of shell as a tempering agent had died out by the end of the 1st century AD, and that this vessel is either residual, or a comparatively long-lived survivor. For a discussion of the possible origins of shell-tempered wares based on the identification of shell inclusions, see above, p 97–8.

Samian (**60**) 5.71% Eves (Fig 54.46–52)
A small quantity of samian was present. The bulk was of Central Gaulish origin, although there was one sherd which may be East Gaulish. Forms include dishes of f18/31 (54.46–50), bowls (54.51), and a residual f29 (51.52). The cup class in the group was exclusively composed of the samian f33 (54.53–55).

Discussion of pottery from pit K90.2

Fabrics and trade (Fig 55)
As always, the most common fabrics represented in the assemblage are the reduced wares of groups **45** and **47** (ie, Romanising grey, and grey wares). Together, these total over 70% of the pit-group (by Eves.) By comparison with the assemblage from ditch K205 (see above), Fabric **45** has declined, while the total of Fabric **47** shows an increase — a pattern evident elsewhere in the town (Going 1987, table 9, p 207). Pottery from elsewhere in Essex, represented in the group, totals only a small proportion of the assemblage. It includes ?South Essex shell-tempered wares (**50**; almost certainly residual), and, more importantly, sherds from early BB2 forms, (**41**), probably from kilns sited in the Thames-side region (2.20% Eves). Wares probably from the Colchester region (**27**) are equally uncommon, and include fragments of two mortaria, but there was no indication of colour-coated fabrics, which appear to have been distributed across Essex only after c AD 160. More distant provincial pottery sources are only represented by a few sherds. Fabric **14** is probably from the Hadham kilns, as, perhaps, are the few sherds of fabric group **37**. Equally rare are sherds from *Verulamium* region

Figure 55   Pottery supply to Chelmsford as evidenced by pit K90.2

sources, and from kilns on the Kentish side of the Thames estuary. Continental imports were almost wholly restricted to samian (5.71% Eves) — the total is very much in line with that from elsewhere in the town at this period (Going 1987, table 9). The only other Continental import evident in the group was three sherds of a beaker, probably from the Lower Rhineland.

Assemblage composition (Table 8, Fig 56.C)
The composition of the assemblage shows minor but perceptible differences from that recovered from ditch K205 (Table 7). The proportion of the jar class has slightly declined (to *c* 67% by Eves), as has platters, while vessels belonging to the two main open classes, (ie, dishes and bowls) have increased their share (to *c* 17% by Eves). New forms in the dish class include bead-rimmed types (Fig 53.15–16), and there were also evident a number of related, bowl-like forms (eg, Nos 17, 32–4), also of a Hadrianic, or early Antonine date. Samian dishes include at least four examples of the f31 (Nos 46–50). Bowl forms include the unusual No 9 (a C15, see above, Fabric **39**), while Nos 10–11 are related to the C2. Mortaria, always rare at Chelmsford, are represented by fragments of *Cam* 496. The presence of large pieces of this vessel here

suggest that Hull's original view of its date range was correct (for further comments, see the discussion of Colchester buff wares above). Fragments of beakers, while fairly common, seem to be restricted to globular, neckless forms or 'poppyhead' types (Nos 3, 5, 7, 8). Only one imported colour-coated example was found. Cups, however, while uncommon, were exclusively in samian, and restricted to the f33 (Nos 53–5). As noted, the jar class is the largest, with types mainly restricted to the G5 (Nos 19, 35, 44 — the last being residual), or more commonly, variants of types G18–20, eg, Nos 21–29). Other vessel classes were barely represented. There were a few pieces of flagons (eg, No 45). No fragments of amphorae were found.

In terms of vessel classes the group is closely comparable with others assigned to Chelmsford Ceramic Phase 3 (dated to *c* AD 125/30–160/75: Going 1987, table 10 and p 110). Comparison with similarly dated material from London (Tyers 1984), show that there is, in general, a higher proportion of jars in the Chelmsford assemblages, and a rather lower proportion of vessels belonging to other classes. This seems to be a well-established and long-lived pattern, although there is little later Roman evidence at present available from London.

Table 8 The quantification details of the Roman pottery from pit K90.2

	Eve	%Eves	Weight (kg)	%weight
Lower Rhineland colour-coated ware (**6**)	0.00	—	0.010	0.042
White-slipped ?Hadham ware (**14**)	0.00	—	0.065	0.277
Verulamium Region ware (**26**)	0.00	—	0.070	0.298
Colchester buff wares (**27**)	0.34	1.439	0.290	1.236
Miscellaneous fine buff/oxidised wares (**21**)	1.82	7.705	2.305	9.825
?North Kent grey wares (**32**)	0.80	3.386	0.340	1.449
White-slipped grey wares (**37**)	0.14	0.592	0.005	0.021
Fine grey wares (**39**)	1.52	6.435	1.250	5.328
Black-Burnished 2 (**41**)	0.52	2.201	0.320	1.364
Storage jar fabrics (**44**)	0.00	—	1.960	8.354
Romanising grey wares (**45**)	11.64	49.28	10.130	43.179
Sandy grey wares (**47**)	5.24	22.18	5.700	24.296
South Essex shell-tempered wares (**50**)	0.25	1.058	0.300	1.278
Central Gaulish samian	1.30	5.503	0.705	3.005
East Gaulish samian	0.05	0.211	0.010	0.042
Total	23.62	99.95	23.460	99.93

While the reasons may be connected primarily with quirks of supply (London being a major port, its inhabitants had access to a much wider range of ceramics), social causes surely also played a part. If the population of Roman Chelmsford was adopting Roman manners, one might expect to see some evidence in the greater variety of forms and classes of vessel in *local* wares, even if the local populace was unable to afford the additional, and probably substantial cost of importing fine wares from such ports as Colchester or London. As Millett has observed (1979, 39), the pattern of ceramic use in sites such as this is still essentially prehistoric. Further quantified data are badly needed, however, before such topics can be properly considered.

The mortaria stamps

Four stamps were found. All were literate, but two were very fragmentary.

57.1 Colchester buff ware (**27**) vessel, stamped with a retrograde die, which reads]CRINA. The stamp

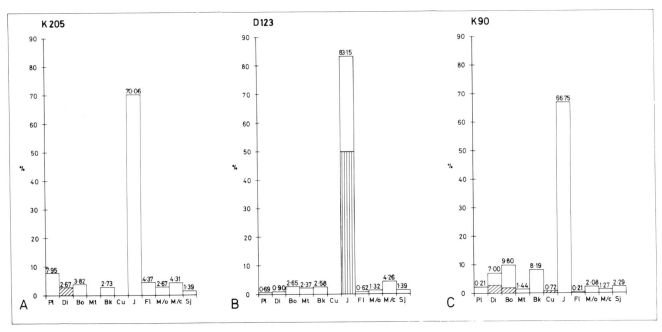

Figure 56   The composition of the assemblages from a) ditch K205 b) pit D123 and c) pit K90.2

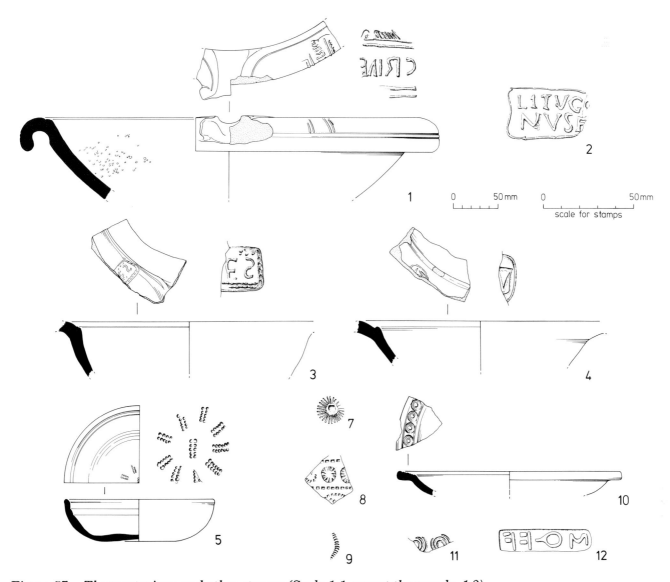

Figure 57   The mortarium and other stamps (Scale 1:1, except the vessels, 1:2)

is not attested from Colchester. K813, V.2–VI.1 (Cat 816).

57.2 Colchester buff vessel (**27**), *Cam* 497, stamped LITVGENVS F. It seems possible that this is the same potter whose stamps on samian are the most prolific at Colchester (Hull 1963, 87, fig 48, No 21a–b). But Hull noted he 'seems more certain of a Hadrianic date, which is....early.' D23, VI.1 (Cat 57).

57.3 Rim sherd of a ?Colchester mortarium (**27**) with a fragmentary die impression which reads]ES (Retrograde). The die has not yet been parallelled at Colchester. Probably Hadrianic–Antonine. K752 (non feature).

57.4 *Verulamium* Region mortarium sherd (**26**), with a fragmentary die impression, probably LVG]V. Counter-stamp. A product of Albinus? *c* AD 70–120. In addition to Albinus, potters using

counterstamps with varieties of this name include Oastrivs, and (Q Rutilius) Ripanvs. In all, some six stamps are known, reading variously LVGD.FEC, LVGVDV, LVGV, LVCD.F (the G being a reversed 'D'), and LVGVD/FACTVS. The fabric is clearly that of the *Verulamium* region, and while products of all three potters have been found on kiln sites at Brockley Hill, the *Sulloniacae* of the *Antonine Itinerary*, the counterstamps clearly indicate another production centre nearby with the name *Lugudunum* or *Lugdunum*. The exact whereabouts of *Lvgvdvnvm* is not known, but a kiln of the potter Oastrius has been excavated at Bricket wood (Saunders and Havercroft 1977), which, on balance would seem the most likely candidate. (For a further discussion of this topic, see K Hartley in Saunders and Havercroft 1977, 139–40). K91 (pit 90, VI).

The other stamps

Native copies of Gallo-Belgic forms (45)

57.5 Stamp comprising two rows of six impressions, impressed ten times on the interior base of a platter, A1.5 (Going 1987); ?Flavian. Ditch K177, IV.2 (Cat 185). Multiple stamp impressions are rare, but have been noted on samian vessels and should be regarded more as decorative than identification marks.

No.6 (not illustrated) Platter base with a low, wide, footring, imitating *Cam* 16, in a fine, quartz-sand-tempered fabric with a red-brown core and dark grey surfaces; burnished. A single central stamp apparently reads INDATIOS (ligatures underlined). Four stamps from the same die have been found at Colchester (Rigby in Symonds and Wade forthcoming, *LTC* 27–30), and one from Kelvedon (Rigby in K Rodwell 1988, fig 75.3, 100), where the platter is a copy of *Cam* 8 (*ibid*, fig 92.292). Ditch K205 LV/IV–III, Period IV.2 (Cats 494–5).

These stamps are difficult to read and assign an origin to. On balance it seems they were manufactured at Colchester in imitation of Gallo-Belgic imports between *c* AD 60 and 95, with a *floruit* of *c* AD 70–85. I am grateful to Valerie Rigby for her comments.

Oxfordshire oxidised wares (3)

57.7 Circular, ribbed stamp with an annular centre, probably from a form C78 (Young 1977, fig 62, *cf* esp C78.4 and 78.6 for varieties of the same stamp, also illustrated in fig 39.12–13). The C78 appears to have been made at two kiln sites, Baldon and Rose Hill, and is dated to *c* AD 340–400. The stamp parallels are also from Baldon. Probably post- *c* 360/75 here. K310, VIII (Cat 343). For the vessel, see Fig 59.8.

57.8 Sherd of an open form, perhaps, like 57.3, a C78, decorated with vertically arranged rosette stamps between vertically placed comb stamps (Young 1977, fig 39.1). See above for comments on the form. Probably post- *c* AD 360/75. K 178 and 390 (post-Roman).

57.9 'Demi-rosette' stamp from a small bowl resembling Oxfordshire form C70. Its size is such, however, that it might be classed as a miniature version of this form, — the C112 (*ibid*, fig 56, esp Nos C112, 2–3, *cf* p 127). Young found only three examples of C112 and thus was unable to date the type, which he felt probably lay within the span of the C70 (ie, post- *c* AD 325). Probably post- *c* AD 360/75 here. K336 (post-Roman). For the vessel see Fig 59.7.

The decoration of Oxfordshire oxidised forms is discussed in Young 1977 (p 128–33). The demi-rosette and rosette stamps, while used on a small scale at an earlier date, are most common only after the mid 4th century. Most of the decorated Oxfordshire sherds found at Chelmsford are stamped. Perhaps significantly vessel forms decorated with paint, a form of decoration which only became really common in the second quarter of the 4th century (*ibid*, 132) while present (see Fig 59.6), are less evident than stamped wares and may be evidence of the comparatively late introduction of the ware in Essex (see Going 1987, Fabric 3, p 3).

Hadham oxidised wares (4) (Fig 57.10–11)

57.10 Triple ring stamp, impressed repeatedly on the top of the rim of a carinated dish of type B10 (Going 1987, fig 2 and p 16). The form is subsumed, with others, under Roberts' type X 37 (Roberts 1982, pl 50 and p 141–3). He does not include this sherd in his *Corpus*. The form was certainly made in the Hadham potteries, and is also known with chevron and dimpled decoration on the rim (I am indebted to Mr B Barr for this information). Probably late 4th century. M46, 54, 59 (VII.2). For a somewhat similar example, see Fig 59.10.

57.11 Triple ring stamp of similar type to 57.10. Impressed on the exterior wall of an uncertain form, probably an imitation f29, K462 (subsoil).

Several other sherds of Hadham oxidised red ware with stamps were recovered from the Temple and other sites, but these have been published by Roberts (1982) and therefore not included here. Most are rather fragmentary and there is some doubt that some of the ring-enclosed bosses are true stamps. These sherds comprise Roberts' ffs A 22.10 (concentric circles); A38.2 (moulded animal); C38.1 (moulded lion, and stamped bosses — this vessel has been published in Going 1987, fig 48.15 as this animal stamp was also found, but in a more framentary state, on Site S (S84)). (See *ibid*, 100–1, with refs). For a discussion of the animal stamps, see Rodwell 1976b; for 'Romano-Saxon' material from the Temple sites in general, see below, p 113–4.

Amphora (Fig 57.12)

57.12 Stamp on a handle of a Dressel 20 amphora in a southern Spanish fabric. The stamp appears to be a retrograde impression. The reading seems to be MQFF[ecit]. Very similar stamps are known in Britain from Cirencester, Corbridge, and Silchester. Continental finds include Arles, Bingen, and Rome. For these and others see Callender 1965, 190 Nr 1165a–b, and fig 11.38–41. An example from Monte Testacchio in Rome has a *dipinto* with a Consular date of AD 149. The date range suggested by Callender is *c* AD 120–160, which agrees with the evidence for this stamp. CR 5.

Graffiti (Fig 58)

Twenty-eight examples of graffiti on pottery vessels were found, bringing the total of graffiti on ceramic objects in the north-east and south-east sectors of the town to 76 — one of the highest totals recovered or at least published, from any small town to date

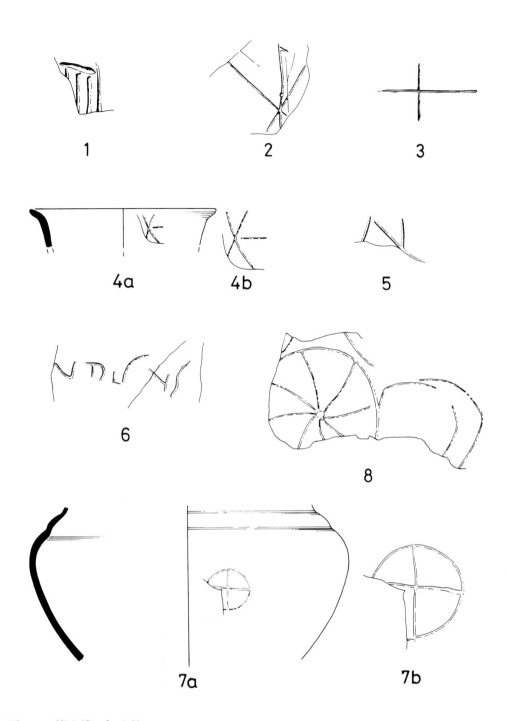

Figure 58   The graffiti (Scale 1:2)

(for the south-east sector graffiti, see Going 1987, figs 49–50, and 102–4).

Pre-firing graffiti on the shoulders of G5 jars
(Fig 58.1)
Four examples of this very distinctive form of graffito were found. They were, with one exception,

in ?South Essex shell tempered ware (**50**). The last was in the highly distinctive fabric of the kiln waste from Site D, (see above), and was almost certainly made there. Its discovery is of some interest and adds to the importance of these insignia. For a discussion of examples from the south-east sector examples see Going 1987, 100 and fig 49.1–10. The examples are from K375, VIII (Cat

379); K885 (post-Roman); D69, subsoil under ovens, IV–V (Cat 70, Fig 58.1); D123, IV–V (Cat 100). The ?local product is from D70.

Simple 'X' (Fig 58.2–3)
Samian, f18/31, CG, stamped PATER.F (see p 92). Post-firing on the exterior base, IX or XI, (for the vessel, see Fig 54.49). K90 (VI); post-firing, scratched on underside of trimmed down samian f33 base, EG, Antonine, reused as spindle whorl (Fig 46.2). D258, rubble, VII.2; post-firing, on the exterior base of a jar in Fabric **45**. 1st and 2nd centuries. Residual in K236 (subsoil); post-firing, on the sidewall of the closed form, probably a jar, in Fabric **47** residual in post-Roman ditch (K339, Fig 58,2); post-firing, lightly scratched on the shoulder of a grey ware (**47**) jar of type G20. Probably later 1st century. Ditch K205 V, IV.2 (Cat 409); post-firing, on exterior of bowl-jar (**4**), probably later 4th century. M65, VII.2 (Cat 67, Fig 58.3); post-firing, on the exterior base of a Hadham oxidised red ware jar (**4**), probably later 4th century (K985, non-feature); jar in Fabric **47**, lightly inscribed on the exterior base, D71, subsoil under ovens, IV–V (Cat 78); deeply scored on the rim of a folded beaker (**47**), probably of 3rd century date, pit M59, VII.2 (Cat 63).

Other marks (Fig 58.4 a–b)
One graffito, post-firing on the shoulder of a jar or folded beaker (**47**) of later 2nd or 3rd century date has a lightly inscribed symbol on the shoulder. At the first sight it resembles an 'X', but a horizontal stroke projecting from the centre makes it a possible symbol for a denarius (M Hassall, pers comm). Unforunately, the sherd is broken away at the edge of the symbol, and no number is visible (M22, subsoil).

Notches (Not illustrated)
Dish (**47**), with two notches scored, post-firing, on the junction of the base of the vessel and its side wall. Probably 2nd century (K440, VIII); Bead rimmed dish, Antonine, in Fabric **47**?, two notches scored, post-firing, on the rim. Ditch D23, VI.1 (Cat 102); IIII notched deeply on abraded footring, samian f18/31, CG, Trajanic–Hadrianic. D subsoil (Cat 15).

Literate graffiti (Fig 58.5–6)
There were only two literate graffiti, and since one of these was pre-firing, there is no evidence that it originated in the town. The first (Fig 58.5) is a single letter, 'N', post-firing on the exterior of a jar sherd in Fabric **47**. Probably 2nd century (K911, subsoil). The second (Fig 58.6), pre-firing inscription, was on the shoulder of a neckless jar (G1–4), in a coarse, lumpy variant of Fabric **45**. It is probably 1st century. The graffito, which is

broken off at the beginning, reads]NDIXVS (M Hassall, pers comm). The terminal letters, while they suggest a comparatively uncommon name, have a variety of possible parallels. K 258, early Roman silt, IV–V (Cat 467).

?Wheel symbols (Fig 58.7–8)
Fig 58.7 a–b: Exterior of a high-shouldered jar (G18–20), in a course variant of Fabric **45**. Inscribed, post-firing, on the shoulder is a cross within a circle. 1st century (ditch K205, IV, 2, Cat 411). Fig 58.8: Base of a dish (**47**), probably 2nd century, with a post-firing graffito on the basal exterior, a circle with a number of curved 'spokes' radiating from a single centre (CR 3). See the discussion, below.

Discussion
The bulk of the inscribed sherds found comprise single marks, and most comprise the motif, 'X', rather than definite letters, numbers, or words. While there is a possibility that these marks are simply capacity estimates or marks of possession, this seems unlikely in view of their ubiquity. To be effective, a name or initials are obviously more useful, or, if the owner of the vessel was illiterate, a more complex symbol, perhaps a rebus, might be expected.

The most probable explanation is that these are symbols with an apotropaic purpose. In a recent discussion of similar marks on metal objects, M Green has suggested that they may be celestial symbols analogous to wheels, or debased 'double axe' motifs, reduced to two intersecting strokes (Green 1984). Wheel symbols, it has been claimed, have funerary or underworld meaning (Lambrechts 1942). If so, the practice of inscribing them on pots seems not to have been very common in Britain. The writer knows of only one fairly unequivocal wheel symbol on a pottery vessel from a funerary context. The vessel is from Ospringe burial CXLII (see Whiting *et al* 1931, pl 38.449, described as an owners mark). It is a close parallel to our No 7 a–b, above. While these graffiti, and especially No 8, seem to depict wheels, most of the symbols, as noted above, are simple crosses. They have been found on a variety of pottery vessels in the region which date to well before the Roman conquest, so it is likely that their significance is rooted deeply in a Celtic *milieu*. The most probable explanation is that they were intended to charm the pot, and to protect their contents from corruption.

Pottery of intrinsic interest (Fig 59.1–60.52)

The pottery published here was largely selected on the basis of its unusual form, rarity at Chelmsford, or rarity elsewhere. In each case a date for the piece has been suggested, and the phase to which the context in which it was found is given. In the absence of coins and the lack of good sequences this

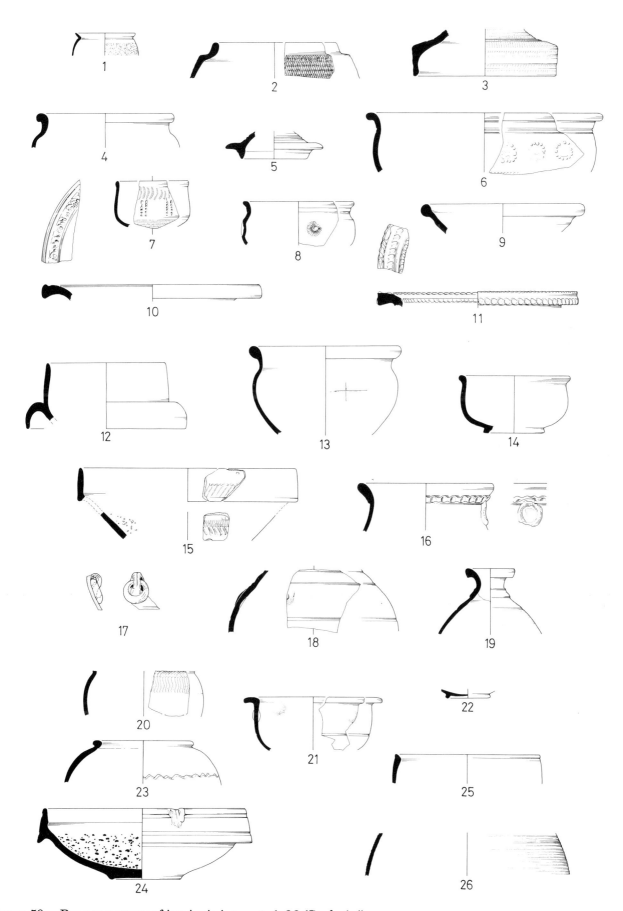

Figure 59   Roman pottery of intrinsic interest, 1–26 (Scale 1:4)

has sometimes been established on the ceramic evidence itself. There is, therefore, the attendant risk of a circular argument, especially with some of the more uncommon pieces for which few, if any, external parallels exist. This is perhaps unavoidable, but it is hoped that in future firmer dating evidence for most of the pieces can be established. Those wishing to check the evidence for any specific context are referred to the site archives.

Lyons Ware (**5**)

59.1 Several sherds from a rough-cast beaker with clay particle rough-casting. The form is Greene 1979, type 20. Pre-Flavian. Ditch K177, IV.2 (Cat 188).

Nene Valley colour-coat (**2**)

59.2 Castor box rim (for the form, see Howe *et al* 1981, fig 7.89). Probably later 4th century AD at Chelmsford. K99 (Subsoil).

59.3 Castor box lid rim (*cf ibid* for parallel). Probably later 4th century. K416 (post-Roman).

59.4 Necked jar rim. (*cf ibid* fig 7.75). The form is rare at Chelmsford. Probably later 4th century. K155 (subsoil).

59.5 Fragment of a lid, probably for use with a jar. *cf ibid*, fig 6.71. Probably 4th century. K420 (subsoil).

Oxfordshire red colour-coat (**3**)

59.6 Young type C77 (Young 1977, fig 62). Few painted Oxfordshire vessels are known at Chelmsford. This motif is not closely paralleled in his series. The form is dated from *c* AD 340, but is probably later 4th century here. (For a discussion of Oxfordshire wares and the date of their introduction at Chelmsford, see Going 1987, 118). K198 (subsoil).

59.7 Large sherds from a form which resembles Young's type C70.2 (*ibid*, fig 61), but with 'demi-rosette' and comb stamps. The type becomes 'most common after *c* AD 340' (*ibid*, 164). It is probably to be dated to after *c* AD 360/75 at Chelmsford, For the demi-rosette stamp, see Fig 57.9. K336 (post-Roman).

59.8 Sherd from a vessel of Young type C78, with circular stamps, as on, eg C78.4 (*ibid*, fig 62). Its date at Chelmsford is probably the same as for 59.6–7 above. For the stamp, see Fig 57.7. K310, VIII (Cat 343).

Hadham Oxidised Wares (**4**)

59.9 Bead rimmed dish form, with a recessed zone on the body. Uncommon.

Probably later 4th century AD. K440, VIII.

59.10 Rim of a carinated dish form (see Chelmsford type B10), decorated with faint stabbing on the exterior. Probably late 4th century AD. For a similar example from *Verulamium*, see Wilson 1972, fig 136.1204, there dated to *c* AD 360–70 (*ibid*, 356). M7, VII.2.

59.11 Carinated dish, same form as above (59.10), with frilled decoration on the rim. Date as for above. K238 (subsoil).

59.12 Rim of a flange rimmed bowl imitating the samian f38. An unusually deep specimen (*cf* Burgh Castle; Johnson 1983, fig 39.66–7). Probably later 4th century. M20 (unplanned late Roman pit). No 59.14 came from the same context.

59.13 Necked bowl-jar, slipped, and burnished overall. For the graffito, see Fig 58.3. Probably later 4th century AD. M65, VII.2 (Cat 67).

59.14 Necked bowl-jar, slipped dull orange. The form is a plain version of Roberts' (1982) type A3, one of the commoner 'Romano-Saxon' vessels of the Hadham repertoire. Probably later 4th century. M20 (Unplanned late Roman pit). No 59.12 came from the same context.

59.15 Fragmentary wall sided mortarium, resembling the Drag f45. It is, unusually, decorated with rouletting on the upper and lower walls. Probably later 4th century AD. K179, VIII/post-Roman (Cat 262).

59.16 Jar with a frilled rim, probably a 'face pot'. The applied, squashed pellet below the rim probably represents a ring handle. The form is probably *Cam* 290. ?Later 4th century. M24 (subsoil).

59.17 Sherd from a jar with a small applied suspension ring attached to a non-functioning ribbed handle. The form is probably also *Cam* 290. Probably later 4th century. M subsoil (P1849).

59.18 Large body sherd from a jar of Roberts' (1982) form C22. It is decorated with pushed-out, moulded bosses. It is not in Roberts' *Corpus*. For a discussion of the 'Romano-Saxon' material from the sites dealt with in this report, see below. Probably later 4th century. K224 (Subsoil).

59.19 Top of a narrow necked jar, slipped a dull reddish-brown. The form is probably *Cam* 296. Probably later 4th century AD. M65 VII.2 (Cat 67).

59.20 Neckless ?beaker form in a bright, yellow-orange fabric, decorated on the shoulder with a faint zone of rouletting. Rare. The Hadham corpus is generally deficient in beaker types.

Probably later 4th century. K385 (post-Roman).

?Local Mica-dusted ware (12)

59.21 Several sherds of a flange-rimmed bowl in an extremely hard-fired, dull orange fabric. The form resembles, save for the body groove, Marsh type 35.18 (Marsh 1978, fig 6.16). The vessel is extensively 'blown' and there is some doubt that it was ever usable. While no trace of production waste of mica-dusted wares has yet been found in or around Chelmsford, this find raises the possibility of local production. Probably Flavian-Trajanic. K752 (Non-feature). No 59.22 came from the same context.

South-East English lead glazed ware (10)

59.22 Base sherd from a footring bowl. While very fragmentary, the form is probably the same as Arthur 1978, fig 8.3, No 7.2 — an imitation f37. Flavian–Trajanic. K752 (Non-feature). No 59.21 came from the same context.

Miscellaneous Oxidised ware (21)

59.23 Neckless beaker resembling type H1. It is decorated with a zone of wavy lines. Probably 1st century AD. K205 I, IV.3 (Cat 446).

Nene Valley 'self coloured' ware (24)

59.24 Wall-sided mortarium. The form is not in Howe *et al* 1981. The spout has been reduced to a small vestigial smear down the side of the rim. Probably later 3rd–mid 4th centuries. M45, VII.

Colchester buff ware (27)

59.25 Neckless closed form with an inturned, bevelled rim. ?1st century AD. K705, IV.2 (Cat 773).

Tilford-Overwey ware

59.26 Fragment of a jar with rilled decoration. The form is probably Portchester type 137 (Fulford 1957b, 253 and fig 191), and a Tilford-Overwey origin seems certain. While no definite examples have been previously identified from the town there was a distinct increase in 'Brockley Hill wares' in Ceramic Phase 8 (Going 1987, table 9). It is now recognised that at least some of these sherds are really from the Tilford-Overwey kilns. The ware is now being recognised elsewhere in Essex and immediately north-east of London, eg, at Leyton (Greenwood 1980, fig 12.7, 13.47–9, 14.89, p 116), Rainham (Greenwood, pers comm), Bow (Sheldon 1971, fig 18.16, p 59), and Mucking (R Jefferies, pers comm). Probably later 4th century at Chelmsford. K417 (post-Roman).

Fine Romanising grey wares (34/45)

60.27 Shallow bowl with a rounded, downturned rim, burnished internally. The type is Chelmsford C2. ?Flavian–Trajanic. K74, VI.

60.28 Shallow bowl, similar to the last in shape. It has an out-turned, bifid rim decorated with a pattern of shallow, burnished impressions. Probably Trajanic–Hadrianic. K90 I (for a discussion of the material from the main pit, see above).

60.29 Bowl, probably an imitation samian f29. ?Flavian–Trajanic. D3, VI.2 (Cat 7).

60.30 Bowl form, similar to last, decorated with faint combed chevrons and rouletting. ?Flavian–Trajanic. D42, V.2 (Cat 16).

60.31 Necked bowl or 'cauldron' form with applied, non-functional 'ring' handles. Luted to the side wall of the vessel is a snake. A possible paralled comes from the site at Garden Hill, Sussex (Dr R Pollard, pers comm). A crested serpent also appears on the handle of a pottery vessel from Carlisle (Ross 1974, 345, 371). Snakes or serpents have many religious connotations. They are chthonic symbols of Mercury (*ibid*, 151), and a 'fairly consistent' attribute of Cernunnos, as well as a 'frequent companion' of the celtic Mars (*ibid*, 153). Interestingly, a flagon from Chelmsford (published in Going 1987 as Chelmsford type J5 1.1) depicts on its handle a creature which may well be a snake. While a variety of zoomorphic forms are used to decorate pottery vessels of this type (and their metal prototypes), the existence of a snake on a similar vessel from Carlisle suggests its use in these contexts may also have some religious significance — for the snake had an early association as a guardian of wells and water. For a discussion of the iconographic significance of the snake, see Ross, 1974 *passim*. It is perhaps significant that this bowl was found on the Temple site. ?Flavian–2nd century+ (The form seems long-lived). M45, 54, VI–VII.2.

60.32 Small open form, resembling a carinated cup. ?1st century AD. K813, V.2–VI–I (Cat 819).

60.33 Small, necked bowl-jar with an out-turned rim. Not closely paralleled

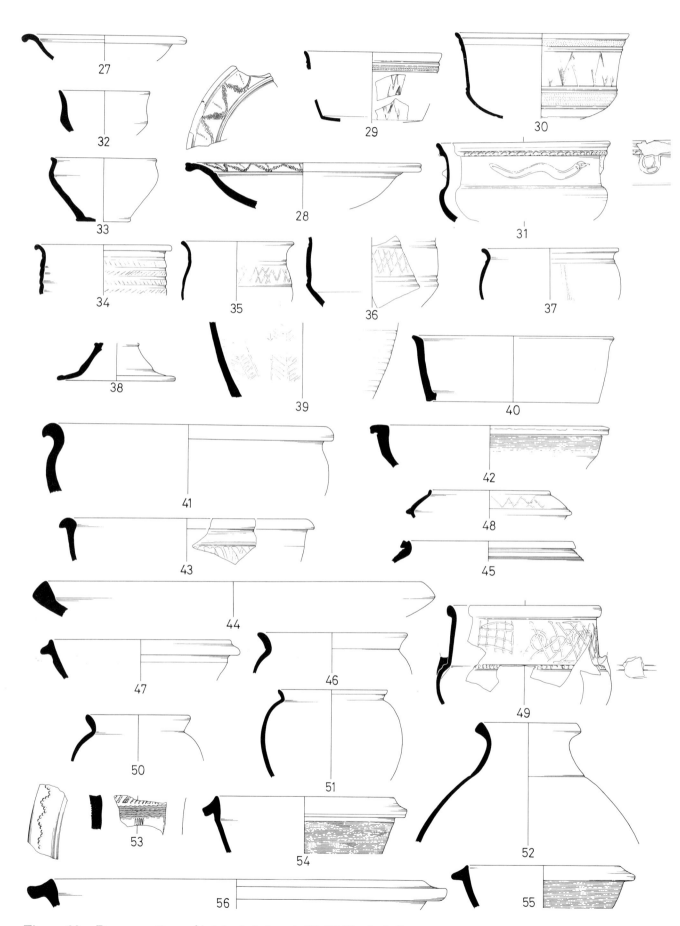

Figure 60   Roman pottery of intrinsic interest, 27–56 (Scale 1:4)

60.34 Multiple-cordoned jar, with burnished line ornament. Probably 1st century AD. K705, IV.2 (Cat 853).

60.35 Fragmentary, slack-profiled jar, probably a variant of Chelmsford type G17. Probably 1st century AD. K719, ?VI (Cat 760).

60.36 Small, carinated bowl form resembling Chelmsford type C22. Probably 1st century AD. K705, IV.2 (Cat 772).

60.37 Necked bowl-jar, with faint combed decoration. 1st–early 2nd centuries. D2 (Trial Trench 2, primary silt). No 59.41 is from the same context.

60.38 Lid, with terminal grip. The form resembles Chelmsford type K3.2. 1st–early 2nd centuries? K753 (early Roman subsoil).

Black-surfaces grey ware (**35**)

60.39 Fragmentary flanged dish? smoothed overall, and decorated on the interior with burnished bands and herring-bone patterns. Vessels like this with internal burnished decoration are rare in Essex generally, but seem to be more common in Hertfordshire (C Partridge, pers comm). *Cf* Wilson 1972, fig 137.1256. Probably later 4th century. K229 (subsoil).

Cream slipped reduced ware (**37**)

60.40 Dish sherd with a canted, flattened rim. Slipped a (now discoloured) dull cream. The form resembles Chelmsford type B8. ?2nd–3rd centuries AD. K765 (subsoil).

Storage jar fabrics (**44**)

60.41 Large bowl (Chelmsford type C28–9), with an undercut rim. ?1st century AD. D2 (Trial trench 2, primary silt). No 59.37 is from the same context.

Sandy grey wares (**47**)

60.42 Rim sherd of a dish, decorated with rilling on the body. Probably 2nd century AD. D36, V–VI.

60.43 Bead rimmed dish, decorated with broad burnished lattice decoration. Hadrianic–early Antonine? D42, IV+ (Cat 40).

60.44 Rim sherd from an open form of uncertain shape — perhaps a large bowl? Probably 1st–early 2nd centuries. K481 (subsoil).

60.45 Ledge rimmed jar resembling Chelmsford type G5.3, decorated with rilling on the shoulder. Probably 1st century. AB 3.1, VI–VII–I.

60.46 Everted rimmed jar, probably later 1st–early 2nd centuries AD. D42, IV+ (Cat 40).

60.47 Flange rimmed dish, slightly concave below rim. Chelmsford type B6. Later 4th century? K147, VIII.

60.48 Closed form of uncertain shape, but similar to one from Colchester Kiln 25 (*cf* Hull 1963, fig 89.8). There is a second parallel from the Colchester temple precinct (Going 1984, fig 16.11). It was suggested there that the Colchester example was datable to the 3rd–4th centuries AD, but its presence in a putative 2nd century context here suggests an earlier date range. K67, VI.

60.49 Handled cauldron or bucket with curvilinear burnished decoration over latticing. The shape is reminiscent of Going 1987, fig 35.20, which is a Moulsham Street product. ?4th century AD. M22 (subsoil).

60.50 Everted rimmed jar, slipped grey and burnished overall. Probably 4th century AD. K425, VIII (Cat 426).

60.51 Neckless, globular beaker resembling Chelmsford type H1. Probably 1st century AD. K813, V.2–VI (Cat 819).

60.52 Large, necked jar with an everted, angled rim. Flavian? K705, IV.2 (Cat 724).

'Rettendon' type ware (**48**)

60.53 Uncertain closed form, decorated with wavy line combing and stabbing. Pedestal jar? Lamp chimney? Probably 4th century AD. M22, 29, (subsoil).

Late shell-tempered pottery (**51**)

60.54 Flange rimmed dish, Sanders type 5 (Sanders 1973). Dish forms are uncommon at Chelmsford, Later 4th century at Chelmsford. M25, 87 (subsoil, unstratified).

60.55 Flange rimmed dish, as above. Probably later 4th century. K180 (subsoil).

60.56 Very large flange rimmed dish, with stabbed decoration on the rim in the form of a wavy line. This is the only example of a stabbed decorated late shell-tempered vessel identified at Chelmsford. Probably later 4th century. M24 (subsoil).

The Romano-Saxon pottery

When William I Roberts published his *Corpus* and survey of the Romano-Saxon pottery (Roberts 1982), the dates of the contexts in which the Chelmsford examples were found had not been determined. Data is now available for the Chelmsford Temple and other material. It is set out

Roberts type	Site Cat no	Published context	Period	Date of context
(A3)	M20	—	—	AD 360/70+
A3.9	K952	—	Subsoil	Post-Roman
A19.8	K486	485	VIII	AD 360–400+
A22.10	K417	—	—	Post-Roman
A38.2	K155	—	Subsoil	Post-Roman
C12.3	K34	21	VII.2	AD 360–400+
C13.1	K152	—	—	Post-Roman
C14.20	K984	72	VII.2	AD 350–400+
C14.22	K190	190	VIII	AD 360–400+
C14.25	M91	?27	VII	AD 360–70+
C19.3	K436	—	Clearing	Post-Roman
C20.11	M88	—	—	Unstratified
(C22)	K224	—	Subsoil	Post-Roman
C38.1	—	—	—	AD 360–400+
C38.7	M54	54	VI–VII.2	2nd–4th century accumulation
D20.6	K915	—	Clearing	Post-Roman
X22.8	K432	432	VIII	AD 360–400+
(X37)	M46	46	VII.2	4th century

below. Sherds found since Roberts' examination of the pottery have been placed in brackets.

Discussion
The dating of contexts in which these sherds appear is very similar to that arrived at for the 'Romano-Saxon' material from Great Dunmow (Going & Ford 1988, 71–3). There too, most, if not all, of the sherds belong to contexts either still accumulating in the middle decades of the 4th century, or dated to after this time. It must be said, however, that the dating is not often based on the inclusion of Valentinianic or later coins, but the prevalence of other wares for which later 4th century dates are fairly secure. While this evidence does not necessarily date to the first production of 'Romano-Saxon' pottery (the main elements of which, as the late J P Gillam noted (1979, 111–2), have perfectly respectable antecedents in the Romano-British ceramic repertoire), it suggests that its general introduction in East Anglia was not much before *c* AD 360–70, which is roughly the date for the widespread use in the region of Hadham wares, to which most of the Romano-Saxon pottery found in East Anglia has been ascribed (*ibid*, 150–1). J N L Myres has recently (1986, 89–96) published a spirited defence of his original hypothesis that this ware is a hybrid of Roman potting and Saxon decorative techniques, intended *inter alia* to satisfy a presumed demand for traditional pottery types and styles by incoming 'Germanic' groups in the 4th century. The general consensus of opinion among Roman pottery specialists and others is that this pottery is a provincial late Roman style, with ceramic antecedents in Britain, and influenced by later Roman metalwork (Dickinson 1978; Gillam 1979; Roberts 1982; Vierck 1978). There is very little evidence to suggest that 'Germanic' groups found this pottery popular, and perhaps significantly, it is absent from the early Saxon cemeteries at Caister by Yarmouth, which Myres would have still as mid 4th century in inception (the town itself produced 22 pieces). None came from the Saxon levels at West Stow (Plouviez in West 1985), which produced a substantial quantity of Roman pottery, much of which probably was sought out by the inhabitants of the site (Going, in prep); and there was none found in Saxon levels at Heybridge, where the possibility that Romano-British pottery was used alongside Saxon material has been discussed (Drury & Wickenden 1982a, 20–5). The distribution of 'Romano-Saxon' pottery closely resembles other wares of suspected Hadham origin (see, eg, Fulford 1975a, fig 61, p 137), and its scarcity in Kent (Myres 1986, map 6; Roberts 1982, pl 54, p 156) is more likely to be a reflection of the general rarity of the fabric, than connected in any manner with the date of the *Adventus Saxonum* in this region (Myres 1986, 91). There is still no good evidence that Saxons ever used 'Romano-Saxon' pottery, anywhere in England.

Summary

The pottery from the north-east sector of
Caesaromagus

The assemblage of pottery retrieved from the sites in the north-east sector of the town, while large (c 1000 kg), did not differ substantially from that recovered from elsewhere in the town, either in terms of forms, or supply patterns. The small number of contexts quantified were useful additions to the body of quantified material from the south-east sector of the town (Going 1987). The breakdown of the classes of vessels in this body of data suggests that the use of pottery at Chelmsford (in comparison with data from London) did not differ greatly from that of sites of the late pre-Roman Iron Age. In this respect, Chelmsford is unlikely to differ much from many 'small towns' in Roman Britain. Indeed, from a ceramic point of view, its apparent poverty — by comparison with such sites as London, *Verulamium*, and Colchester, makes it important, for its pattern of pottery use is likely to be repeated elsewhere.

However, there remains much work to be done on both this aspect of ceramic use, and, where sufficiently large areas of settlements have been excavated, on site patterning. Contexts producing assemblages which are substantially different from the site 'norm' are undoubtedly susceptible to statistical enquiry, and may yield a considerable amount of information, for example, about the comparative wealth of certain sites. At Exeter, an attempt has been made to see if medieval ceramic assemblages reflect the wealth or otherwise of the town as defined by Hearth Tax returns (Allen 1985). These have yielded encouraging results, which suggest that a similar effort could be expended on Romano-British material. However, a very much greater data base is required before this sort of work can be interpreted with much confidence, but there are signs that it could produce worthwhile results.

VIII The Faunal Remains, by R M Luff

Introduction

Six thousand, four hundred and fifty-eight animal bone fragments were recovered from the Roman levels of Sites D, K and AB. Approximately 50% of the assemblage was identifiable and this low figure mainly reflects the highly fragmentary nature of the material, particularly from Site D (710 identifiable fragments; 2,454 unidentifiable fragments). Site K produced the largest number of identifiable bones (2,357 identifiable fragments; 835 unidentifiable fragments) and provided the principal data for this report since both Sites D and AB yielded small samples. Site M was also part of the temple excavation but the faunal data has not been included in this report due to contamination and uncertainty of dating of many of the features.

Bone retrieval and preservation dictate the nature of the archaeological questions to be answered. Sieving was not undertaken during excavation and it is therefore likely that some smaller bones were not recovered. The Site K assemblage mainly consists of ovicaprid bones and their preservation was heavily biased towards the more durable parts of the skeleton, for example the jaws, while smaller bones, for example carpals, tarsals and phalanges, rarely occurred. The long bones were represented more by shaft fragments than proximal or distal epiphyses. This probably resulted from canid gnawing and at least 10% of the sheep/goat bones showed evidence of this from Periods IV and VI.

Thus a detailed analysis of the jawbones was undertaken in order to ascertain the following information:

1 Was the emphasis on sheep or goat butchery?
2 Were the slaughter patterns different from contemporary domestic sites?
3 Is there any evidence that killing was seasonal?

Additional post-cranial data together with information from other species was utilised in determining whether the assemblage was normal as opposed to 'ritual'.

A. Site K

Introduction

Seventy-four percent of a total sample comprising 3,192 fragments was identified to species level. The mammalian bone fragments (2,271) consisted of cattle, sheep, goat, pig, horse, dog, fox, red deer and roe deer (Table 9). Domestic chicken, woodcock, mallard and a shoveler duck are represented by 86 bird bones (Table 10). In addition ten human bones were recovered.

Table 9 Numbers and percentages of bone fragments identified by period from Site K

Period	Cattle	Sheep/ goat	Pig	Horse	Horse/ cow	Dog	Other
IV	175 (20.7)	616 (73)	34 (4)	19 (2.2)	4	7	1 red deer (antler)
V	34 (30.1)	70 (61.9)	4 (3.5)	5 (4.4)			
V–VI	31 (28.7)	59 (54.6)	8 (7.4)	10 (9.3)	1	9	1 fox
VI	126 (17.3)	508 (69.6)	96 (13.2)		2	8	1 roe deer
VI+	18	35	4		1		
V–VII	2	1					
VI–VII+	11	15	4				
VII	123 (59.4)	57 (27.5)	21 (10.1)	6 (2.9)	3	5	1 fox
VIII	80 (60.2)	38 (28.6)	13 (9.8)	2 (1.5)		2	

Numbers in brackets represent percentages

Table 10 Numbers of bird bone fragments identified by period from CH K

Period	Chicken	Wood cock	Mallard	Duck sp
IV	9		1	
V	17 (headless cock)			
VI	52	1		2
V–VI	1			
VII	1	1		1 (?shoveler)

The excavated bone was generally in good condition allowing some measurement. Tooth loss from the mandibles and maxillae was low in all instances, both for cattle and sheep/goat which is suggestive of primary dumping. Much of the bone recovered had been excavated from two features, ditch 205 (IV.2) and pit 90 (VI). This enabled an investigation into whether there was continuity in the treatment of the Temple animals through time.

Relative frequency of species occurrence

Quantification of species was achieved by simply counting the bone fragments with allowances being made for bones which occur in different numbers in different species; for example dogs, cattle, pigs and horses have dissimilar numbers of metacarpal bones per leg and hence these were weighted for.

The use of Minimum Number of Animals (MIN) as a quantification technique depends on judging whether it is likely that bones from the same animal could occur in different features and/or layers. It is impossible to be sure which features and/or layers to combine in calculating MIN. Table 11 shows the MIN for Periods IV, VI and VII; the contexts for each period were amalgamated. Thus the MIN figures could be larger since bones from different contexts may not relate to each other.

The earlier samples of bone from Site K are interesting in that they show sheep/goat predominating both with the Number of Bone

Table 11 Minimum numbers of animals by period from Site K

(Minimum Distinction Method after Grayson 1984, using mandibles)

Period	Cattle	Sheep/goat	Pig
IV	15 (23.1)	48 (73.8)	2 (3.1)
VI	5 (9.8)	35 (68.6)	11 (21.6)
VII	7 (50)	4 (28.6)	3 (21.4)

Table 12 Relative percentages of meat weights from Site K

Period	Cattle	Sheep/goat	Pig
IV	(67.8)	(30.2)	(2)
VI	(40.6)	(39.5)	(19.9)
VII	(85.1)	(6.8)	(8.1)

Fragments method (Periods IV, V, V–VI and VI) and MIN (Periods IV and VI). In Periods VII and VIII, cattle become the commonest species followed by sheep/goat and then pig. This is a trend exhibited by other sites in the area (Luff 1982). Pig and horse are of minor significance during all periods at Chelmsford.

Few other sites in the Trinovantian canton have this overwhelming predominance of sheep/goat. Bone samples from the post-Boudican fort at Chelmsford (Luff 1982, 222) had sheep/goat ranking first in order of importance (47.7%), using the Number of Bone Fragments Method but this does not compare with the much higher percentages found on Site K particularly in Periods IV and VI. In Roman Britain as a whole, a few sites are sheep/goat dominated but these are mainly confined to the 1st and 2nd centuries, for example the 1st century villa at Frocester. However, apart from the Harlow Roman Temple bone assemblages, the percentages are nowhere near as high as those from the Chelmsford Temple samples (Luff 1982, tables 3:24–3:26). The Harlow bone deposits for the Belgic and Roman periods revealed the presence of sheep exceeding approximately 80% of the combined faunal samples (Legge & Dorrington 1985).

If meat-weights are considered as in Table 12, the pre-eminence of beef in the diet is seen. The MIN figures have been multiplied respectively by 7.2 for a cow, 1 for a sheep and 1.1 for a pig representing the ratios of meat weight for these species (Carter et al 1965).

Distinction of sheep and goat bones

The adult ovicaprid bone assemblages were represented mainly by sheep; the criteria of Boessneck et al 1964 were used for distinguishing the two species. Pit 90 (VI) provided the only recognisable goat remains: two male horn-core fragments and a right innominate. Further confirmation was sought from the metrics. Figure 61 shows Payne's method of utilising the metacarpal condyle and trochlea measurements to distinguish sheep and goat. No goat was present in this distribution.

Ditch 205 (IV) provided an interesting assemblage of sheep skulls. Most of the fragments signified males (at least seven skulls) whilst two skull fragments were female. Two sheep crania were also found in the Period V–VI well deposit 813.

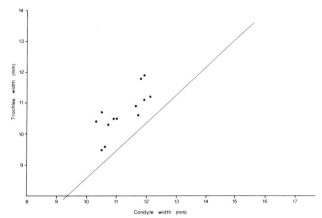

Figure 61 Graph of sheep/goat metacarpal trochlea width against condyle width

The immature ovicaprid assemblages, as with the adult ones, appeared to consist mainly of sheep. Payne's method of a species distinction based on the deciduous mandibular dentition worked well (Payne 1985). The most useful points of identification were the patterns of enamel ridging on the occlusal surfaces of the deciduous premolar 3, the extra enamel pillars on the buccal surface of the deciduous premolar 4 together with the angle of the enamel-cementum junction. Only one immature goat was identified from the enamel configuration of the deciduous premolar 3.

Sheep slaughter patterns

Table 13 illustrates the sheep slaughter patterns for Period IV and VI from Site K. Payne's method of ageing was utilised which has the distinct advantage of being able to record the individual wear patterns of the deciduous premolar 4 and molars 1–3 (Payne 1973).

In both Periods IV and VI, the emphasis is on the slaughter of sheep at Payne's stage C (molar 1 in wear, molar 2 unworn) which according to Payne is

Table 13 Sheep/goat ageing data from Site K

Age/Period	IV	Ditch 205	VI	Pit 90
2–6 months	2	5		1
6–12 months	5	37	1	14
1–2 years		9	1	11
2–3 years	1	3		5
2–4 years		1		
3–4 years	1	10		12
4–6 years				7
6–8 years		3		

Ageing was achieved using the methods of Payne 1973 and Silver 1969

Table 14 Identification of sheep jaw bone side by period and age

Wear stage (after Payne 1973)	Period IV		Period VI	
	R	L	R	L
B	3	5	1	
C	20	19	10	9
D	4	4	4	6
E	1	2	1	4
F	4	10	12	4
G	1	1	4	5
H	1	1		

R = Right mandible
L = Left mandible

when beasts are 6–12 months of age. However, the assemblages do differ in that less animals are killed at this stage in Period VI than Period IV and also there is a higher percentage of older animals in the later sample. Thus it would appear that there is no real continuity in the pattern of slaughter between the two periods.

Table 14 shows the separation of left and right mandibles for each wear stage. Since the jaws had been butchered, significant differences between the occurrence of rights and lefts may have resulted in an under estimation of particular age groups. However, certainly for stages C and D there is a realistic matching of rights and lefts.

Most of the sheep at Harlow were similarly killed off at Payne's stage C (85%) and Legge and Dorrington claimed evidence of seasonal killing (Legge and Dorrington 1985). They summarised clearly the evidence for the times of eruption of sheep teeth through a sound appraisal of 19th century and modern data and concluded that much earlier work had been misleading. A reliable observation of sheep teeth eruption times is given by Simonds 1854. The deciduous premolar 4 erupts shortly after birth while the first, second and third molars erupt at 3, 9 and 18 months respectively with the premolars emerging after the eruption of the third molar.

Figure 62a illustrates the relative wear stages of the third milk molar and first permanent molar for Harlow (after Legge & Dorrington 1985). Most of the jaws have the first molar in wear stages 5–7 and at stage 7 the second molar had not erupted. Since the first molar was not in its earliest stage of wear but showed moderate wear, Legge and Dorrington suggested that the beasts were slaughtered closer to 6–9 months of age rather than 6–12 months. Further they identified another group of sheep with worn second molars and either very late wear on the milk molars or erupting premolars. They judged these animals to be c 18 months of age at death. Hence it was suggested that seasonal slaughter had taken place.

Sheep mandibles from Harlow Temple showing relative wear stages of third milk molar and first permanent molar

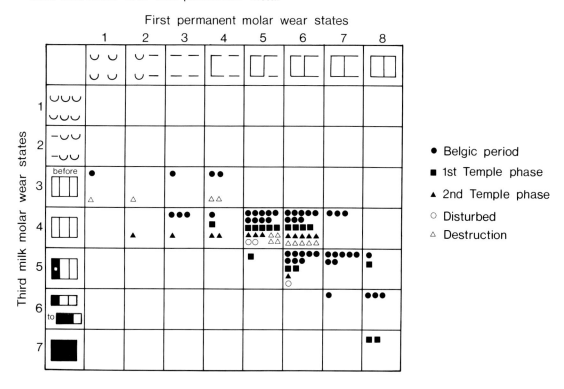

Sheep mandibles from Chelmsford Temple showing relative wear stages of third milk molar and first permanent molar

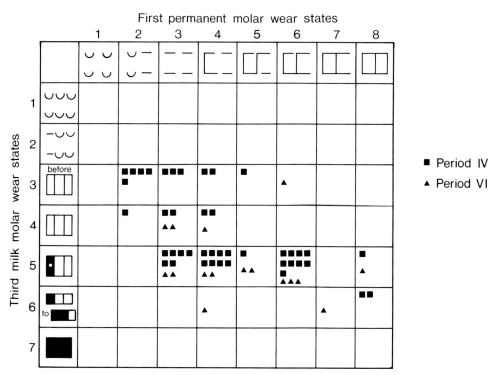

Figure 62   Relative wear stages of the 3rd milk molar and first permanent molar at a) Harlow, b) Chelmsford temple

With respect to the Chelmsford Temple data, Figure 62b shows that for the same wear stages of the milk molar 3, 4 and 5, the first molar showed earlier stages of wear suggesting that the animals were slightly younger than those from Harlow. It is tentatively suggested that the Chelmsford sheep were approximately 4 to just over 6 months of age at slaughter. Unlike Harlow only four jaws exhibited moderate wear on the second molar and late wear on the milk molars. Most of the second molars exhibited a well worn fourth premolar. Further, third molars were not found in the state of erupting or in early stages of wear. Therefore at Chelmsford, no evidence of seasonal slaughter can be proposed.

Much older animals were identified at the Roman Temple site at Witham, also in the Trinovantian canton; 20% of the sheep were less than 12 months old, 26.5% were 1–2 years old, 30.6% were 2–4 years old and 40.8% were 4–8 years old (Luff forthcoming). Here there are reflections of a wool and meat economy.

Metrical data

Table 15 summarises the sheep/goat metrical data. Sheep metapodial measurements show animals of a large size, eg, metatarsal lengths of 148, 149 and 150mm for Period VI. The Witham Roman Temple site has produced some very large sheep of comparable size to Site K, Period VI. Measurements pertaining to Period IV include average and large-sized animals. Tibia distal widths are illustrated in the same table. No significant differences were found between measurements for Periods IV and VI.

Mandible morphology and pathology

Fifty-one out of 89 Period IV mandibles (57.3%) exhibited a secondary mental foramen which generally occurred below the first and second deciduous or permanent teeth on the buccal side, sometimes along the diastema. This contrasts with Period VI where only 21 out of 69 mandibles have a secondary foramen (30.4%). Most of the Period IV mandibles belonged to ditch 205 and most of the Period VI mandibles belonged to pit 90. One additional mandible from Period VI exhibited in addition to the main mental foramen twin foramina below the second and third deciduous molars on the buccal side. The following periods illustrated very small jaw samples: 4 out of 7 mandibles for Periods V–VI show this secondary mental foramen, 4 out of 4 for Period V, 0 out of 3 for Period VI, and lastly 1 out of 2 for Period VI+.

Three mandibles revealed an agenesis of a second premolar from Period VI; two of these exhibited a secondary foramen.

Overall, the mandibles from the two main samples originated from good mouths; only 8.9%

Table 15 Sheep/goat metrical data from Site K

Greatest length of sheep metacarpal (mm)

Period	n	r	x̄	s
IV	2	122–126		
V–VI	2	121–131		
VI	9	114–137.5	126.6	8.8

Sheep: metacarpal greatest distal width (mm)

Period	n	r	x̄	s
IV	2	23.9–24.1		
V–VI	2	24–24.6		
VI	10	21.6–25.6	24.3	1.22

Greatest length of sheep metatarsal (mm)

Period	n	r	x̄	s
IV	2	127–144		
VI	9	138.5–150	143.1	4.27

Sheep: metatarsal greatest distal width (mm)

Period	n	r	x̄	s
IV	2	21.5–25.2		
VI	8	22.1–25.1	23.7	1.01

Sheep/goat: tibia distal width (mm)

Period	n	r	x̄	s
IV	14	20.2–26.7	23.9	1.93
V	3	22.1–26.3	23.5	1.98
VI	15	22–27.2	25.1	1.62
VI+	2	23.5–24.1		
VIII	1	24.3		

Key: n = number of specimens
 r = range
 x̄ = mean
 s = standard deviation

showed calculus deposits for Period VI and 42% for Period IV. The latter figure is interesting since most of the sheep were less than 12 months old. Twelve out of 89 Period VI mandibles showed evidence of tooth crowding (13.5%) while 14 out of 69 showed it for Period IV (20.3%). Furthermore 23.3% of the Period IV jaws exhibited calculus deposits on the teeth as well as a secondary mandibular foramen while only 6.5% of the Period VI jaws showed this phenomenon. It is possible that different breeds are represented between Periods IV and VI as illustrated by the increased percentage of jaws exhibiting both calculus/double mental foramina and tooth crowding in Period IV.

The only mandible showing severe periodontal disease belonged to a 6–8 year old animal of sub-Roman date.

Sheep butchery patterns

Table 16 shows the counts for the different skeletal elements by period.

Table 16 Relative occurrence of skeletal elements by period from Site K: Sheep/goat

		Period IV	Ditch 205	Period VI	Pit 90
Horn-core		2.0	3.8	6.7	5.2
Skull		6.5	7.9	2.2	2.5
Hyoid					
Maxilla		5.4	6.9	1.2	1.6
Mandible		24.9	24.6	26.1	26.3
Scapula		5.8	5.4	6.9	7.7
Humerus	P				
	S	2.7	1.6	1.6	1.1
	D	0.5	0.6	0.8	0.2
	W			0.2	0.2
Radius	P	1.3	0.6	1.4	1.1
	S	12.8	11.7	7.7	7.3
	D	0.9	0.6	0.6	0.9
Ulna		1.3	1.6	2.6	3.9
	W	0.5	0.8	1.8	2.0
Metacarpal	P	1.3	0.8	2.8	2.9
	S	2.2	1.4	4.3	4.3
	D	0.4	0.4	2.0	2.0
Carpal					
Pelvis		0.9	1.4	3.8	4.1
Femur	P	0.2		0.2	0.2
	S	5.2	4.8	2.4	2.5
	D	0.2		0.6	0.7
Tibia	P				
	S	12.6	15.3	6.3	6.1
	D	3.1	2.2	3.0	3.4
	W	0.5	1.2	2.4	2.7
Metatarsal	P	1.3	1.2	4.0	3.9
	S	4.0	1.8	5.1	5.2
	D	0.2	0.2	0.2	0.2
Tarsal		0.5			0.7
Phalanx	1	0.4	0.4	0.4	0.7
	2			0.2	0.2
	3			0.4	0.4
Atlas					
Axis				0.6	0.7
Cervical vert		0.4	0.6	0.6	
Thoracic vert		2.0	1.8	0.8	0.7
Lumbar vert				0.2	0.2
Caud vert					
Sacrum					
Calcaneus		0.2	0.2	0.2	0.2
Astragalus					
Patella					

Figures represent percentages

Period IV

The whole assemblage shows a striking abundance of mandibles, a lack of the more fragile late-fusing bones (for example, proximal tibiae and humeri), and a shortage of smaller bones (for example, carpals and tarsals). Meat-bearing bones are reasonably well represented (for example, scapulae, radii, and femorae), while non meat-bearing bones (for example pelves, metapodials, and vertebrae) are noticeably low. The metapodials are fairly robust bones and could have been left attached to the skins after skinning. There is some evidence that beasts were skinned. One metacarpal exhibited three knife-cuts at the extreme proximal lateral shaft edge. The meat-bearing bones showed knife-cuts and chop-marks indicative of flesh removal for food.

Table 17 Numbers of bone fragments by species for each layer from ditch 205 (Period IV)

Layer	Horse	Cattle	Sheep/goat	Pig	Dog
1		4	18	1	
2			19		
3	1	3	33 (cranium)	4	
3/4					skull
4		4	26 (4 male skulls)	2	
5		3	25 (3 male skulls)	6	
6		2	47	1	
7		12	45	2	
8		10	14	4	6
9	4	12			
10	1	2			
11		14	2		
12			1		

Surprisingly few skulls and horn-core remains were found; seven male skulls occurred in ditch 205. Table 17 shows ditch 205 split up into its component layers. Sheep/goat is the predominant species in practically all the layers. Most of the male sheep skulls emanate from layers 4 and 5 while the remains of an isolated dog skull was found in layer 3/4. Sheep heads were severed from the main body by chopping through the occipital condyles. As at Uley Roman temple (Ellison 1980) there was an intentional removal of frontals and horn-cores from the sheep skulls. The other Period IV enclosure ditch, 705, was unusual in that it contained pony and large horse bones together with a human infant tibia.

Period VI

Thirty-five animals are represented by the mandibles, but again there is little representation of skull and horn-core fragments. There are greater numbers of metapodial bones than in Period IV and even fewer meat-bearing bones. However, both deposits show a lack of small bones, vertebrae and loose teeth. The Period VI deposits appear more like waste material than IV.

The Period VII assemblage is very small and shows a tendency towards waste bone.

Other species

Cattle

Metrically, the cattle remains provided few measurements, but all fall within the Romano-British range of variation:

Bone	Period	Greatest Length (mm)	Sex
Metacarpal	VI	171	female?
Metacarpal	VII	183	female
Metatarsal	VII	213.5	female

Male animals also occurred as evidenced by horn-core from Period IV (ditch K 205). A female pelvis was identified from the Period IV levels of ditch 705 and a castrate horn-core with basal diameters of 59.5 and 45 mm occurred in Period V+.

Few mandibles were available for ageing but the general impression was that the animals were just mature; and indeed the post-cranial material revealed very few unfused epiphyses.

The relative percentages of skeletal elements show that the Period IV deposit is dominated by mandible fragments and scapulae (Table 18). Skull and horn-core fragments are scarce, the later having been chopped off at the base with one exhibiting a saw-mark, possibly indicative of horning. The Periods VI and VII deposits show a dominance of mandibles and horn-cores.

Most of the bones from all the deposits exhibited butchery marks indicative of primary butchery (dismemberment of carcass) and secondary butchery (flesh removal for eating).

Horse

The following intact long-bones allowed measurement and estimation of withers heights after Vitt in Boessneck and von den Dreisch 1974:

Period	Feature	Bone	Greatest length (mm)	Shoulder hds height
IV	705	metacarpal	218	12.9 (pony)
IV	705	metacarpal	233.5	12.1 (pony)
IV	705	metatarsal	288	15.0 (horse)

Table 18 Relative occurrence of skeletal elements by period from Site K: Cattle

		IV	VI	VII
Horn-core		2.6	19.8	16.3
Skull		9.1	9.1	1.6
Hyoid		1.3		
Maxilla		1.3		1.6
Mandible		31.8	17.4	13.8
Scapula		28.6	5.8	10.6
Humerus	P			
	S	1.3	2.5	
	D		1.6	1.6
Radius	P			1.6
	S			
	D		2.5	2.5
Ulna		1.3		3.2
	W			0.8
Metacarpal		3.2	3.3	1.6
	S	0.6		0.8
	D	0.6	0.8	0.8
Carpal				0.8
Pelvis		3.2	5.0	6.5
Femur	P	0.6	0.8	1.6
	S		1.6	
	D	0.6		0.8
Tibia	P		0.8	0.8
	S	0.6	2.5	0.8
	D	0.6		1.6
Metatarsal	P	1.3	4.1	1.6
	S	1.3	0.8	0.8
	D	1.9	3.3	2.4
Tarsal			1.6	0.8
Phalanx	1	1.9	4.1	3.2
	2	1.3		0.8
	3	0.6		1.6
Atlas				
Axis			0.8	1.6
Cervical vert			2.5	1.6
Thoracic vert		1.9	5.8	5.7
Lumbar vert				
Caud vert				
Sacrum		0.6		
Calcaneus		0.6		2.4
Astragalus			3.3	5.7
Patella				

Figures represent percentages

Table 19   Chicken bone length measurements (mm)

Tarsometatarsus greatest length

V	80.5	male
VI	83.5	male
VII	62.7	female

Ulna greatest length

VI	63.4, 64.9

Radius greatest length

VI	66.0, 66.2

Tibiotarsus greatest length

VI	116.4

Carpometacarpus greatest length

VI	34.9

Humersus greatest length

VI	64.2
V	71.0

Horse was butchered for food in Period V; a left radius excavated from F771 exhibited numerous knife-cuts along the proximal anterior and posterior portions of the shaft. However the majority of bones recovered from the site were non meat-bearing bones (metapodia, astragali, and calcanea) and showed no signs of butchery.

Although not a huge amount, the largest quantity of butchered horse bone occurring in the Trinovantian *civitas* was from the Roman temple at Witham. It is possible therefore, that a religious connotation can be attached to the remains found in ditch 705 and F771. For a possible votive horse burial from Chelmsford, see Wallis 1988.

Pig
Too few bones were available for a close scrutiny of butchery practices, but Periods IV, VI, and VII show a mixture of meat-bearing and non meat-bearing bones.

Bird
The identified bird species are shown in Table 10. Table 19 shows their length measurements. The largest number of bones came from pit 90 (Period VI). At least five carcasses were found of the domestic chicken; the fact that they were headless is perhaps indicative of the fragile nature of the skull. They are not interpreted as votive offerings since whole carcasses are quite commonly found on domestic sites. Both male and female birds occurred and one tibiotarsus exhibited a heavy chop-mark. Period V contained the next largest collection of domestic chicken and included a headless cock.

The domestic chicken measurements are not unduly large and fit within the range of variation for Romano-British specimens.

Dog
A partial dog burial occurred in F820 (Period VVI). The following measurements were taken and the shoulder height was estimated after Harcourt 1974:

Bone	Greatest length (mm)	Shoulder height (mm)
Femur	116	35.1
Humerus	109	34.7
Tibia	117	35.1

These measurements are within the range of Romano-British variation. Another partial burial (four fragments) was recovered from pit 90 (Period VI). The remains of a dog skull were found in ditch 205 (layer 3/4) and may have some ritual significance. Few dog bones occurred on the site; however, the presence of dog was attested by the following percentages of chewed bones:

Period IV	sheep/goat	13.3%
	cattle	3.4%
	pig	5.9%
Period VI	sheep/goat	11.4%
	cattle	4.0%
	pig	8.3%
Period VII	sheep/goat	7.0%
	cattle	8.0%

Human
Apart from one adult ankle bone from ditch 705 (Period IV), the human remains were those of infants. A partial burial of four unfused long-bones was excavated from the well pit 820 (Period VVI) and a single unfused tibia was found in ditch 705 (Period IV). Feature 2 (Period VI) contained an infant facial bone.

Conclusion

One of the most significant features of this bone assemblage is the dominance of sheep in Periods IV, V, and VI. No other Romano-British site in Essex has yielded such high percentages of sheep remains. The sheep kill-off pattern, however, is not unusual; lamb was popular at the post-Boudican fort at Chelmsford and several contemporary domestic sites at Colchester (Luff in prep) show similar slaughter. Thus a 'ritual' connotation for interpretation of the bone is not upheld.

Table 20 Numbers of bone fragments by period from Site D

Period	Cattle	Horse	Pig	Sheep/goat	Cattle/horse	Dog	Other
IV	14			1	6		
IV–V	78	1	3	23	14		1 chicken
IV–VI	16						
V	110	2		20	3	2	3 chicken
V–VI	5	2					
VI	176		10	39	10	1	2 red deer (ant), 1 chicken
VII	108	2	11	14	18		15 human frags 1 chicken

While there is an emphasis on lamb slaughter in both Periods IV and VI at Site K, more mature sheep were killed in Period VI. The Period VI bone samples consisted of more waste bone than those from Period IV. Hence there does appear a lack of continuity of site usage through time.

No evidence of seasonal sheep slaughter was evinced. Differences in mandible morphology and pathology could possible represent differences in breed between Periods IV and VI.

B. Site D

Seven hundred and ten bone fragments were identified out of a total of 3164 fragments and assigned to a phase. Table 20 shows the number of identified bones for each species. It appears that cattle was the predominant species in all periods but very few measurements could be taken due to the fragmentary nature of the material. The majority of animals were mature. Fifteen human cranial fragments came from contexts 241 (three

frags), 244 (10 frags), and 261 (two frags) of Period VII.

C. Site AB

The bones comprised a very small sample. Feature 3, a Period VI–VII pit, provided the only sizeable amount of bone:

Horse	Cattle	Sheep/goat	Pig	Dog	Unidentified
2	11	14	64	5	6

It is interesting to note that one of the dog bones, a distal tibia, had been butchered; it exhibited four heavy chop-marks into the distal medial third of the shaft. A cattle scapula had longitudinal butchery marks on the superior and inferior surfaces, characteristic of meat filleting. One female chicken tarsometatarsus measured 66.7 mm in total, which fits well within the range of variation found at 1st century Sheepen (Luff 1985).

IX Discussion

Introduction

The analysis of the Roman pottery from the *mansio* sites (Going 1987; Drury 1988, 125–6) made it clear that there was no sign of activity on them before about AD 60/65, when a small military road station was erected in the immediate aftermath of the Boudican revolt, overlooking the nodal confluence of the Rivers Chelmer and Can. The road itself which forms the main north-south axis of the town is the main London–Colchester road, and was built around, or before *c* AD 60/65 (Drury 1988, 128). That part of the town discussed in vol **3.1** — the south-eastern sector — underwent a major Hadrianic expansion, as part of his major reorganisation of the *cursus publicus*, involving the construction of a *mansio*, first in wood, and soon after in stone, so sited as to utilise a pre-existing, ?military bath-block and masonry *laconicum*. A new street was laid out to link the *mansio* with the London-Colchester road (Drury 1988, 130), and it is in the 120s that we find a rapid development of the road frontages with long, narrow strip houses, with gables facing the street, of a type well known, for instance, at *Verulamium* (Frere 1972; 1984). Some of these commercial buildings were demolished *c* AD 160/75 to clear a site for the construction of major earthen defences enclosing the *central* nucleus of the town; these appear to have been partly refurbished around AD 200, and finally levelled *c* AD 200–220. Some copper alloy objects (Wickenden in Drury 1988, fig 63.17–19) hint at a military presence in the town in the later 2nd century, whilst several assemblages of burnt daub have been taken as evidence for a major fire at the end of the 2nd century (Rodwell 1975, 93; Drury 1988, 135–6). In the later Roman period, the *mansio* probably continued in use into the 4th century, providing the major (perhaps only) reason for the survival of the town, which never developed economically beyond a 'small town' status. One suspects that *Caesaromagus* became something of an economic disappointment to the administration which had presumably awarded it its grand name (see Drury 1988, 137). Nevertheless, its possession of a *mansio*, as opposed to a lesser *mutatio*, gives it a position of respectability on the *Antonine Itinerary* (Fuentes 1986), and its road system appears to have an air of town planning, not so well developed in other small towns in Essex. This will be considered in greater detail below.

The excavations under discussion here produced several finds relating to the immediately post-Boudican military occupation, albeit lasting probably no more than a decade, and these add to a growing corpus of military small finds from Chelmsford and other small towns in the *civitas* (eg *mansio*, Wickenden in Drury 1988, fig 65, 66, 71; Heybridge, Wickenden 1987, fig 10.4; Dunmow, Wickenden 1988 b, fig 63; Kelvedon, K Rodwell 1988; Wickford, in prep; Chelmsford frontage sites, in prep). The present sites add a legionary apron strap (Fig 39.2), a stud with quatrefoil decoration (Fig 39.3) and other quasi-military objects. In addition, the coin list has produced six Claudian issues, one die-linked to a coin from Lincoln, and one issue of Tiberius. For a complete catalogue of all these military finds see Wickenden 1988a.

Drury discerned three major trends in the alignment of the principal topographic features of the Roman settlement (Drury 1988, 126); firstly the rectilinear pattern of land division established in the late Iron Age south of the rivers Can and Chelmer. *Caesaromagus* was established largely on agricultural ground — the nearest major LPRIA settlement was probably a village at Little Waltham, 6 km to the north (Drury 1978), although post-excavation analysis of road frontage sites south of the Chelmer indicate the existence of a small nucleus of round-houses (in prep). Important to the present discussion is the conformation to this alignment of the two major east-west streets. (Compare Drury 1988, fig 85 with Fig 2). Secondly the London–Colchester road itself which was superimposed on the late Iron Age landscape around or before *c* AD 60/65. Thirdly, an approximately east-west alignment which the *mansio* follows, as does a boundary on Site T (see Fig 1), and the religious complex dealt with here: the 1st century ditches, K205 and K705; the 2nd century 'corridor' structure; Structure 11; the gravel pathway and the 4th century temple itself. How these three alignments are reflected on the sites under discussion here will unfold below.

1st–2nd Centuries (Figs 63–5)

The earliest features on Sites D and K are large, amorphous hollows dug to exploit the natural brickearth deposits (presumably for daub) which form a band, *c* 0.40–50m thick, above the gravel (Fig 4.S3, 6). They were backfilled with a leached brickearth and loam mixture, containing mid–late 1st century pottery sherds and tile fragments, as well as part of a wide copper alloy bracelet (Fig 39.15) and a ribbed glass bowl (Fig 44.7). The pottery from Pit D123 appears in part to have been production waste from a nearby, unlocated, kiln, making ledge-rimmed jars.

The ovens

On Site D, an oven was built over a backfilled brickearth pit at the very end of the 1st century, and was then replaced by a second oven, built on a slightly different alignment immediately to the north (Fig 8). For similar remains of ovens from Site S, see Drury 1988, fig 47.

126

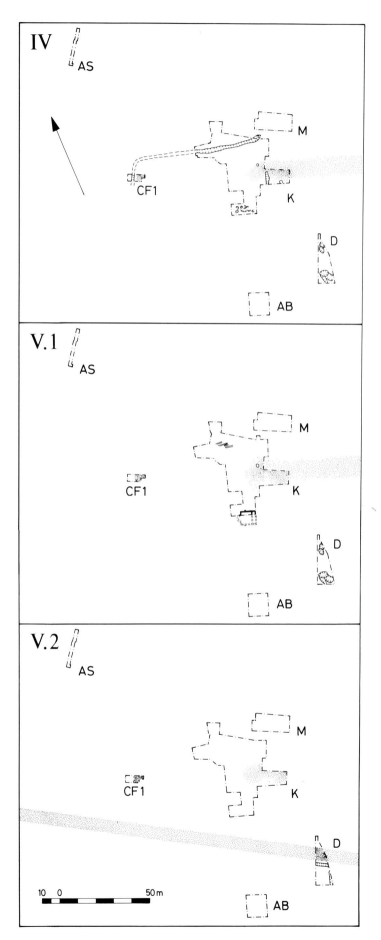

Figure 63 The north-eastern sector of Caesaromagus.
Periods IV–V

Parallel to the second oven, and only 0.15m to the north was built a masonry cill wall (Structure 1, Fig 8). Pottery evidence suggests that it was built in the later 2nd century, but this might be the date of a second phase of the building. Certainly a second wall, mostly robbed out, meets it at an angle, and cuts the second oven. The section (Fig 4.S3) shows the footings built on the level of the demolished second oven. Such masonry footings are presumably the ground-level cills for a timber-framed superstructure. It is impossible, given such limited evidence, to suggest any form of re-construction. The wall, 124, terminates in a wider plinth at its eastern end, and there is a pad of similar masonry to the north, on the projected line of 113. Importantly this line is perpendicular to the road ditch 186 (see below).

A similar situation occurs in Period V in the southern part of Site K, where clay-reddened vestiges of one oven were found c 1.20m away from, and parallel to, a second more complete oven — presumably its replacement (Fig 16). This was set in a hollow, was lined with brickearth of which three successive firings are visible in section (Fig 14.S47), and had walls of flint and tile. Though it was not possible to establish a relative chronology, the oven lay within, and was perhaps contemporary with, a building (Structure 11) with masonry cill walls, discussed below. It was subsequently cut by Structure 12 (evidenced by a shallow gulley) which significantly follows Drury's Alignment 1 and which will be discussed below.

It is interesting that there is such a high concentration of activity in the later 1st century, so far from the London–Colchester road, and its military road station (Drury 1988), and emphasises the existence at this time of an east-west route, if not an actual road, leading to the port of Heybridge on the east coast (Wickenden 1987). The occupation along this road and its junction with the London–Colchester road will be the subject of a third Roman report (in prep).

The enclosures

Two ditched enclosures were found on Sites K/CF1, and D. Both follow Drury's Alignment 3. The former, comprising ditches 205 and 705 on Site K and ditch 81 on CF1 (Fig 32) was dug sometime after the Boudican revolt, and backfilled again c AD 80 (spanning Period IV.2). It was also closely associated, or at least contemporaneous, with the 1st century votive deposits made on and/or around the 'totem' post-193 (see below). The ditches on Site K form the north-east corner of an enclosure, leaving a gap between them (a putative entrance) of 19.5 m. The north–south extent of the enclosure is not known; Drury reconstructed a southern ditch, totally obliterated by the post-medieval drainage ditch 133 (1972, fig 2). There is some evidence to suggest that ditch 205 terminates or turns an angle just south of the limit of excavations (p 19 above), in which case we find that the 1st

century enclosure has as its central focus the site of the 4th century temple, ie, whatever preceded this, perhaps a sacred grove. The east–west extent between Site CF1 and Site K, ditch 205, was 72 m.

The enclosure, however, was short-lived, probably little more than a decade. The line of ditch 205, once backfilled, was not reflected by any later features. The 2nd century corridor slot, 658, however, closely follows the southern lip of ditch 705. Further south, Structure 11 follows the same alignment.

The latter enclosure on Site D is also evidenced only by its north-east corner with a gap between the two ditches of 1.5m, though the corresponding banks, probably on the inside, could well have been continuous; thus it is by no means certain that there was an entrance at this point. The ditches D23 and 173 were dug in the early decades of the 2nd century, cutting the two ovens and the early road ditch 186. Like these on Site K they appear to be relatively short-lived, being backfilled towards the mid 2nd century on pottery evidence, after which Structure 1 was built on the site.

The early religious complex

We have already seen how on Site K the enclosure ditch 205 and the early temple pathway, 257, follow Drury's Alignment 3, which originated soon after the Boudican revolt when a military road station was first established. The 4th century temple was built partly over a series of lobed hollows, and these may represent a grubbed-out group of trees (?sacred grove). Such a feature might equally have been the focus of religious attention in the early Roman period (cf Ross 1974, 59–65).

Veneration in the Roman period took the form of the votive deposit of brooches and other copper alloy jewellery pieces, possibly hung on a totem-like post, the pit of which was excavated (F193, Fig 12). Much trouble seems to have been taken with this pit including bringing in estuarine clay for its packing. The votive objects include an incised bar (Fig 37.5; Wickenden 1986), fragments of a decorated buffware oil lamp, 13 brooches plus several more from Site CF1 (Fig 34), a complete bracelet, several finger rings, pins and a few coins. Of special interest is a decorated stud (Fig 39.3) of a well-known mid 1st century military type, found with a coin of Claudius I in the primary gravel paving K257. These objects were found scattered near the post-pit and in the fill of ditch 205, along with broken pieces of a buffware decorated 'lamp chimney' of a type similar to one from Verulamium (Wheeler & Wheeler 1936, fig 32; Fig 46.13). It is not possible to suggest the form or subject of this veneration; the practice does not, however, continue beyond the last quarter of the 1st century, when the votive pit went out of use, and ditch 205 was filled in. The discovery of an 'X' graffito, and a post-firing graffito of a cross within a circle from the bottom of ditch 205 (Fig 58.7), are also highly relevant. Miranda Green has suggested these symbols are

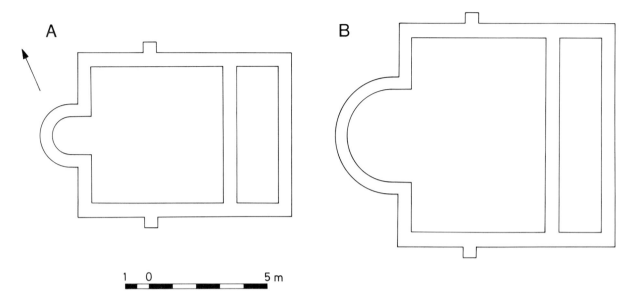

A

B

1 0   5 m

Figure 64   Site K, Structure 11: alternative reconstructions of 1st century AD temple

wheels, and as such have an underworld meaning. They dovetail closely with the snake-applied pot from Site M (Fig 60.31). This is a remarkable object with few known parallels. The snake is closely connected with the underworld, for obvious reasons, and is also an attribute of Mercury (see below).

Other examples of votive posts can be cited: At West Hill, Uley, an early 1st century AD ditch was dug with an associated focal circular pit, F251, 1.4m in diameter and 1.6m deep, which yielded a number of iron projectile heads, eight Dobunnic fine-ware vessels, unusual bone tools and the articulated rear limb of a cow (Ellison 1980, 307–8). Remains of a contemporary post-holed rectangular building were found beneath, and aligned on, the 4th century stone temple (*ibid*). The pit was recut in the late 1st century AD. At Springhead, Kent, a large post-hole was found, surrounded by animal bones, adjacent to a square (?altar) base, suggesting some form of sacred post or image (Harker 1980, 287–8, with references to Penn's articles in *Archaeol Cantiana*).

Contemporary with the post-pit, and following alignment 3, was a timber-framed square well (K558), but its sludge fill had been cleaned out (possibly ceremonial deconsecration) and it was deliberately backfilled with gravel and brickearth.

Two further pieces of information serve to indicate the special nature of activity in Periods IV and V on Site K. The use of samian is predominantly Flavian (75%) (see p 92), and appears to stop with Trajanic forms, apart from a few later pieces, indicating a different usage of the site in Period VI. This is apparently unique to Site K, and differs from a more normal supply, eg, Site S (Going 1987, Section VIII). Even the samian from Site M, only 20m north of the temple site, continues into the Antonine period, and this helps confirm the

difference in the nature of the two sites, Site M being largely an area of rubbish pits. Only the snake-decorated pot from M (Fig 60.31) hints at the close proximity to a religious precinct.

Secondly the analysis by Dr Luff of the faunal remains has revealed that a remarkably high percentage of bone in K Period IV was sheep (73%). This drops slightly in Period VI to 69.6%, but falls dramatically in Periods VII–VIII to 28%, replaced by cattle (60%) and pig (10%). Where the Period IV sheep statistics differ from those of Period VI are the higher number killed in their first year (49%, as opposed to 22%) and in the higher number of mandibles with secondary foramina (57.3% as opposed to 30.4%), especially mandibles with a calculus deposit (42% as opposed to 8.9%). This possibly isolates a specific breed of sheep, bred perhaps primarily for sacrificial purposes in Period IV. Ditch 205 also yielded nine sheep skulls and a dog skull, whilst ditch 705 produced pony remains, a human ankle bone and a baby's tibia. Single human bones can be deliberate votive deposits, ie at Uley (Ellison 1980, 308), where infant burials were also found (*ibid*). At Maiden Castle, pony bones (associated with harness fittings), and brooches *inter alia* were found in Belgic levels near the circular shrine (Wheeler 1943, 274; Ellison 1980, 309).

Structure 11 (Figs 16, 64)

This is here reconstructed as a two-celled structure with an external square buttress (possibly as support for a small upper storey) at the centre of each wall of the larger cell, and an apsidal end in the centre of the western wall. Since the surviving masonry is incomplete, and the length of curvature of the apse is very short, two possible reconstructions are illustrated in Figure 64. In Figure 64a, the larger cell is a square with sides of 6m, whilst in Figure 64b the entire structure (without the apse) forms a square with sides of 9m. The longitudinal proportion of smaller cell to the larger is 1:2.6. Whilst the walls which survive are of masonry, these may be only low cill walls, on which a timber and clay superstructure rested. There is no evidence for the nature of the roofing materials.

The building is not easily paralleled. One 2nd century, apsidal-ended, two-celled structure is Building 4 at Wood Lane End, Hemel Hempstead, part of a larger complex of buildings, and which Neal interprets as a possible *schola*, 'used to hold ceremonies associated with a guild of worshippers' (Neal 1984, 199, figs 1 and 4). However the plan is complicated by two side wings. Two further rectangular buildings with apsidal exedrae at Corbridge were interpreted as *scholae* by Richmond (1943, 132–3). A small one-, or possibly two-celled classical temple with a three-sided niche for a statue in the centre of its northern side stood to the west of the first forum in London (Marsden 1980, 43–4).

One strikingly similar parallel is a 'cult building' in Neckarburken, Baden-Württtenberg, Germany (Schallmayer 1987, 134–7). The building, with masonry cill walls, is approximately 6m x 10m with an additional small central apse in the short western wall. However, the building is only one-celled, and does not have any external buttresses. It is interpreted as possibly a mithraeum or *schola*, but definitely as a place of worship, and part of a larger complex. Its construction is put in the early 2nd century, and its main use to the mid 2nd century. Of greatest interest is the stone setting in its eastern half for a large oven, reminiscent of the two smaller versions in the Chelmsford example. Nearby at Neckarburken were fragments of the upper portion of a bunker sandstone Jupiter Column, again reminiscent perhaps of the Chelmsford 'totem pole' (Fig 12, F193).

I am grateful to Mr R Isserlin for drawing my attention to this and other possible parallels.

The Chelmsford building stands within or immediately to the south of the Flavian ditched enclosure and focus of religious attention that may be associated, at least in origin, with the post-Boudican military foundation of the town. Whilst its construction is put in Period V, on the grounds that it overlies Period IV brickearth pits, its plan and parallels may indicate a military origin and usage. The two successive ovens within it may suggest a short-lived primary function, quickly re-used, though see above for a parallel at Neckarburken. What is clear that its alignment is that of the temple precinct, and not that of the east-west road immediately to its south. However, the gulley which cuts the cill wall of Structure 11 and which dates its demise, *is* aligned on the road, suggesting the road had only then been constructed.

The Corridor Structure, and 3rd Century Occupation

The main 2nd century emphasis on Site K is on a long 'corridor' structure. A series of charcoal-filled, near vertical-sided slots precede this phase, and all follow the same general alignment closely mirroring the line of ditch 705. Their function is unknown; it is tempting to see them as troughs in which fires were lit, possibly connected with the sacred rites practised. They appear to be replaced by a group of storage-jar hearths nearby, slightly later in date, one of which overlies one of the charcoal-filled slots. The whole of the 'corridor' complex is devoid of anything of a religious nature; but given the 1st century religious emphasis — and the 4th century temple — it is likely that the complex does represent a continuation of worship; indeed similar building ranges have been excavated at Pagans Hill, Uley, and Thistleton (see below) and are clearly part of an overall complex, though peripheral to the main focus temple. The 'sacred grove' at Chelmsford, if one accepts such a feature, appears not to have been destroyed until the end of the 3rd century.

The 3rd century is fraught with difficulties. It will be noticed that very few features are assigned to this Period, and the same is true of other sites as well. 3rd century coinage is infrequent as a general rule, and is of little help. Given the shallow stratigraphy, most phasing is based on spot dating the Roman pottery from the contexts. Since specifically 3rd century pottery forms are rare in Essex (Going 1987), this is reflected in the spot dating, and ultimately in the site phasing. We are left with two equally feasible hypotheses. One is that there is a real decline in 3rd century occupation on sites in Essex; the other is that pottery production becomes stagnated, and 2nd century forms continue to be produced, with some additions, for much of the 3rd century. However the samian evidence agrees with a dwindling of the supply at the end of the 2nd century.

The 'corridor' structure on Site K comprises a number of parallel slots, aligned east–west; these are narrow and shallow, and could have held a hedge, or sleeper beams. Only in a few instances was there any evidence of post-in-slot construction. The southern slot, 619, had been recut twice (as 617 and 624) and terminates in post-holes 615 and 655. The slot is cut on the west by the temple robbing trench, and terminates just short of the eastern limit of excavation. The overall length is not, therefore, known, but a short length of slot further west might indicate its continuing outside the western limit of excavation; indeed the parallel slot to the north, 658, does extend further west. If the slots all belong to one structure, it would be at least 30m long x 6.80m wide. Whilst no easterly extension of the northern line 658 was found, it is conceivable that this was not recognised in the similar black loamy fill of the underlying ditch 705. Post-holes mainly within the two lines of slots are possibly associated smaller structures (Structure

130

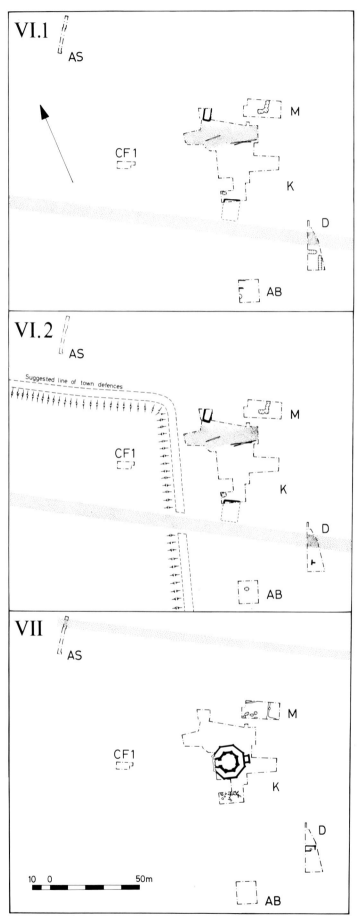

Figure 65 The north-eastern sector of Caesaromagus.
Periods VI–VII

6–7) within a portico, and it is feasible that the walls were hedges and/or fences.

At the east end of the corridor, one structure's outline is preserved by external paving levels, with only a thin scatter of pebbles internally (largely obliterated by later pits). Post-holes 734 and 979 might form part of its presumed wall, but otherwise it is suggested that its walls rose from a ground-level cill, no evidence of which survives. Its alignment is due east–west, virtually parallel with ditch 705 at this juncture. Three square post-holes to the south were thought by Drury to be a verandah (1972, 20); they are perhaps more likely, on the basis of alignment, to be associated with sSlot 637, than with the above mentioned structure. Only one contained any finds; another had been recut; the gravel paving was laid around the standing posts.

Within the main body of the corridor, a number of post-holes seem, on dating grounds, to be contemporary, though their inter-relationships are mostly dubious. Three appear to belong to a four-post structure (Structure 6); others may belong to a trapezoidal structure built against the southern corridor slot (Structure 7). One line of post-holes, 1.20m inside the northern slot 658, possibly forms an aisle, or a replacement line for 658 using posts instead of a beam slot (or a fence instead of a hedge). If 658 represented a hedge, the posts could form the wall of a building inside.

The densely gravelled area within the main slots, with several phases apparent, is very distinct from the sparse external metalling. At the western end, however, the compact gravel was extended to the north and beyond the limit of excavation. No structural evidence survives, unless a gulley (containing a post-hole) is interpreted as a foundation slot or eaves drip. Another structure found directly under the alluvial silts in the northern extension of the excavated area consisted of lines of closely laid flints and septaria (Structure 8). Gaps in this packed stone base indicate the position of posts, possibly the provision of *external* support for walls rising from ground-laid cills (Drury 1972, 21), unless the stonework itself represents low cills for the superstructure, with structural timbers set into them. The plan appears trapezoidal — though incomplete — with an apparently open northern side, although Drury suggests this may have been the centre of the building with an eastern entrance and outwardly-extended porch. An obvious parallel, also in a religious context, is Phase 2 of the shrine at Great Dunmow (Wickenden 1988 b, fig 33), dated to the last years of the 4th century AD. This is also trapezoidal in plan, with posts set in a stone raft of an uneven and rough-and-ready nature (Fig 66). Unfortunately the recording of the Chelmsford structure was curtailed due to the road building programme; no dating evidence was recovered. The building was however constructed on a pre-existing gravel paved area.

The recutting of the southern line of slots, the number of gravel surfaces and the replacement of the northern slot 658 by a row of posts all indicate building and rebuilding on the same plot over a century or more. What these timber structures were, whether they were peripheral to the main 2nd–3rd century religious focus, cannot be determined. Little in the way of finds, whether liturgical or secular, was deposited, making improved dating difficult. However, an examination of the complex at Pagans Hill discussed below (Lewis 1966, fig 114) reveals many similar features.

The Roads

It has been noted above that Structure 12, in the southern part of Site K, replaced Structure 11 in the mid 2nd century (Period VI) and was marked by a shallow gulley which cut through the earlier masonry cill wall and ovens. It turns southward at its western end where it appears to be cut by pit 2. This gulley may well be an eaves drip, or even a property boundary rather than actually structural, but would still reflect the position and alignment of Structure 12. The alignment, noticeably different to that of Structure 11 and the 1st century enclosure, is Drury's Alignment 1, which the main east-west road to Heybridge and the Dengie peninsula follows. This road runs parallel to Structure 12, c 13.80m to the south, so that the structure is likely to be the rear of a frontage building.

Assuming that the road was not in existence by the time Structure 11 was built (though see below), a date range for the construction of the road of AD 90/125–150/80 is indicated, perhaps suggesting a Hadrianic or later reorganisation of the town. Structure 1 on Site D appears to be aligned on the enclosures (Alignment 3). But a second wall at an angle to it, partly robbed in the later 2nd century is significantly aligned at right angles to the road ditch 186. This may well indicate a second phase to the building, added *after* the construction of the road. Ditch 186 was the southern road ditch, running approximately 3m to the south of the metalled road surface (5m wide). A gulley 215 containing pottery of AD 90–130 was later covered by the road surface and may have been a marking-out trench. The ditch silted up and was partly cut into by ditch 173 (enclosure), whilst the road surface was widened. In the later Roman period, the road width was reduced, as dark loams and silts (261) accumulated where the metalling settled over the underlying earlier hollow 346 (Fig 4.S10). The metalling 220 to the south of the agger was used as flooring for frontage structures in Period VII, which reveal a distinct change of alignment from the Period V ditch 186, following instead the Period VI.1 enclosure.

Sections of what should be the same road have been observed at several points to the west of Site D (Cables Yard, 1969; the Prince of Orange, 1961/71; Mildmay Road; Site V 1972, 1975; Site AF, 1974; Site AJ, 1975), though initial work on all these sites indicates a 1st century date for the road. Significantly it ran at a different angle further west, and comprised several distinct metallings and

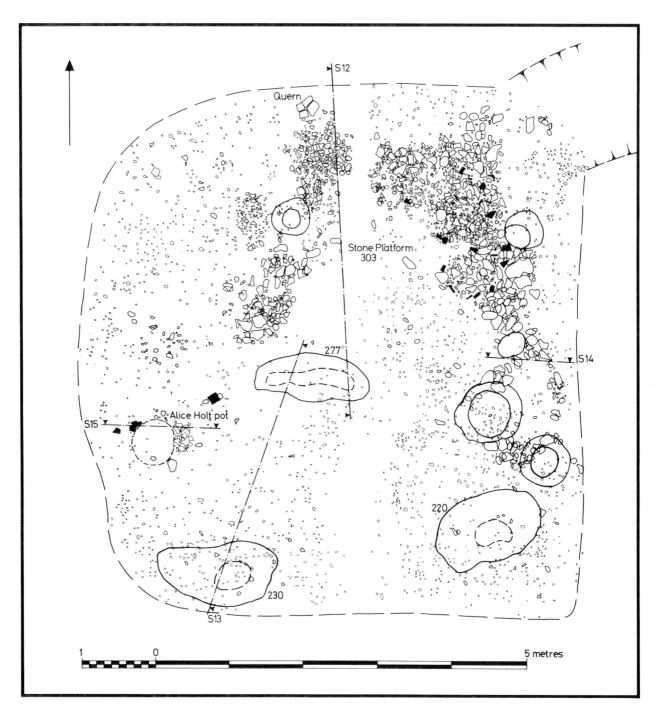

Figure 66   The late 4th cenury shrine at Great Dunmow, Essex

intermediate silts. This is clearly at variance with the date of the road section on Site D; the explanation may be that the road as excavated on the sites further west was immediately post-Boudican in origin, part of the military fort and did not at that time extend as far east as Site D perhaps stopping near the Prince of Orange Public House; under the Hadrianic reorganisation, the 1st century road was incorporated into a major east-west route, hence the change in alignment. Preliminary work on Sites V 1972 and 1975 (in prep) indicates a further change in alignment in the 4th century when two crude, apparent frontage

structures were built, one on each side of the road, which had clearly shifted direction to a more true east-west line. The reason for this becomes clear when the line is extended, and is seen to lead directly to the 4th century temple. This will be discussed in full in the Frontage report (in prep).

The second road running parallel, and *c* 200m to the north of, the above-mentioned road, was located only after Drury's interims of 1972 and 1975, and appears to be heading for presumed riverside wharves and the confluence of the Can and Chelmer. It was located in Site AS (16–18 Baddow Road, p 49, Figs 28–30), where Robin Turner has suggested a metalled, cambered surface, c 4.2m wide, was laid down in the early 3rd century on a thin bedding layer of sandy gravel. A shallow roadside ditch was found on the north side. In the 4th century a second road surface, 3.5m wide, was laid down after a black silty soil had accumulated. Another short section of the same metalled road was observed in a watching brief for a sewer trench in July 1970 (CR 35), whilst a holloway on Site Q may well be due to a heavy medieval use of the same route. The little dating which survives from Site AS would suggest an early 3rd century date for the road, and it seems unlikely that it can be part of the Hadrianic reorganisation of the town. Its character appears much less substantial than its southern counterpart.

Trade and Industry

A summary of the finds from the *mansio* indicated that 'Caesaromagus ..... acted as a market centre, where the produce of the countryside could be exchanged for goods and services originating in the town or goods imported wholesale from outside its hinterland' (Drury 1988, 136). Drury goes on to list *stili* and graffiti indicating a degree of literacy; iron smithing debris and smith's tools suggesting ironware manufacture and repair; copper alloy working and pottery manufacture. In other words, Chelmsford developed along lines similar to other small towns in Essex, of which some study has been made based on excavations in the 1970s, ie, Heybridge, Great Dunmow, Braintree and Kelvedon. This standard development was despite the presence in the town of a *mansio*, despite its grandiose name, *Caesaromagus*, and contrary to early published reports in the 1970s, when it was believed the town was a Claudian foundation, designed to be a new *Civitas* capital for the Trinovantes (eg, Wacher 1974, 198). More recently, Nicholas Fuentes has made a study of the size of towns in Essex, as part of an attempt to locate *Durolitum* at Romford, and concludes that Chelmsford had a 'town zone' of one mile, making it a 'large town'. This is largely derived by an examination of the *Antonine Itinerary* and the *Peutinger Table* (Fuentes 1986, 18–21), but he appears to select certain mileage figures whilst disregarding others as presumed errors, which, 'it must be expected, ... will have been made' (*ibid*, 18).

It is not here intended to reassess the status of the town, merely to see where finds from the excavations reported on here can shed new light on the discussion published by Drury (1988).

The assemblage of copper alloy objects is biased by a 1st century group of votive deposits, and a large number of brooches. A similar situation occurred in the 4th century at Great Dunmow (Wickenden 1988 b, 53), where shrine offerings of ribbon strip bracelet fragments and finger rings, and especially coins, biased the assemblage. The votive assemblage at Chelmsford also contained fragments of an oil lamp (surprisingly rare in the town), and part of a lamp chimney. Copper alloy objects are often difficult to date with any certainty, so that it is helpful to find, for instance, Figure 39.11, in a good 1st century context; also Figure 39.15, another distinctive 1st century form. Late 4th century finds include an interesting mount decorated with ring-and-dot (Fig 39.6), a rosette disc attachment often associated with 'Germanic belt sets' (Fig 41.50), a small silver buckle (Fig 38.1), part of a decorated bone comb (Fig 43.1), and the bone plaque carved with a human bust (Fig 43.2; *cf* Wickenden 1986). The worked bone assemblage is small when compared to the *mansio*, which produced a large group of pins. Since animal bone preservation is fairly good, this scarcity of worked bone must be regarded as real. The glass assemblage includes a useful group of late, olive-green, bubbly, flame-rounded vessel rims, of types found elsewhere in Essex, eg, Heybridge (Wickenden 1987, fig 12.52–3) and Great Dunmow (Wickenden 1988 b, fig 32.21–3), but is otherwise uninteresting. Not enough pieces of window glass were recovered to suggest the temple was glazed, though it remains a possibility; more was recovered from the *mansio* excavations (Drury 1988, 114). If Figure 44.11 really is a glass paste *tessera*, it is an interesting addition to a fairly small number of sites which have yielded them (eg, *Verulamium*, Colchester).

Of the ironwork, the most interesting piece is a woolcomb (Fig 42.1) with 13 teeth surviving, remarkably similar to one from Great Dunmow (Wickenden 1988 b, fig 40.14). Others have recently been excavated at Harlow and Kelvedon, and do not appear to be of the standard East Anglian type. These four examples are the only known from Essex, in what must have been a very rich agricultural area. Wild (1982, 117) suggests that woolcombing implies specialised cloth production, it being natural to connect it with the rearing of fine-wool jacketed sheep. The fired clay triangular loomweights from Site K, are further evidence for the textile industry, interestingly recovered from the main temple site. So too were many other domestic objects, such as corn-grinding quern stones, and some copper alloy fish-hooks, indicating that non-liturgical objects were finding their way in to the temple precinct.

The fired clay assemblage is worthy of comment: Figure 46.8 from a Period V hollow in the north-western corner of the site, might either be the terminal of a fire dog or large fire bar. From the same area, associated with the charcoal-filled slots and a localised charcoal-rich subsoil, came smaller fragments, as well as part of an unpierced triangular loomweight (Fig 46.7), and fragments of a ?pedestal and a thick 'plate' (?fire bar grid) in a very different fabric, much less compact and full of coarse vegetable matter, almost certainly brique-tage (Fig 46.9). Pieces of thin-walled pans of a more distinctive briquetage nature with the typical cream and purple colouring also came from in and around the well, and from ditch K 205, and were thus clearly deposited in the 1st century AD. This raises two questions. Firstly what was briqetage doing so far inland, and on a religious site? and secondly what meaning does the concentration of atypical fired clay objects in an area dense with charcoally loam and charcoal-filled slots have? Briquetage pan fragments were also found on Site AB (p 88) and on Site V (in prep; in a mid 1st century 'military' deposit) as well as on Site S (Drury 1988). It is possible that these were brought inland from the salt production sites on the east coast either as salt-lick for cattle (Paul Barford, pers comm), or as salt containers, which were subsequently discarded and broken up. Their association with other ?briquetage objects — a possible pedestal and hearth wall/firebar grid — might suggest the former solution, their presence on a religious site being purely fortuitous. Their further association with a firebar and unpierced loomweight, assuming that is what it is, in a denser fabric, might also be fortuitous. One hesitates to suggest that the charcoal and strange slots indicate industrial manufacture of some sort, as far more material evidence would be expected to survive if this were the case.

The Romano-Celtic Temple

Much has been written on the subject and definition of Romano-Celtic temples in recent years (Lewis 1966; Wilson 1975; Muckelroy 1976; Rodwell 1980a) and it is not intended to add to that discussion in any detail here. The Chelmsford example survives only as robbing trenches with a few remnants of masonry, mainly in the semi-circular pier bases, and has already been discussed in print (Drury 1972; Rodwell 1980b, 223–8). For a reconstruction of the plan, see Figure 69 (after Rodwell 1980b, fig 10.4), though note that his interpretation of the plan differs to Drury's (1972, fig 3). Much of what is written below is unashamedly extracted from the pages of Drury (1972) and Rodwell (1980b).

The term 'Romano-Celtic' may be applied without hesitation, since the temple comprised two concentric units, and the ambulatory does surround at least three-quarters of the circumference of the cella, despite the apsidal projection and later porch. It also conforms to an octagonal genre, well known both in this country and on the continent, and parallels will be examined below. Nevertheless, save for conforming to the traditional Romano-Celtic plan, there is nothing to suggest any non-Roman element in the temple.

Whilst dating evidence for the temple's construction is scant and disturbed by later robbing and flooding, it seems apparent that it was built in the first quarter of the 4th century, and that prior to construction, large amorphous lobed hollows, possibly the site of an earlier focal grove, had been backfilled with stone and tile rubble, containing painted plaster and mortar, all presumably from an earlier, nearby masonry building — the temple's

3rd century predecessor, missing from the excavated area?

Rodwell (1980b, 224) points out that the new temple was, in Romano-British terms, a very sophisticated building, purporting to be Architecture, yet built not of ashlar and marble, but of flint, tile and stucco. Its importance in the architectural milieu of 4th century Britain cannot be overstated; its inspiration must have been imported, unless prototypes elsewhere in the south east await discovery. The period of its erection also saw the great octagonal baptisteries, mausolea and martyria being built on the continent. Indeed, it appears to be a British phenomenon that at a time when Christianity was being widely and officially embraced by the Roman authorities, pagan Roman-Celtic temples were still being built and clearly flourishing (Frend 1955).

Little plasterwork survives, and what does is mostly from pre-temple make-up. Drury noted a small patch of lime-rich mortar adjoining one of the piers on the south side, probably representing the last remains of a mortar-mixing pit, sunk into the ground against a completed section of the wall; it was too deep to indicate ground level at the time of construction, and in any case rested on clean brickearth (1972, 22). One thinks of the large dump of oysters nearby (Fig 2), apparently not a domestic midden, but possibly a source of lime.

The dimensions

The building was c 17.70m overall, with a cella c 11.00m. The cella walls were c 1.00m thick at foundation level, with rectangular piers internally and semi-circular piers externally at the angles; masonry of some of these piers has survived, perhaps because walls were robbed by following the straight lines 'blind', and hence protruding piers were missed. They were of flint rubble, with some septaria, greensand and tile, in a hard lime mortar. The trenches were c 0.50m deep and bottomed on the stiff natural gravel below the brickearth, making further penetration superfluous. On the west the foundations terminated in relatively heavy pier bases, one of which partly survives. Much of the ground in the immediate vicinity is disturbed, but the piers define an opening c 2.50m wide. Beyond lay an alcove, reconstructed as apsidal. An intact block of undisturbed natural brickearth rules out a smaller rectilinear alcove.

The ambulatory walls were c 0.70m thick at foundation level. While the plan of most of the external ambulatory piers was destroyed, they have been reconstructed as semi-circular, on the basis of the east/south-east and the north/north-east examples. However, the robbing trench of the south/south-east pier is rectangular. This is either a simple irregularity of the robbing trench, or may possibly truly indicate a rectangular pier on this corner. If this were the case, there is a possibility that the external ambulatory piers were alternatively semi-circular and rectangular, though this cannot be proved.

On the east, two additional attached columns were provided at the outer quarter points, clearly flanking the entrance; at an unknown later date, a rectangular porch was added, projecting forward some three metres. The north porch wall foundation trench was clearly misaligned, revealing the prior existence of the column foundation at that point. Note that structural additions to the entrances of Romano-Celtic temples are not at all uncommon, eg, at Uley, where a timber doorcase appears to have been replaced by a colonnaded antechamber (Rodwell 1980b, 229–30, fig 10.2). The two rubble-packed post pits, 294 and 586, thought by Drury to be part of two lean-to sheds belonging to the robbing phase (1972, 25) may be vitally important here. The flint and tile packing is no different to that used in the construction make-up levels, and hence are as likely to be contemporary with the temple, as to post-date it. The roofing-tile mortar bedding surviving from a third associated pit 423, cannot, therefore, be taken as evidence for the temple roof having been tiled (*ibid*, 23) — although it surely was. The evidence for a robbers' squatting phase will still be examined, but appears to consist of shallow stake-hole construction, a low quality method at odds with large, well-packed post pits. Divorced from this association, the two pits' importance becomes apparent. They are directly in line with the eastern wall of the 'porch', and may be assumed to be part of the building's new facade, similar to the development at Uley (above). The third rubble-packed post pit, 423, lay immediately east of the south east corner of the 'porch'. A corresponding pit on the north side may also have originally existed.

It is probable, though proof is lacking, that the walls were constructed of similar materials to the foundations, and totally rendered. Little building material survived in later features; no architectural fragments were found, and only a small quantity of a coarse two-coat plaster predominently red in colour (Drury 1972, 23). Rodwell (1980b, 224) uses the word 'stucco', which should be treated with caution — it is a rather grand word for a plain plaster; indeed wholesale rendering, though likely, cannot be proven at all, from the small amount of plaster surviving in robbing levels.

Floor levels had been totally eroded. Lack of *tesserae* in later features, though not conclusive, seems to militate against a mosaic floor; concrete is possible (small amounts of *opus signinum* were found); gravel on brickearth would surely be inconsistent with the standard of the remainder of the structure. The continuity of the walls of the portico and ambulatory through the entrances may argue for the floors being raised somewhat above the general ground level — a wise precaution in a fairly low-lying area such as this, possibly liable to occasional flooding. A raised floor in the cella could have been in timber, but this would be difficult to visualize in the ambulatory or portico. The matter

cannot satisfactorily be resolved on the evidence available.

When we turn to a reconstruction of the main structure, the relative wall thickness of *cella* and ambulatory suggests a tall *cella* with clerestorey lighting, rising through an ambulatory with low external solid walls and a lean-to roof supported on attached columns at the angles (Drury 1972, 22). Muckelroy certainly found that virtually all Romano-Celtic temples in Britain had closed ambulatories rather than open porticoes (1976, 188), in contrast to the continental *genre* — perhaps a concession to British weather. Rodwell writes:

> the internal angles of the *cella* were given definition by shallow flat pilasters, and while these might have run straight up to a plain string-course at about the point where the ambulatory roof adjoined, it is far more likely that they assumed a more emphatic architectural role. Their most probable function would have been to flank broad arches which communicated with the ambulatory [as is envisaged at Pagans Hill (1980, 226)]. Thus we may imagine that the pilasters rose to the springing level of the arches, where they would have been surmounted by imposts from which curved strip-work sprung to outline the heads of the arches. In the ambulatory the arches were flanked by semi-circular pilaster strips, or engaged columns, set at the angles of the octagon. Similar features decorated the outer angles of the ambulatory wall (1980, 223–4).

Drury again suggests that the structural form indicates a *cella* roof (probably tiled) based on a system of radial main beams transmitting the weight to the piers. Whilst the presence of piers shows that the walls of the *cella* were of masonry, at least to ambulatory roof, it is possible that the structure above this level was wholly of timber.

The reconstruction of the western recess as an apse does present problems. In filling the space between the *cella* and ambulatory walls, it must have totally blocked through access in the ambulatory, unless the latter wall extended out in parallel. Drury originally reconstructed the apse as a curving wall (based on a columnar ambulatory); Rodwell more realistically reconstructs it as apsidal internally, but with straight external walls leaving the pier corners and abutting the western ambulatory wall (Fig 67). Perfect symmetry is maintained with the entrance to the east, utilising the long gravel pathway.

West Hill, Uley: an association with Mercury?

The development of the religious complex at Chelmsford is paralleled remarkably closely at West Hill, Uley in Gloucestershire, despite the latter's grander scale. Both sites had 1st century phases, and ditched enclosures closely associated with the religious complex, though the Uley enclosure was dated to the pre-Dobunnic Iron Age in origin. Nevertheless a 1st century element (Ellison 1980, 306: F264) was present, along with a *focal circular pit* (F251, *ibid*, fig 15.1), containing a group of votive objects (see above). In this phase at Uley there were also elusive traces of a post-holed rectangular building, 7m x at least 8m. Two ranges of stone buildings were subsequently constructed within the second century, *demolished* by the opening years of the 4th century (Ellison 1980, 310; my italics). Whilst not actual temples themselves, these two buildings were not domestic in character, but rather resembled the 'guest house' at Lydney (Structure X; see Wheeler & Wheeler 1932). They indicate the former existence of a 2nd or 3rd century Roman religious building at Uley (Ellison 1980, 310; ie, the main temple of this date was not found, in exactly the same way as the main 2nd–3rd century focus at Chelmsford was not recovered, merely what are presumed to be subsidiary buildings — the 'corridor' structure). The main temple at Uley, a rectangular Romano-Celtic temple with an ambulatory on only three sides, was erected in the second quarter of the 4th century, had a colonnaded porch extension added, and appears to have been dismantled in the early 5th century, though occupation continued. The similarity with Chelmsford is striking.

The whole complex at Uley was dedicated to Mercury, many classes of evidence agreeing on this. One of these was the presence in large numbers of ovicaprid remains in the temple rubbish deposits, possibly resulting from sacrifical activities. '*Mature male goats seem to have been preferred, and the deliberate removal of frontals and horn cores seem to have been a characteristic of the cult*' (Ellison 1980, 312; my italics). The goat was of course one of the main attributes of Mercury. Another attribute was the cockerel, bones of which were found at Uley; whilst no bones were found on the temple site in Chelmsford, cockerel bones have been found elsewhere in the town (Luff 1982), and a copper alloy figurine was found in the *mansio* (Drury & Wickenden 1982b). The pottery bowl from Site M (Fig 60.31) may also be relevant here. An appliqué snake is depicted slithering along with its jaws open. Another appliqué snake from Garden Hill, near Hartfield, East Sussex, (unpubl) appears to have no religious connotations, but given the context at Chelmsford, it is possible that both were votive, the snake having an apotropaic attribute — by renewing its skin every year it represents eternal rebirth. Two entwined snakes are always depicted around the head of the staff of Mercury, in his capacity as Messenger of the Gods, but one also recalls the Pompeian paintings in *lararia* showing snakes approaching a central altar with open jaws (eg, Claridge & Ward-Perkins 1979, 52, 58). For a discussion of the snake in Roman art, see Toynbee 1973, 223–236.

Returning to the high percentage of ovicaprid remains at Uley, the animal bones assemblage from

Site K shows an equally high percentage of ovicaprid, at least in the early periods (73%, Period IV; 61.9%, Period V; 69.6%, Period VI). Unfortunately only a small number of fragments could be positively identified as goat, all coming from pit 90 (Period VI), see Section VIII. A very high number of mandibles was present, *but surprisingly very few skull and horn-core remains were found, seven male skulls occurring in ditch 205*. Indeed, ditch 205, already identified with votive practices in the 1st century (above), contained a very high number of ovicaprid remains, as well as an isolated dog skull. The corresponding ditch 705 was also unusual in that it contained pony and large horse bones, as well as a human ankle bone and infant tibia (note that infant burials were found in the late 1st century enclosure deposits at Uley (Ellison 1980, 308)).

Bearing in mind the relatively small size of the Chelmsford excavations compared to Uley (1100 sq m, as opposed to 2150 sq m), it might be assumed that Chelmsford too was part of a much larger religious complex, and a similar dedication to Mercury also cannot be ruled out.

Similarly high ovicaprid remains have been found at the Romano-Celtic temple at Harlow (France & Gobel 1985), where Legge suggests that sheep between 6 and 9 months old, carefully selected on dental examination, were being slaughtered seasonally, in the autumn following a spring lambing (*ibid*, 122–33). The Chelmsford assemblage of ovicaprid might even indicate different breeds, represented by the differing number of mental foramina, and the amount of calculus present, in the mandibles: in Period IV, for example, mainly comprising bone from ditch 205, 51 out of 89 (57.3%) mandibles exhibited a secondary foramen (Section VIII).

Octagonal temples: Britain and the Continent

Polygonal Romano-Celtic temples occur both in Britain and on the continent; among them the octagonal plan is by far the most common. A study in 1933 listed eight, including two in this country, at Caerwent and Weycock Hill (Koethe 1933). The polygonal form, in effect, is a sophisticated development of the circular plan, the change being due perhaps to the innovation in the Iron Age of a segmental carpentered wall plate in place of a woven ring beam of withies (Drury 1978, 118–22; 1980, 72). Certainly at Little Waltham in Essex, a number of Iron Age round-houses were excavated which took the form of irregular polygons (Drury 1978). No polygonal shrines have yet been reported from pre-Roman Britain, though a structure excavated at Trisov in Czechoslovakia has been claimed as a potential prototype for the polygonal form of Romano-Celtic temple (Drury 1980, 70; Bren 1976, 92).

A gazetteer of polygonal Romano-Celtic temples in Britain was recently published by Rodwell in the

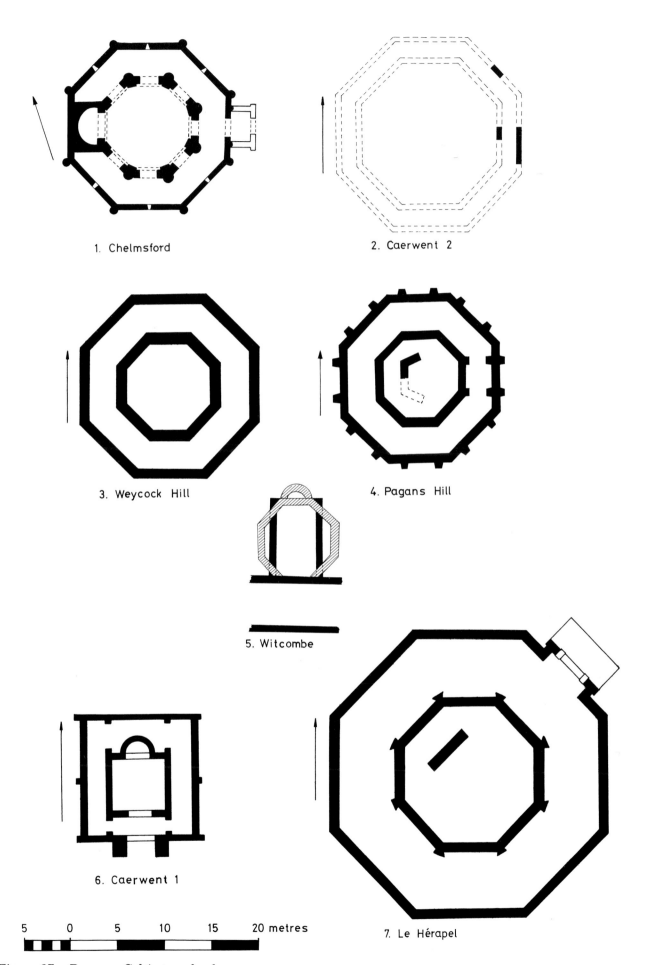

1. Chelmsford

2. Caerwent 2

3. Weycock Hill

4. Pagans Hill

5. Witcombe

6. Caerwent 1

7. Le Hérapel

5   0   5   10   15   20 metres

Figure 67   Romano-Celtic temple plans

Table 21 Comparative measurements of Romano-Celtic temples
(after Lewis 1966, 13, converted into metres (feet in brackets))

| | Short diameter | | Wall thickness | |
	Ambulatory	*Cella*	*Ambulatory*	*Cella*
British				
Chelmsford	16.00 (52ft 6")	9.14 (30ft)	0.70 (2ft 3")	1.0 (3ft 3")
Caerwent 2	20.12 (66ft)	16.15 (53ft)	0.46 (1ft 6")	?0.46 (1ft 6")
Pagans Hill	17.22 (56ft 6")	9.75 (32ft)	0.91 (3ft)	0.91 (3ft)
Weycock	19.38 (63ft 7")	10.95 (35ft 11")	1.17 (3ft 6")	1.07 (3ft 6")
Continental				
Le Hérapel	30.20	14.00	0.90	1.20

proceedings of the 1979 conference which has rapidly become the standard work on religious structures in Roman Britain (1980c, 565–6). Eight examples are listed, of which five are octagonal. The Nettleton example is a triple concentric structure, but the remaining three are close parallels for Chelmsford (Caerwent 2; Pagans Hill, Somerset; Weycock Hill, Berkshire). The Caerwent 2 temple (Fig 67.2; Hudd 1913; Lewis 1966, figs 33, 115; Wacher 1974, fig 82) is very incomplete, but lay inside a circular *temenos*. Indeed an inner octagonal *cella* is reconstructed on a very short length of wall, excavated in difficult circumstances (Hudd 1913, 449–51 and fig 9); if it is a *cella*, the ambulatory is remarkably narrow (5ft between walls), and perhaps a greater degree of uncertainty should be attributed to the interpretation of this building than has hitherto been made. As at Chelmsford, the temple lay outside the town walls to the east. It has no associated dating evidence but apparently lay over the ditch of the city wall, dated to the mid–late 2nd century at the earliest (Frere 1984 b, 70; *contra* Lewis 1966, 54, who dates it to c AD 75). It is worth noting that the square Romano-Celtic Caerwent 1 temple (Fig 67.6; Lewis 1966, fig 3; Wacher 1974, fig 84), is the only other Romano-Celtic temple in the province with an apse attached to the *cella*. It has recently been shown to date after c AD 330 (Frere 1986, 369; 1987, 308). At Witcombe Villa, Gloucestershire, an octagonal room, c 8.00m overall, also has an apse, and the excavator, Mr E Greenfield, interpreted the room as a shrine (Fig 67.5, after Wilson 1970, 294). Indeed simple octagonal temples or shrines in the province number a further nine (Rodwell 1980c, 570–1, with refs).

The Weycock Hill temple (Fig 67.3; Neville 1849; Cotton 1956; Lewis 1966, fig 36) was built in the early 4th century within a rectangular *temenos*:

Both walls were of equal thickness and apparently survive to a height of 2.44m (8ft) from the bottom of the foundations. None of this height can have been above temple floor level, since no gaps for doors were recorded; but as it is too deep for foundations alone, some of the 8ft probably represents the height of a podium. Otherwise no architectural deductions can be made. (Lewis 1966, 31).

Pagans Hill, Chew Stoke, Somerset (Fig 67.4, 68), has been fairly comprehensively discussed (Rahtz 1951; Lewis 1966, 30; Rodwell 1980b, 224–8). The ambulatory wall is shown by 16 external rectangular buttresses and by plaster to have been substantially solid; the absence of any plaster from the *cella* walls has been taken as a sign that they supported full columns in turn supporting a clerestorey (but see below). Both the inner and outer walls are of the same thickness, c 0.91m (3ft). The entrance to the *cella* was perhaps flanked by engaged columns, forming a small vestibule between the two walls. Inside the *cella*, a three-sided screen was added, probably as a backing to the cult statue. Over 237 coins were recovered, trodden into the path leading to the entrance. Large numbers of coins were also found at Weycock: it is interesting that coins were not being deposited in votive contexts at Chelmsford, unlike the shrine at Great Dunmow (Wickenden 1988 b, 44). The Pagans Hill temple is dated to the later 3rd century, surviving into the 5th century after a late 4th century rebuild. The temple was enclosed on the north and eastern sides by ranges of buildings, possibly dormitories or assembly rooms (Rahtz & Harris 1958, fig 1). These include long narrow porticoes or corridors, and it is possible that the Chelmsford 'corridor structure' is a part of such a range of buildings. A similar long hall with a corridor on its west side appears on air photographs at right angles to the temple axis at Thistleton 2 (Lewis 1966, 94). Such structures suggest deliberate planning not just of the temple itself, but of the whole precinct (Rodwell 1980b, 224).

Rodwell suggests a different reconstruction for the *cella* at Pagans Hill (1980b, 226), based on the responds flanking the doorway indicating a pair of lateral arches, in which case the *cella* must have had a solid wall, rather than being colonnaded. 'Communication with the ambulatory would have

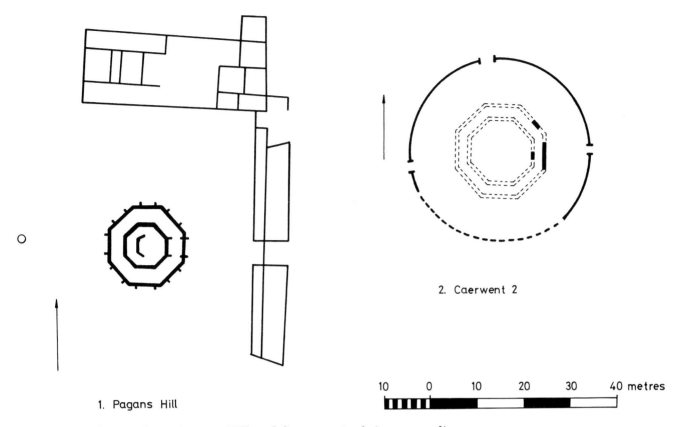

1. Pagans Hill

2. Caerwent 2

10   0   10   20   30   40 metres

Figure 68   *The temples at Pagans Hill and Caerwent in their surroundings*

been via a series of round-headed arches, as at Chelmsford' (*ibid*). The external buttresses, placed opposite the angles of the *cella* walls, must be to a containment of an outward thrust from vaulting across the width of the ambulatory. The Chelmsford external buttresses on the other hand are placed at the salient angles, and must have taken the thrust exerted on the tops of the walls by the ambulatory roof.

At the time of writing, a new Romano-Celtic octagonal temple has been discovered in London.

What is clear from Table 21 and Drury 1972, 23–4, is that the Chelmsford temple (232 sq m floor area) is much smaller than the average size of polygonal Romano-Celtic temples in Britain (310 sq m), and the continental average of 365 sq m. Nevertheless, the continental octagonal temples appear closest to the same architectural form as Chelmsford, the nearest parallel being Le Hérapel, near Cocheren, Moselle (Fig 67.7; Koethe 1933, No 14; Horne & King 1980, 419, fig 17.26.2). The temple is set within a *temenos*, with its entrance facing north-east; the *cella* wall has slight external buttresses or pilasters on the salient angles, and painted wallplaster survives in the exterior of the *cella*, suggesting a solid wall. The ambulatory wall survives to a height of 1.5m. Gaulish and Roman coins date between the 1st and the late 4th century, and includes a possible hoard of Arcadian issues. Other continental octagonal temples are listed and illustrated by Horne & King (1980, figs 17.25–27).

The Temenos

The majority of those Romano-Celtic temples discussed above, appear to lie within a religious enclosure, or *temenos*, defined by a wall or line of buildings. At Chelmsford, no clear evidence for a *temenos* was found, one reason being the excavated area was virtually restricted to the temple itself and the 'corridor structure' lying to the north. Several boundaries, however, would indicate the possible extent of the religious precinct. Firstly, roads to the north and south, running in an east-west direction are obvious boundaries defining what we may loosely term an *insula*. The 1st century gravel path extends eastwards and appears to stop where a small length of a mortared tile and flint wall, c 0.30m wide, was found in watching briefs, perhaps running at right angles to the roads (Fig 3; CR 7, F2). The line approximately coincides with the western limit of the oyster dump, perhaps indicating that the latter was deposited immediately outside the eastern *temenos* wall. If these boundaries are correct, the *temenos* would be approximately 94m wide x at least 132m long, enclosing 1.24 hectares.

South of the Drainage Ditch, 133

The area to the south of the post-medieval drainage ditch, 133, was of a different nature to the northern area, and was much more 'domestic' in character,

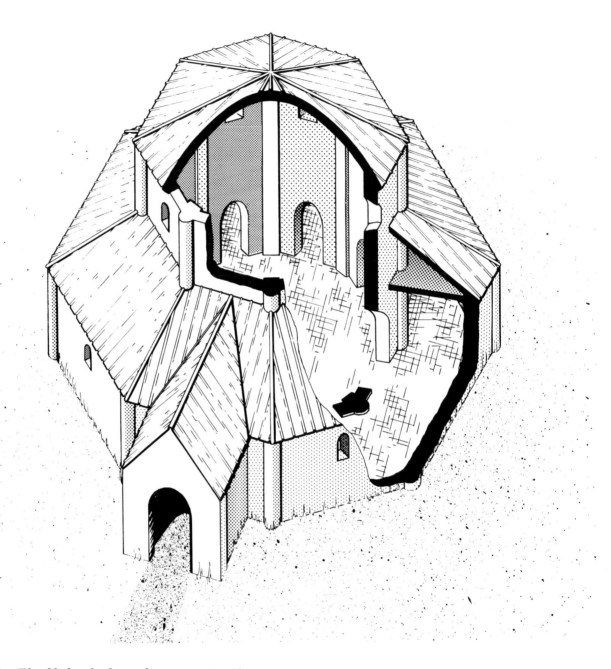

Figure 69   The Chelmsford temple: a reconstruction

similar to Sites D and M, comprising building foundations fronting the Roman road leading south-east out of the town, intercutting rubbish pits and ovens. Nevertheless it appears to have had close links with the precinct in that the rubbish pits, whilst containing little refuse, did yield a high number of coins (41) and other small finds. Of the 41 coins, nine were AD 43–268; four were 268–273; seventeen were Constantinian (310–330, 6; 330–360, 11); ten were Valentinian, and one was Theodosian. It is abundantly clear from these rubbish pits that there was a great deal of activity in the 4th century between *c* AD 310 and *c* 378, in a relatively small area. The 'activity' *could* be, and probably was, connected with the usage of the octagonal temple, although similar coin densities were not *directly* associated with the temple itself; nevertheless as Reece points out (1980, 118), all British sites show a major loss of coin between 330 and 378. What is equally interesting is the lack of Theodosian issues in these pits; if they do reflect the usage of the temple, it strongly suggests that the temple was no longer functioning by the last decade of the 4th century.

Other Religious Evidence in Chelmsford

The corner of a building excavated on Site AR in 1977 was defined by cill beam trenches apparently with a portico c 3.2m wide on both facades, and has been tentatively interpreted as a double square Romano-Celtic temple (Drury 1988, 134–5). It appeared to face south-eastwards towards the *mansio*. Since nothing of a 'votive' nature was found, and since the evidence is perfectly consistent with its being the corner of a secular building, its identification as a Romano-Celtic temple cannot be definite. Material evidence is not great: a copper alloy cockerel figurine was found in the *mansio* (Wickenden in Drury 1988, fig 63.20), and a gilded copper alloy sheet, possibly depicting the wheel of Taranis has also been published (*ibid*, fig 66.84). A near complete pipeclay Venus figurine was found off Moulsham Street in 1972 (unpublished), and several smaller fragments of pipeclay figurines have also been recovered during excavations in the town. A well shaft, recut at least six times *above* the water table and filled with faunal remains clearly deposited in a votive context, was published from Site AR (Drury 1988, 19–20). More recently, a votive context has been suggested for a horse burial in the south of the town (Wallis 1988, 43–5).

Sub-Roman Activity and the Temple Aftermath

There is not enough evidence, given the absence of surviving contemporary floor levels, to say at what stage the temple fell into disuse and was subsequently plundered for its valuable masonry. The robbing, however, was virtually total, leaving only pockets of masonry *in situ*, mainly some of the rectangular and semi-circular pilasters and buttresses. This suggests that final robbing of the foundation trenches was done when no masonry survived above ground, so that in following the trenches 'blind', many of the projecting areas were missed. Evidence in the archaeological record of a two-phase dismantling is sadly lacking; three late 13th century sherds were found in the temple robbing trenches 442 and 534 (see p 42).

Late Roman finds include rim, base and body sherds of eight glass vessels from Site K in an olive green metal with many pinhead bubbles (Fig 44.16–21). Five cone beakers and a hemispherical bowl are represented and are dated to the decades just before and after AD 400. Unfortunately all the pieces were found either in the main medieval north-south boundary ditch 264 or in medieval subsoil. A copper alloy ring-and-dot decorated mount (K, Fig 39.6) is regarded by Professor Vera Evison as of late 4th century manufacture, whilst a rosette disc attachment from Site M (Fig 41.50) should be dated to c AD 400. The silver buckle from Site K (Fig 38.1) and a decorated glass bead (Fig 44.22) are of a similar date. Two bone objects are probably also late 4th century: part of a comb (Fig 43.1) from oven K485, and a plaque incised with a human figure (Fig 43.2; Wickenden 1986) from a pit which cut oven 485. The same pit cut another pit, itself containing late shell-tempered pottery dated post- c AD 360/70. Other sherds of late shell-tempered pottery, as well as Oxfordshire red colour-coat, late Nene Valley colour-coat, and oxidised Hadham ware all come from the robber trenches of the temple walls. The coin sequence for Site K includes 59 Constantinian issues (40% total) and 35 Valentinian (24%), representing the probable main period of use of the temple. There were 16 Theodosian coins (11% total for Site K), and a further three on Site D. The K examples came from subsoils, medieval silts, the medieval boundary ditch, and the Period VIII post-hole 745 (two Arcadius, two House of Theodosius).

The ambulatory wall in the north-east quarter must have been removed to ground level by the time a stake-built structure, c 4m x 3m, was built against the still extant *cella*. This rather flimsy sub-rectangular building consisted of a number of small stakes, penetrating the subsoil, with a possible internal support along the long axis. Associated pottery was residual. The structure resembles a Saxon *grubenhaus*, and may be 5th century in date, though no early Saxon pottery was found on site. A similar structure from Fladbury in the West Midlands was thought to be middle Saxon (Peacock 1977).

Drury also postulated the existence of two lean-to structures to the north and south of the porch (1972, 24). The stone-packed post-holes are now thought to be part of the porch facade (see above), but the lean-to structures are still credible, their plans comprising a number of small stake-holes, identical in nature to the sub-rectangular hut. These may well have been contemporary, and concerned with the temple demolition, though we are no nearer knowing for what end the masonry was robbed than when Drury wrote in 1972. Saxon remains are still elusive in Chelmsford, though a major settlement and cemetery has been investigated at Springfield (Buckley & Hedges 1987), and mid-Saxon pottery has been found at Great Waltham (CHMER). Note also the major princely burial at Broomfield nearby (VCH 1903, 320–31). The Roman town of *Caesaromagus* itself appears to have been deserted.

The Roman levels were subsequently eroded and sealed by a layer 0.60m thick of alluvial flood silt deposited in the medieval period, probably also putting an end to limited medieval occupation of the site (to be dealt with in a later report), comprising a boundary ditch and possible 13th century dyer's tanks. By the close of the 16th century the area was under cultivation, as illustrated by the 1591 Walker map of Moulsham (ERO D/DM P.2). A post-medieval ditch destroyed the boundary between temple and frontage structures to the south, whilst the site is crossed by two modern sewer trenches, unfortunately laid by the road contractors between the two principal phases of work.

Bibliography

Allason-Jones, L, & Miket, R, 1984 *The Catalogue of small finds from South Shields Roman Fort*

Allen, T P, 1985 *Medieval and Post–medieval finds from Exeter, 1971–1980*, Exeter Archaeol Rep, **3**

Arthur, P, 1978 The lead glazed wares of Roman Britain, in Arthur & Marsh, (eds), 1978, 293–356

Arthur, P, & Marsh, G, (eds), 1978 *Early fine wares in Roman Britain*, Brit Archaeol Rep, **57**

Bateson, J D, 1981 *Enamel-working in Iron Age, Roman and Sub-Roman Britain*, Brit Archaeol Rep, **93**

Bedwin, O, 1980 Excavations at Chanctonbury Ring, Weston, West Sussex 1977, *Britannia*, **11**, 173–222

Boessneck, J, Muller, H-H, & Teichert, M, 1964 *Osteologische Unterschiedungsmerkmale Zwischen Schaf (Ovis aries Linne) und Ziege (Capra hircus Linne)*, Kuhn Archiv, Arb aus d Landw der Martin Luther Univ, **78** Band, Heft 1/2, 1–129

—— & Driesch, A, van den, 1974 Kritische Anmerkungen Zur Widerristhohenberechnung aus Längen- massen vor- und Frühgeschichtlicher, Saugetierkundliche Mitteilungen, **22**.4, 325–48

Böhme, H W, 1974 *Germanische Grabfunde des 4 bis 5 Jahrhunderts*

Boon, G C, (Rev ed), 1974 *Silchester: The Roman Town of Calleva*

Brailsford, J W, 1962 *Hod Hill 1: Antiquities from Hod Hill in the Durden Collection*

Bren, J, 1976 Earliest settlements with urban character in Central Europe, in Cunliffe, B W, & Rowley, R T, (eds), *Oppida: the Beginnings of Urbanisation in Barbarian Europe*, Brit Archaeol Rep, **S11**, 81–94

Brodribb, A C C, Hands, A R, & Walker, D R, 1972 *Excavations at Shakenoak*, **3**

——, ——, & ——, 1973 *Excavations at Shakenoak Farm, near Wilcote, Oxfordshire*, **4**

Brown, D, 1975 A fifth-century burial at Kingsholm, *Antiq J*, **55**, 290–4

Buckley, D G, & Hedges, J D, 1987 *The Bronze Age & Saxon Settlements at Springfield Lyons, Essex. An Interim Report*, Essex County Council Occas Pap, **5**

——, & Major, H, 1983 Quernstones, in N Crummy 1983, 73–6

Bushe-Fox, J P, 1926 *Second Report on the excavation of the Roman fort at Richborough, Kent*, Res Rep Soc Antiq London, **7**

——, 1932 *Third Report on the excavation of the Roman Fort at Richborough, Kent*, Res Rep Soc Antiq London, **10**

Callender, M H, 1965 *Roman amphorae*

Carter, P L, *et al*, 1965 The Iron Age farmstead at Hawk's Hill, *Surrey Archaeol Collect*, **62**, 40–2

Chancellor, F, 1857 On Roman remains lately discovered at Chelmsford, *Trans Essex Archaeol Soc*, **1**, 59–63

Charlesworth, D, 1972 The glass in Frere 1972, 196–215

——, 1978 The Roman glass, in A Down, *Chichester Excavations*, **3**, 267–73

——, 1981 The Roman glass, in A Down, *Chichester Excavations*, **5**, 293–8

Claridge, A, & Ward-Perkins, J, 1979 *Pompeii AD 79*

Cotton, M A, 1956 Weycock Hill, 1953, *Berks Archaeol J*, **55**, 48–68

Crummy, N, 1979 A chronology of Romano-British bone pins, *Britannia* **10**, 157–63

——, 1983 *The Roman Small Finds from Excavations in Colchester, 1971–9*, Colchester Archaeol Rep, **2**

Cunliffe, B W, (ed), 1968 *Fifth Report on the Excavations of the Roman Fort at Richborough, Kent*, Res Rep Soc Antiq London, **23**

——, 1971 *Excavations at Fishbourne 1961–9*, Res Rep Soc Antiq London, **27**

Cunningham, C M, & Drury, P J, 1985 *Post Medieval Sites and their Pottery: Moulsham Street, Chelmsford*, CBA Res Rep, **54**, Chelmsford Archaeol Trust Rep, **5**

Curle, A O, 1923 *The Treasure of Traprain, a Scottish hoard of Roman silver plate*

Detsicas, A, 1974 Finds from the pottery kiln(s) at Eccles, Kent, *Antiq J*, **54**, 305–6

Dickinson, T M, 1978 British Antiquity: post-Roman and Pagan Anglo-Saxon, *Arch J*, **135**, 332–44

Down, A, & Rule, M, 1971 *Chichester Excavations*, **1**

Downey, R, King, A, & Soffe, G, 1978 *The Roman Temple on Hayling Island* (2nd interim)

Drury, P J, 1972 Preliminary report: the Romano-British settlement of Chelmsford, Essex: *Caesaromagus*, *Essex Archaeol Hist*, **4**, 3–29

——, 1976 Braintree: excavations and research, 1971–6, *Essex Archaeol Hist*, **8**, 1–143

——, 1978 *Chelmsford Excavations I: Excavations of Little Waltham 1970–71*, CBA Res Rep, **26**

——, 1980 Non-classical religious buildings in Iron Age and Roman Britain: a review, in W J Rodwell 1980, 45–78

——, 1988 *The mansio and other sites in the South-Eastern Sector of Caesaromagus*, CBA Res Rep, **66**, Chelmsford Archaeol Trust, **3**.1

——, & Rodwell, W J, 1973 Excavations at Gun Hill, West Tilbury, *Essex Archaeol Hist*, **5**, 48–112

——, & Wickenden, N P, 1982a An Early Saxon settlement within the Romano-British small town at Heybridge, Essex, *Medieval Archaeol*, **26**, 1–40

——, & ——, 1982b Four bronze figurines from the Trinovantian *Civitas*, *Britannia*, **13**, 239–43

Ellison, A, 1980 Natives, Romans and Christians on West Hill, Uley: an interim report on the excavation of a ritual complex of the first millennium AD, in W J Rodwell 1980a, 305–28

Evison, V I, 1967 The Dover ring-sword and other sword-rings and beads, *Archaeologia*, **101**, 63–118

——, 1968 Quoit brooch style buckles, *Antiq J*, **48**.2, 181–250

——, 1988 *An Anglo-Saxon cemetery at Alton, Hampshire*, Hampshire Field Club Monog, **4**

Fitch, S E, 1864 Discovery of Saxon remains at Kempston, *Ass Architect Soc Rep pap*, **7**.2, 295–7

France, N E, & Gobel, B M (eds), 1985 *The Romano-Celtic Temple at Harlow*

Frend, W H C, 1955 Religion in Roman Britain in the fourth century AD, *J Brit Archaeol Assoc, 3 ser*, **18**, 1–18

Frere, S S, 1972 *Verulamium Excavations* I, Res Rep Soc Antiq London, **28**

——, 1984a *Verulamium Excavations*, **3**, Oxford Univ Comm Archaeol Monog, **1**

——, 1984b British urban defences in earthwork, *Britannia*, **15**, 63–74

——, 1986 Roman Britain in 1985. I. Sites Explored, *Britannia*, **17**, 363–427

——, 1987 Roman Britain in 1986. I. Sites Explored, *Britannia*, **18**, 302–59

Fuentes, N, 1986 Durolitum found, *Essex J*, **21**.1

Fulford, M G, 1975a *New Forest Roman pottery*, Brit Archaeol Rep, **17**

——, 1975b The pottery, in B W Cunliffe, *Excavations at Portchester Castle*. I. *Roman*, Soc Antiq Res Rep, **32**, 270–366

Galloway, P, 1976 Note on descriptions of bone and antler combs, *Medieval Archaeol*, **20**

Gibson, A V B, 1970 A Roman steelyard from Bishops Stortford, *Hertfordshire Archaeol*, **2**, 109–10

Gillam, J P, 1979 Romano Saxon pottery, an alternative explanation, in J Casey, (ed), *The end of Roman Britain*, Brit Archaeol Rep, **71**, 103–18

Going, C, 1984 Pottery, in Drury, P J, The Temple of Claudius at Colchester reconsidered, *Britannia*, **15**, 46–9

——, 1987 *The mansio and other sites in the South-Eastern Sector of Caesaromagus: The Roman Pottery*, CBA Res Rep, **62** Chelmsford Archaeol Trust Rep, **3**.2

——, & Ford, B, 1988 The Roman pottery, in Wickenden, N P, 1988b, 60–76

Goodburn, R, 1984 The non-ferrous metal objects, in S S Frere 1984 a, 19–67

Grayson, D K, 1984 *Quantitative zooarchaeology*

Green, M J, 1984 The wheel as a cult symbol in the Romano-Celtic world, *Coll Latomus*, **183**, 66–71 (Brussels)

Greene, K, 1979 The Pre-Flavian fine wares. *Report on the excavations at Usk 1965–1976*

Greenwood, P, 1980, The cropmark site at Moor Hall Farm, Rainham, Essex, *London Archaeol*, **4**.7, 185–93

Guido, M, 1978 *The glass beads of the Prehistoric and Roman periods in Britain and Ireland*, Res Rep Soc Antiq London, **35**

Gurney, D A, 1986 *Settlement, religion and industry on the fen- edge; three Romano-British sites in Norfolk*, E Anglian Archaeol, **31**

Haberey, W, 1942 Spätantike Gläser aus Gräbern von Mayen, *Bonner Jahrbucher*, **147**, 249–84

Harcourt, R A, 1974 The dog in prehistoric and early historic Britain, *J Archaeol Sci*, **1**, 151–75

Harden, D B, 1971 Glass, in A C C Brodribb, A R Hands & D R Walker, *Excavations at Shakenoak Farm, Near Wilcote, Oxfordshire*, **2**, 98–108

——, 1983 The glass hoard, in S Johnson 1983, 81–8

Harden, D B, & Price, J, 1971 The glass, in B Cunliffe 1971, 317–68

Harker, S, 1980 Springhead — a brief re-appraisal, in W J Rodwell 1980, 285–8

Hawkes, C F C, & Hull, M R, 1947 *Camulodunum*, Soc Antiq Res Rep, **14**

Hawkes, S C, & Dunning, G C, 1961 Soldiers and settlers in Britain, fourth to fifth century, *Medieval Archaeol*, **5**, 1–70

Healey, E, Wickenden, N P, & Brown, N, forthcoming *Prehistoric sites in Chelmsford: their flintwork and pottery*

Horne, P D, & King, A C, 1980 Romano-Celtic temples in Continental Europe: a gazetteer of those with known plans, in W J Rodwell, 1980a, 369–555

Howe, M D, Perrin, J R, & MacKreth, D F, 1981 *Roman pottery from the Nene Valley: a guide*, Peterborough City Mus Occas Pap, **2**

Hudd, A E, 1913 Excavations at Caerwent, Monmouthshire, on the site of the Romano-British city of *Venta Silurum*, in the years 1911 and 1912, *Archaeologia*, **64**, 437–52

Hull, M R, 1958 *Roman Colchester*, Soc Antiq Res Rep, **20**

——, 1963 *The Roman potters' kilns of Colchester*, Soc Antiq Res Rep, **21**

Isings, C, 1957 *Roman Glass from Dated Finds*

Johnston, S, 1983 *Burgh Castle: excavations by Charles Green, 1958–61*, E Anglian Archaeol, **20**

Jones, M U, & Rodwell, W J, 1973 The Romano-British pottery kilns at Mucking, *Essex Archaeol Hist*, **5**, 13–47

Koethe, H, 1933 Die Keltischen Rund- und Vieleck-tempel der Kaiserzeit, *Bericht der Rom-Germ Kommission*, **23**, 10–108

Lambrechts, P, 1942 *Contributions á l'étude des divinités Celtiques*, 64–80

Legge, A, & Dorrington, E J, 1985 The animal bones, in France & Gobel (eds), 1985, 122–33

Lewis, M J T, 1966 *Temples in Roman Britain*

Lowther, A W G, 1948 *A Study of the Patterns on Roman Flue-Tiles and their Distribution*, Surrey Archaeol Soc Res Pap, **1**

——, 1976 Romano-British chimney-pots and finials, *Antiq J*, **56**, 35–48

Luff, R M, 1982 *A Zooarchaeological Study of the Roman North- Western Provinces*, Brit Archaeol Rep, **S137**

——, 1985 The fauna, in Niblett, R, 1985, *Sheepen: an early Roman Industrial site at Camulodunum*, CBA Res Rep, **57**, 143–9

——, forthcoming The animal bone, in B R G Turner forthcoming, *Excavations of an Iron Age settlement and Roman religious complex at Ivy Chimneys, Witham, Essex, 1978–83*, E Anglian Archaeol

Manning, W H, 1966 Caistor-by-Norwich and *Notitia Dignitatum, Antiquity*, **XL.157**, 60–3

——, 1972 The iron objects, in S S Frere 1972, 163–95

——, 1976 *Catalogue of Romano-British Iron Work in the Museum of Antiquities, Newcastle upon Tyne*

Margary, I D, 1967 *Roman Roads* (rev ed)

Marsden, P, 1980 *Roman London*

Marsh, G D, 1978 Early second century fine wares in the London area, in Arthur & Marsh (eds), 1978, 119–224

Meaney, A L, 1981 *Anglo-Saxon Amulets and Curing Stones*, Brit Archaeol Rep **96**

Menghin, W, 1983 *Das Schwert im frühen Mittelalter*

Millett, M, 1979 An approach to the functional interpretation of pottery in M Millett (ed) *Pottery and the Archaeologist*, Univ London Inst Archaeol Occ Publ, **4**, 35–48

Myres, J N L, 1986 *The English Settlements*

Muckelroy, K W, 1976 Enclosed ambulatories in Romano-Celtic temples in Britain, *Britannia*, **7**, 173–91

Neal, D S, 1974 *The Excavation of the Roman Villa in Gadebridge Park, Hemel Hempstead 1963–8*, Soc Antiq Res Rep, **31**

——, 1984 A sanctuary at Wood Lane End, Hemel Hempstead, *Britannia*, **15**, 193–216

Neville, R C, 1849 Memoir on remains of the Anglo-Roman Age, at Weycock, in the parish of Laurence Waltham, Berkshire; and on the excavations there made in 1847, *Archaeol J*, **6**, 114–23

Partridge, C, 1977 Excavations and fieldwork at Braughing, 1968– 73, *Hertfordshire Archaeol*, **5**, 22–108

——, 1981 *Skeleton Green. A late Iron Age and Romano-British Site*, Britannia Monog Ser, **2**

Payne, S, 1973 Kill-off patterns in sheep and goats; the mandibles from Asvan Kale, *Anatol Studies*, **23**, 281–303

——, 1985 Morphological distinctions between the mandibular teeth of young sheep, ovis, and goats, capra, *J Archaeol Sci*, **12**, 139–47

Peacock, D, 1977 Fladbury, *Current Archaeol*, **5**, 123–4

Pirling, R, 1966 *Das Römisch-Frankische Gräberfeld von Krefeld-Gellep*

Piton, D, 1985 *La Nécropole de Nouvion-en-Ponthieu*, Dossiers archéologiques, historiques et culturels du Nordet du Pas-de-Calais, **20**

Priddy, D, (ed), 1982 Work of the Essex County Council Archaeology Section, 1981, *Essex Archaeol Hist*, **14**, 111–32

Raddatz, K, 1957/8 Zu den magischen Schwertanhängerndes Thorsberger Moorfundes, *Offa*, **16**, 81–4

Rahtz, P A, 1951 The Roman Temple at Pagans Hill, Chew Stoke, Somerset, *Proc Somerset Archaeol Nat Hist Soc*, **96**, 112–42

——, 1985 *An Invitation to Archaeology*

——, & Harris, L G, 1958 The temple well and other buildings at Pagans Hill, Chew Stoke, North Somerset *Proc Somerset Archaeol Natur Hist Soc*, **101–2**, 15–51

Reece, R, 1980 Religion, coins and temples, in W J Rodwell 1980b, 115–28

Richmond, I, 1943 Roman Legionaries at Corbridge ...., *Archaeol Aeliana*, **21**, 132–3

Ritterling, E, 1913 *Der Frühromische Lager bei Hofheim im Taunus*

Roberts, W I (IV), 1982 *Romano-Saxon Pottery*, Brit Archaeol Rep, **106**

Robinson, H R, 1975 *The Armour of Imperial Rome*

Rodwell, K A, 1988 *The prehistoric and Roman settlement at Kelvedon, Essex*, CBA Res Rep **63**, Chelmsford Archaeol Trust **6**

Rodwell, W J, 1975 Trinovantian towns and their setting, in Rodwell & Rowley (eds), 1975, 85–102

——, 1976a Coinage, Oppida and the rise of Belgic power in south-eastern Britain, in Cunliffe & Rowley (eds) 1976, 181–367

——, 1976b A relief-moulded vessel, in P J Drury, Rettendon Ware kiln debris and other material from Sandon, *Essex Archaeol Hist*, **8**, 253–8

——, 1978 Stamp-decorated pottery of the early Roman period in eastern England, in Arthur & Marsh, (eds), 1978, 225–92

——, 1979 Iron age and Roman salt winning on the Essex coast, in Burnham & Johnson (eds), 1979, 133–176

——, (ed), 1980a *Temples, Churches and Religion: Recent Research in Roman Britain*, Brit Archaeol Rep, **77**

——, 1980b Temple archaeology: problems of the present and portents for the future, in W J Rodwell 1980a, 211–42

——, 1980c Temples in Roman Britain: a revised gazetteer, in W J Rodwell, 1980a, 557–85

——, 1982 The production and distribution of pottery and tiles in the territory of the Trinovantes, *Essex Archaeol Hist*, **14**, 15–76

—— & Rowley, R T, 1975 *The Small Towns of Roman Britain*, British Archaeol Rep, **15**

Ross, A, 1974 *Pagan Celtic Britain*

Sanders, J, 1973 *Late Roman Shell-gritted Ware in Southern Britain*. Unpubl London Univ BA thesis

Saunders C & Havercroft, A D, 1977 A kiln of the potter Oastrius and related excavations at Little Munden Farm, Bricket Wood, *Hertfordshire Archaeol*, **5**, 109–56

Schallmayer, E, 1987 Ein basilikäahnlicher Gebäudegrundriss in Neckarburken, Gemeinde Elztal, Neckar-Odenwald-Kreis, *Archäologische Ausgrabungen in Baden-Württemburg 1986* (Stuttgart)

Sheldon, H, 1971 Excavations at Lefevre Road, Old Ford, E3. *Trans London Middlesex Archaeol Soc*, **23.1**, 54–64

Silver, I A, 1969 The ageing of domestic animals, in Brothwell, D R, & Higgs, E S, (eds), *Science in Archaeology*, 283–302

Simonds, J B, 1854 *The Age of the Ox, Sheep, and Pig*

Stead, I M, 1976 *Excavations at Winterton Roman Villa*

Symonds, R, 1983 *Cataloguing Pottery at Colchester.* Privately circulated

——, & Wade, S, forthcoming *The Roman pottery from excavations in Colchester, 1971–1985,* Colchester Archaeol Rep, **10**

Tempelmann-Maczynska, M, 1985 *Die Perlen der römischen Kaiserzeit und der frühen. Phase der Völkerwanderungszeit im mitteleuropäischen Barbaricum,* Röm-German Forsch, **43**

Thompson, I, 1982 *Grog-tempered Belgic pottery of south-eastern England,* Brit Archaeol Rep, **108**

Thorpe, W A, 1935 *English Glass*

Toynbee, J M C, 1973 *Animals in Roman Life and Art*

Tyers, P, 1984 An assemblage of Roman ceramics from London, *London Archaeol,* 4.14, 367–74

Vanderhoeven, M, 1958 *Verres Romains tardifs et Mérovingiens du Musée Curtius*

VCH, 1903 *Victoria County History of Essex, Vol 1*

Vierck, H, 1978 Noel [*sic*] Myres und die Besiedlung Englands, *Praehistorische Zeitschrift,* **51,** 43–55

Wacher, J, 1974 *The Towns of Roman Britain*

Wallis, S, 1988 On the outskirts of Roman Chelmsford: excavations at Lasts Garage 1987, *Essex Archaeol Hist,* **19,** 40–6

Walters, H B, 1914 *British Museum: Greek and Roman Antiquities: Catalogue of the Greek and Roman lamps*

Webster, G, 1950 A Romano-British burial at Glaston, Rutlandshire, *Antiq J,* **30,** 72–3

Wedlake, W J, 1958 *Excavations at Camerton*

Werner, J, 1956 *Beitrage zur Archäologie des AttilaReiches,* Bayerische Akademie der Wissenschaften Philosophisch-Historische Klasse, Abhundlungen Neue Folge Heft, **38**

West, S E, 1985 *West Stow: The Anglo-Saxon village* (2 vols), E Anglian Archaeol, **24**

Wheeler, R E M, 1928 The Roman amphitheatre at Caerleon, Monmouthshire, *Archaeologia,* **78,** 111–218

——, 1930 *London in Roman Times,* London Mus, **3**

——, 1943 *Maiden Castle, Dorset,* Soc Antiq Res Rep, **12**

Wheeler, R E M, & T V, 1932 *Report on the Excavation of the Prehistoric, Roman, and Post-Roman Site in Lydney Park, Gloucestershire,* Soc Antiq Res Rep, **9**

——, & ——, 1936 *Verulamium: A Belgic and two Roman Cities,* Soc Antiq Res Rep, **11**

Whiting, W, Hawley, W, & May, T, 1931 *Report on the excavation of the Roman cemetery at Ospringe, Kent,* Soc Antiq Res Rep, **8**

Wickenden, N P, 1986 A copper alloy votive bar and a carved bone plaque from Chelmsford, Essex, *Britannia,* **17,** 348–51

——, 1987 Prehistoric Settlement and the Romano-British small town at Heybridge, *Essex Archaeol Hist,* **17,** 7–68

——, 1988 a, Some military bronzes from the Trinovantian *civitas,* in J C Coulston (ed), *Military Equipment and the identity of Roman Soldiers,* Brit Archaeol Rep, **S 394,** 234–56

——, 1988 b, *Excavations at Great Dunmow, Essex: a Romano-British small town in the Trinovantian Civitas,* Chelmsford Archaeol Trust Rep, **7,** E Anglian Archaeol, **41**

Wild, J P, 1982 Wool production in Roman Britain, in Miles, D, (ed), *The Romano-British Countryside. Studies in Rural Settlement and Economy,* Brit Archaeol Rep, **103,** 109–22

Wilkinson, P, & Clarke, F, 1985 The coarse pottery, in France & Gobel, (eds), 1985, 106–22

Wilson, D R, 1968 Roman Britain in 1967, *J Roman Stud,* **58,** 177–206

——, 1970 Roman Britain in 1969, *Britannia,* **1,** 269–315

——, 1975 Romano-Celtic temple architecture, *J Brit Archaeol Ass* (Ser 3), **38,** 3–27

Wilson, M G, 1968 Other objects of bronze, silver, lead, iron, bone and stone, in B W Cunliffe, 1968, 93–110

Wilson, M, 1972 The other pottery, in S S Frere 1972, 263–370

Young, C J, 1977 *Oxfordshire Roman Pottery,* Brit Archaeol Rep, **43**

Index

by Susan Vaughan

Antonine Itinerary, 125, 133
apron strap, 15, 73, 125, Fig 39

Baddow Road, 3, 53, 57–8
    Site AS, 1, 3–4, 49–54, 92, 132–3, Figs 2, 28–30
    see also Chase, The (Site M); Salvation Army
        (Site Q); Site CR
bangles *see* bracelets
bank, 49
bath-block, 125
beads,
    glass, 15, 41, 86, 141, Fig 44
    jet, 86, Fig 45
    melon, 18, 23, 86, Fig 44
bonding tile *see* tile
bone,
    animal, 19, 26–7, 29, 35, 42, 58, 61–2, 116–24,
        128, 133, 136, Figs 61–2, *see also* shells
    cremated, 6, 9, 25–6, 57–60
    human, 13, 15, 19, 29, 33, 61, 116, 121, 123–4,
        128, 136
bone objects, 42, 58, 61, 82–3, 133, 141, Fig 43, Pl
    IX, *see also* comb; needles; pins
Boudican revolt, aftermath of, 125, 127, 129
box flue tile *see* tile
bracelets, 19–20, 23, 33, 35, 38–9, 46, 58, 77, 79,
    86, 88, 125, 127, Figs 39–40, 45
Braintree, 91, 133
brick, 60, 63
briquetage, 27, 64, 88–9, 133–4, Fig 46
brooches, 1, 3, 18, 20, 23, 25, 29, 36, 42, 44, 46,
    56–7, 71–3, 79, 82, 127, 133, Figs 34, 37–8, 42
Broomfield, 141
buckle, 41, 71, 133, 141, Fig 37
building materials, 63–4, *see also* brick; daub;
    mortar; *opus signinum*; plaster; *septaria*; tile
buildings, 6, 13, 16–17, 26, 30–3, 46–9, 125, 127–9,
    131–2, 140–1, *see also* corridor structure;
    frontage structures; temple
burials,
    dog, 29, 35, 123
    horse, 123, 141
    human, 29, 61, 141
    see also cremations

Cables Yard, 131
Caerwent, 136, 138, Figs 67–8
cella see temple
Cernunnos, 111
Chanctonbury Ring, 60
Chase, The,
    Site L, 3, 49, 79, Fig 2
    Site M, 1, 3–4, 44–7, 63, 65–6, 69, 71, 77, 79–80,
        82–3, 85–6, 88–9, 91, 106, 108, 110–11,
        113–14, 116, 128, 140–1, Figs 2, 23–4
chatelaine fitting, 35, 77, Fig 39
Cherry Garden Lane, 98
chimney pot, 89, Fig 46

Christianity, 134
cills, 10, 13, 26, 31, 127, 129, 131
clay pipe, 32
cobbles, 9–10, 13, 57, 60, 62, *see also* hoggin;
    metalling
coins, 3, 9–10, 13, 15, 19, 23, 25, 29, 35–6, 38–42,
    44, 46–7, 49, 56–8, 61–2, 65–71, 125, 127, 140–1
comb, 42, 82–3, 133, 141, Fig 43
Congregational Church, 61
copper alloy objects, 1, 18–19, 30, 35, 40–2, 46,
    56–7, 73–80, 125, 127, 133, Figs 34, 37–41, *see
    also* apron strap; bracelets; brooches; ferrules;
    figurines; finger-rings; *ligulae*; mirror; needles;
    pins; *spathomela*; studs; *stili*; tweezers; votive
    bar
Corbridge, 129
corridor structure, 17, 29–32, 36, 125, 127, 129,
    131, 136, 138–9, Pl IV
counters, 63, 88, Fig 46
cremations, 6, 9–10, 25–6, 57–60
cult statue ?, 37
cursus publicus, 125

daub, 13, 64, 125, Fig 36
defences, 1, 125
Dengie Peninsula, 9, 131
ditches, 1, 6, 9–10, 13, 15, 17–20, 23, 25–6, 29–33,
    41–2, 50, 54, 56–8, 60–1, 127, 129, 131, 133,
    136, *see also* gulleys
drains, 17, 23
Durolitum, 133

earscoop, 77, Fig 39
enclosures, 1, 10, 17, 19, 23, 57, 127, 131, 136, Fig 8

ferrules, 36, 38, 79, Fig 41
field boundary, 49
figurines,
copper alloy, 136, 141
pipeclay, 60, 89, 141
finger-rings, 19, 23, 56, 77, 127, Figs 34, 39
fire bar, 29, 88, 133–4, Fig 46
fire dog *see* fire bar
flint (worked), 6, 16–17, 44
floor tile *see* tile
floors, 9–10, 13, 17, 26, 29, 31, 36–7, 42, 63–4, 131,
    135, *see also* mosaics; *opus signinum*; *tesserae*;
    tiles (floor–tile)
fort, 117, 123, 132
frontage structures, 1, 13, 33, 71, 125, 131–2,
    140–1, Pl II

gaming pieces *see* counters
gems, 86, Fig 44
glass,
    bangle, 86
    beads, 15, 18, 23, 41, 86, 141, Fig 44
    pin–head, 36, 79, 86, Fig 40

post-medieval, 30
tesserae, 17, 64, 86, 133
vessels, 6, 18, 23, 38, 41–2, 46, 58, 61–2, 83–5,
125, 133, 141, Fig 44
window, 49, 85–6, 133
Goldlay Road, 3, 57–8, 62
Site AB, 3, 47–9, 63, 65, 79, 85, 88–9, 92–3, 113,
116, 124, 134, Figs 2, 25–6
Site P, 3, 58, 61–2, Fig 2
Site Q, 1, 3, 49, 133, Figs 2, 27
see also Site CR
graffiti *see* pottery
Great Dunmow, 20, 73, 83, 85, 91, 99, 113, 125,
131, 133, 138, Fig 66
Great Waltham, 141
grubenhaus, 42–3, 141
gulleys, 6, 9–10, 13, 19, 26–7, 29–30, 32–3, 35–6,
44–7, 60, 127, 129, 131, *see also* ditches
Gun Hill, 97–8

Hadham, 99, 102, 106, 110, 114
Harlow, 99, 102, 117–20, 133, 136
Hayling Island, 60
hearths, 19, 26, 29, 32, 35, 82, 88, 129, 134, Fig 19,
Pl V, *see also* ovens
Hemel Hempstead, 129
Heybridge, 1, 9, 20, 69, 83, 91, 114, 125, 127, 131,
133
hoggin, 46, 62
hollow-way, 49, 133
Hunsdon, 102

imbrices see tile
iron objects, 18, 42, 80–2, 133, Fig 42, Pl X, *see also*
knife blades; linch pin; nails; woolcomb
iron-working, 133, *see also* slag

jet and shale objects, 46, 86, 88, Fig 45

Kelvedon, 69, 125, 133
kilns,
local, 6, 42, 49, 95–9, 111, 125, 133, Fig 52
others, 63, 95, 97–9, 102–3, 105–6, 111, 113–14
knife blades, 82, Fig 42

laconicum, 125
lamp chimneys, 18–20, 23, 47, 89, 113, 127, 133,
Fig 46
lamps *see* oil lamps
Le Hérapel (France), 139, Fig 67
lead, 38, 80
leather, 20, 50, 62, 91, *see also* tanning
ligulae, 35, 73, 77, Fig 39
lime, 59, 63, 134
linch pin, 9, 82, Fig 42
Lincoln, 69
Little Waltham, 20, 125, 136
London, 129, 139
loomweights, 27, 64, 88, 91, 133–4, Figs 46–7
lorica squamata, 80, Fig 41
Lynmouth Avenue, 61

M & S Motors, 62
Maiden Castle, 128

mansio, 1, 3, 9, 32–3, 42, 63–4, 73, 125, 133, 141
Mars, 111
medieval period, 1, 3, 15, 17, 30, 41–2, 47, 49,
53–4, 56, 141
Melbourne Farm Estate, 98
Mercury, 111, 128, 135–6
metalling, 9, 13, 15, 17–20, 23, 25, 31, 47, 49–50,
54, 56, 59–60, 62, 131–3, *see also* cobbles; roads
middens *see* shells
Mildmay Road, 131
Site CF1, 1, 3–4, 19, 54–7, 127, Figs 2, 31–4
Site CR, 57, 60, Fig 2
Mildmay Terrace, Site AB, 1, 3, 47–9, 63, 65, 79,
85, 88–9, 92–3, 113, 116, 124, 134, Figs 2, 25–6
military presence, 125, 129, 132, *see also* fort
mirror, 56
mortar, 20, 32, 36–8, 42, 57–9, 61, 63, 134–5, 139
mosaics, 99, 135, *see also tesserae*
Moulsham, 141, Fig 1
Moulsham Street, 49, 98, 141
Mucking, 97–8, 102

nails, 31, 38, 49, 73, 79–80, 82
Neckarburken (Germany), 129
needles,
bone, 83
copper alloy, 58, 73, 79
Nettleton, 138

oil lamps, 18–20, 23, 88, 127, 133, Fig 46
opus signinum, 37, 42, 44–5, 47, 62–4, 99, 135
Orchard Site, 69
ovens, 6, 9–10, 13, 26, 32, 42, 45, 63–4, 125, 127,
129, 131, 140–1, Figs 8, 16, Pls I, III, *see also*
hearths oysters *see* shells

Pagans Hill, 36, 129, 131, 135, 138–9, Figs 67–8
pathway, 17, 20, 23, 25, 32, 36–7, 49, 54, 56, 125,
127, 135, 139
Peutinger Table, 133
pigment, 64
pins,
bone, 58, 61, 83, 133, Fig 43
copper alloy, 9, 19, 23, 32, 35–6, 40, 49, 56, 58,
60, 79, 86, 127, Fig 40
pipe clay figurines *see* figurines
pits, 1, 6, 9–10, 13, 15, 17, 19–20, 23, 25–6, 29–33,
35–6, 38–9, 41–2, 44–9, 54, 56–61, 125, 131,
134–6, 140–1, *see also* post-pits; quarries
plaster, 32, 36, 44–5, 47, 59, 63–4, 134–5
post *see* votive post
post-holes, 9–10, 13, 15–17, 19–20, 23, 25–6,
29–32, 35, 42, 48, 60, 129, 131, 141, *see also*
post-pipes; post-pits; stake-holes
post-medieval period, 3, 6, 15, 32, 47–9, 53–4, 127,
141
post-pipes, 19–20, 30–1, 38
post-pits, 10, 19–20, 23, 30, 38–9, 43, 127–8, 135
pottery, 3, 6, 9–10, 13, 15, 17–20, 23, 25–7, 29–33,
35–6, 38–42, 44–50, 53–8, 60–2, 69, 92–115,
125, 127–9, 136, 141, Figs 35, 49–60
amphorae, 29, 35, 58, 61, 106
graffiti, 6, 18, 23, 58, 61, 88, 93, 96, 98, 106–8,
110, 127–8, 133, Fig 58

148

manufacture of *see* kilns
medieval and post-medieval, 29, 42, 44, 49
mortaria, 6, 10, 23, 29, 35, 40, 44, 58, 60–1, 99, 102–5, 110–11, Fig 57
prehistoric, 16–17, 44, 61, 115
'Romano-Saxon', 110, 113–14
samian, 3, 6, 9–10, 17, 20, 23, 25–7, 29, 31–2, 35–6, 44, 46–7, 49–50, 58, 60–2, 92–3, 96, 102–4, 108, 128–9, Fig 48
prehistoric period, 1, 6, 16–17, 44, 54, 61, 115, 125
Prince of Orange, 69, 131–2

quarries, 45, 47, 57, 125
querns, 10, 49, 58, 60, 89, 91, 133, Fig 47

Rivenhall, 69
river access, 1, 132
roads, 1, 6, 9–10, 13, 15, 32–3, 35, 49–50, 53, 59, 62, 125, 127, 129, 131–3, 139–40, *see also* hollow-way; metalling; pathway
robber trenches, 6, 13, 16, 41–2, 63, 129, 134, 141
Rochford Road,
    Site D, 1, 3–4, 6–15, 63–5, 69, 71, 73, 75, 77, 79–80, 82–3, 85–6, 88–9, 91–3, 97–8, 105–6, 108, 111, 113, 116, 124–5, 127, 131–2, 140–1, Figs, 2, 4–9, Pls I–II
    Site K, 1, 3–4, 16–43, 47, 63–4, 66–9, 71–3, 75, 77, 79–80, 82–3, 85–6, 88–9, 91–7, 99–106, 108, 110–11, 113–14, 116–25, 127–9, 131, 133–4, 136, 141, Figs 2, 10–22, 64, Pls III–VIII *see also* Site CR

sacred grove, 17, 23, 25, 36, 54, 127, 129, 134
salt production, 134, *see also* briquetage
Salvation Army, Site Q, 1, 3, 49, 133, Figs 2, 27
Saxon Period, 42–3, 113–14, 141
septaria, 10, 13, 20, 31, 36–8, 49, 63, 131, 134
shale *see* jet and shale
shells, 27, 29, 35, 42, 58–61, 134, 139
shoes, 91
silver objects, 41, 71, 133, 141, Fig 37
Site AB, 1, 3, 47–9, 134, Figs 2, 25–6
    finds from, 63, 65, 79, 85, 88–9, 92–3, 113, 116, 124
Site AF, 131
Site AJ, 131
Site AR, 141
Site AS, 1, 3–4, 49–54, 92, 132–3, Figs 2, 28–30
Site CF1, 1, 3–4, 19, 54–7, 127, Figs 2, 31–4
Site CR, 1, 4, 57–62, 89, 91–2, 106, 108, Figs 2, 35
Site D, 1, 3–4, 6–15, 125, 127, 131–2, 140–1, Figs 2, 4–9, Pls I–II
    finds from, 63–5, 69, 71, 73, 75, 77, 79–80, 82–3, 85–6, 88–9, 91–3, 97–8, 105–6, 108, 111, 113, 116, 124, Fig 52
Site K, 1, 3–4, 16–43, 125, 127–9, 131, 133–4, 136, 141, Figs 2, 10–22, 64, Pls III–VIII
    finds from, 63–4, 66–9, 71–3, 75, 77, 79–80, 82–3, 85–6, 88–9, 91–7, 99–106, 108, 110–11, 113–14, 116–24
Site L, 3, 49, 79, Fig 2
Site M, 1, 3–4, 44–7, 128, 140–1, Figs 2, 23–4

finds from, 63, 65–6, 69, 71, 77, 79–80, 82–3, 85–6, 88–9, 91, 106, 108, 110–11, 113–14, 116
Site P, 3, 58, 61–2, Fig 2
Site Q, 1, 3, 49, 133, Figs 2, 27
Site S, 125, 128
Site T, 125
Site V, 131–2
Skeleton Green, 99
slag, 6, 17–19, 29, 61, 82, 133
slots, 6, 13, 15, 17, 19, 23, 26–7, 29–31, 46, 48, 54, 127, 129, 131, 133–4
spathomela, 32, 77, Fig 39
spindle whorls, 88, 93, 108, Fig 46
Springfield, 141
Springhead, 128
stake-holes, 15–17, 25, 42–3, 135, 141, *see also* post-holes
statuettes *see* figurines
stili, 79, 133, Fig 40
stone (building material), 63
stone objects, 10, 49, 58, 60, 89–91, 133, Figs 35, 47, *see also* loomweights; querns; whetstones
streets *see* roads
studs, 18–19, 25, 35, 73, 79, 127, Figs 39, 41

tanning, 59
Taranis, 141
tegulae see tile
temenos see temple
temple, 1, 4, 16–43, 47, 49, 57, 59–60, 63–4, 117–20, 125, 127, 132–41, Figs 2, 20–2, 65, 67, 69, Pls VI–VIII
    ambulatory, 40, 42, 134–6, 138–9, 141
    cella, 16, 37, 40, 42, 134–5, 138–9, 141
    parallels, 135–6, 138–9, Figs 66–8
    temenos, 57, 59–60, 139–40
    see also corridor structure; pathway; sacred grove; votive deposit; votive post
tesserae, 17, 38, 58, 61, 64, 86, 99, 133, 135
textile industry, 133, *see also* loomweights
Thistleton, 129
Thomas John's Alms Houses, 16
tile, 6, 10, 13, 15, 18–20, 26–7, 30, 32, 36–8, 42, 44, 46–50, 58–61, 63–4, 98, 125, 127, 134–5, 139, Figs 36, 64
    bonding, 18, 26, 36, 58, 61, 63
    box flue, 20, 49, 58, 61, 63
    floor tile, 36–7, 42, 63–4
    imbrices, 10, 18, 36, 38, 58, 61, 63
    tegulae, 17–20, 26, 36, 38, 49, 58, 61–3, 88
trackway *see* pathway
trade and industry, 133–4
Trinovantes, civitas of, 117, 125, 133, Fig 3
tweezers, 39, 49, 58, 60, 73, 77, Fig 39

Uley, 38, 121, 128–9, 135–6

Venus (pipe clay figurine), 141
votive bar, 18–20, 23, 73, 75, 127, Fig 39, Pl IX
votive deposit, 18–20, 32, 36, 57, 71–3, 89, 127–8, 133, 136, 141, Fig 12
votive post, 19–20, 127–9

wall plaster *see* plaster
walls, 1, 10, 13, 26, 29, 31, 36–8, 42, 57, 59, 63,
    127, 129, 131, 134–5, *see also* cills; daub;
    plaster; slots; wattle
watching-briefs, 57–62
water tanks, 35, 49
wattle, 64, *see also* daub
wells, 19–20, 23, 26–7, 29, 31–2, 48–50, 57, 61–2,
    111, 128, 133

Weycock, 36, 136, 138, Fig 67
whetstones, 58, 91, Fig 47
Wickford, 20, 69, 83, 91, 125
Witcombe, 138, Fig 67
Witham, 83, 91, 120, 123
wood, 20, 27, 29, 50, 59, 62, 128
woolcomb, 82, 133, Fig 42, Pl X
worked bone *see* bone objects